RESEARCH FOR DESIGNERS

RESEARCH FOR DESIGNERS

A Guide to Methods and Practice

GJOKO MURATOVSKI

Los Angeles | London | New Delhi
Singapore | Washington DC

Los Angeles | London | New Delhi
Singapore | Washington DC

SAGE Publications Ltd
1 Oliver's Yard
55 City Road
London EC1Y 1SP

SAGE Publications Inc.
2455 Teller Road
Thousand Oaks, California 91320

SAGE Publications India Pvt Ltd
B 1/I 1 Mohan Cooperative Industrial Area
Mathura Road
New Delhi 110 044

SAGE Publications Asia-Pacific Pte Ltd
3 Church Street
#10-04 Samsung Hub
Singapore 049483

Editor: Mila Steele
Assistant editor: James Piper
Production editor: Imogen Roome
Copyeditor: Solveig Gardner Servian
Proofreader: Leigh C. Timmins
Indexer: Adam Pozner
Marketing manager: Michael Ainsley
Cover design: Jen Crisp
Typeset by: C&M Digitals (P) Ltd, Chennai, India
Printed and bound by CPI Group (UK) Ltd,
Croydon, CR0 4YY

Library of Congress Control Number: 2015939731

British Library Cataloguing in Publication data

A catalogue record for this book is available from the British Library

MIX
Paper from
responsible sources
FSC www.fsc.org FSC® C013604

ISBN 978-1-4462-7513-9
ISBN 978-1-4462-7514-6 (pbk)

At SAGE we take sustainability seriously. Most of our products are printed in the UK using FSC papers and boards. When we print overseas we ensure sustainable papers are used as measured by the PREPS grading system. We undertake an annual audit to monitor our sustainability.

To Ekaterina and Ella

CONTENTS

7 Applied Research 189

8 Research and Design 203

9 Conclusion 227

LIST OF IMAGES, FIGURES, TABLES AND ILLUSTRATIONS

LIST OF IMAGES

LIST OF FIGURES

LIST OF TABLES

LIST OF ILLUSTRATIONS

ABOUT THE AUTHOR

Gjoko Muratovski has more than 20 years of global, multidisciplinary design experience. He holds a PhD in Design Research with focus on Branding and Corporate Communication Strategies. In addition to this, he is trained in a range of design fields such as Graphic Design, Visual Communications, Industrial Design, Architectural Design, Interior Design, and Furniture Design and Manufacturing. His formal education and professional development spans across 11 countries.

Over the years Dr Muratovski has been working with a broad range of corporate, governmental and not-for-profit organizations from around the world. This includes Deloitte, Toyota, Greenpeace, NASA Johnson Space Center, UNESCO World Cultural Heritage, World Health Organization, United Nations Association of Australia, Department of the Premier and Cabinet of South Australia, Auckland Council of New Zealand, and Melbourne International Design Week, to name a few. He is also regularly retained as an advisor by various design firms and advertising agencies on issues ranging from strategic design to brand development strategies.

In addition to having broad industry experience, Dr Muratovski also has a significant academic experience that ranges from teaching and curriculum development, to research, education management, and academic leadership. Currently, he holds senior academic roles at the Shanghai-based College of Design & Innovation at Tongji University – one of the oldest and most prestigious universities in China, and at the School of Art & Design at Auckland University of Technology – the leading design school in New Zealand.

ENDORSEMENTS

Today, designers design services, processes and organizations; craft skills no longer suffice. We need to discover, define and solve problems based upon evidence. We need to demonstrate the validity of our claims. We need Design Research, but as a special kind of research, with methods appropriate to the applied, constructive nature of design. We need a book on research for designers that can educate students and be a reference for professionals. And here it is: Gjoko Muratovski's masterful book for 21st century designers.

Don Norman, Professor and Director: Design Lab, University of California San Diego and former Vice President: Advanced Technologies, Apple

Inspiring and engaging. Gjoko Muratovski gives us a visionary preview on the future of design. He argues that design is transforming from 'problem-solving' to 'problem-finding' – something every company, from startups to multinationals, needs in today's hyper-connected and fast-changing world. Muratovski provides the context and more importantly, the implications of the rise of design as a powerful competitive advantage. If you want to know more about the role of design in the past, present and where design is headed, start here. If you've ever wanted to become a 'design-driven' company, read this book.

David R. Butler, Vice President: Innovation & Entrepreneurship and former Vice President: Global Design, The Coca-Cola Company

Today, as designers, we are exploring a new vision; a vision that seeks to apply creativity to challenges of our age, namely digital technology and information. The designer of today is involved with designing experiences, not just looks and appearances. Gjoko Muratovski's *Research for Designers* gives the reader a pair of wings to transcend limitation and do original work.

Suresh Sethi, Vice President: Global Consumer Design – South Asia, Whirlpool Corporation

Research for Designers clearly explains how effective cross-disciplinary discovery and delivery of strategic solutions to complex problems needs to begin with targeted and credible research of the problem area, the ecosystem, the context, and the stakeholders involved. While the book provides a great overview for designers that are interested in learning about research methods and how to use them, the book is also useful to strategists and decision-makers as it can expand their problem-solving toolkit to incorporate design research and practice in the pursuit of new, original and better outcomes. This is an excellent resource for both students and developing design practitioners.

Jane Treadwell, Practice Manager: Governance Systems, The World Bank Group and Advisor: Clinton Foundation Climate Initiative

Gjoko Muratovski has written the definitive compendium that not only covers 'how' to best conduct design research but 'why' it is such a vital ingredient to success. Although intended for design students, I believe Muratovski's manual offers a far broader appeal. Strategists, business leaders, policy makers, anyone who wants to enhance and advance their research proficiency to achieve a better outcome should read this book. I know I'll be sharing copies with my colleagues.

Maureen Thurston, Corporate Strategy Executive and Principal: Design Leverage, Deloitte Australia

Research for Designers is a welcome contribution to the world of design academia as it discusses methods for carrying out systematic design research. This book allows the reader to choose methods for design research according to different types of design problems and not only for the different stages of the design process. In this respect, this will be useful not only to postgraduate students and academics engaged in serious design research, but also to practicing designers dealing with large-scale, complex and cross-disciplinary design problems.

Kun-Pyo Lee, President, IASDR – International Association of Societies of Design Research. Professor and Head of Department: Industrial Design, KAIST and former Executive Vice President / Head of Corporate Design Centre, LG Electronics

Design's importance in social, cultural and economic terms has never been greater. So it's a surprise that the design research community has waited so long for an authoritative and comprehensive handbook on research methods which further our understanding and knowledge of the process of designing. *Research for Designers* fills this gap in the literature. There's no doubt it will become a seminal reference for those seeking to undertake research in the field.

Seymour Roworth-Stokes, Chair, Design Research Society. Professor and Dean: School of Art and Humanities, Coventry University

Research for Designers explores design research based on a panorama of the evolution of design. It is a useful book for designers, educators and researchers. It is also a meaningful book, as it opens the window for enriching and improving the rationalities between design and a possible better world. While facing a new era of design activism, a new culture of knowledge creation should be involved as part of the agenda. Gjoko Muratovski's work makes a concrete step forward.

Yongqi Lou, Professor and Dean: College of Design and Innovation, Tongji University and Vice President, CUMULUS

Flexible production technology and new business models enable companies to make almost anything. The unintended consequences include consumers confused by too many choices and managers not knowing what to make. Design offers new ways for executives to understand and fulfil people's needs and aspirations; however, the informality of design knowledge prevents design operating at the speed and scale that is needed. *Research for Designers* is a major contribution to giving structure to design knowledge. This book will help companies succeed by helping people have better lives.

Patrick Whitney, Steelcase/Robert C Pew Professor and Dean: IIT Institute of Design

Gjoko Muratovski's *Research for Designers* provides a structured approach to introducing design students and new researchers to design research. Designers embarking on research have often found it to be challenging to find books that are able to provide them with the necessary advice and guidance for success. This book helps to overcome this challenge by taking the reader through the research process from defining the research problem through to the literature review on to data collection and analysis. With such practical and useful chapters this book should prove to be essential reading in design schools across the world.

Tracy Bhamra, Professor and Pro Vice Chancellor: Enterprise, Loughborough University

With *Research for Designers*, Gjoko Muratovski has put together a highly valuable resource for designers who want to better understand how to do design research. Designers, but also those who teach designers, will find these resources extraordinary useful.

Erik Stolterman, Professor and Chair: Informatics, Indiana University Bloomington and Professor: Institute of Design, Umeå University

A brilliantly written and wonderfully comprehensive book on the wide array of research methods available that can, ultimately, help us design a better world. As companies, organizations and even governments turn to designers to solve a wide range of problems, a more evidence-based approach to design will certainly be in design's future. This book is an invaluable contribution to that effort. Appropriate for students and professional designers alike, Gjoko Muratovski's *Research for Designers* should be required reading for anyone creating anything!

Dan Formosa, Award-Winning Designer and Founding Partner, Smart Design

In *Research for Designers*, Gjoko Muratovski provides a comprehensive and insightful guidance to designers on how to find answers to well articulated design related questions, in a methodical and systematic way. Given that the design field have suffered a lack of well grounded literature on research methods and research methodology this book is a welcome contribution and fills a gap for everyone that aims to approach the field in a methodologically proper way. This book is an excellent contribution to the knowing of 'how' to do design research – a knowledge critical not only for researchers but for everyone operating in the design field. With *Research for Designers*, Gjoko Muratovski makes a long awaited contribution to the professionalization of the design field.

Göran Roos, Professor: Strategic Design, Swinburne University of Technology

The need for conducting rigorous knowledge-based inquiry is a central theme of this very timely and relevant book by Gjoko Muratovski. *Research for Designers* is an extremely valuable 'how to' book that arms designers with practical knowledge on how to conduct and communicate research in order to create even greater value from the work that they currently do.

Swee Mak, Professor and Director: Design Research Institute, RMIT University

Research for Designers is a highly valuable book for anyone who engages with the design process, regardless of whether they are designers, engineers or business developers. This book introduces research with a strong practical focus and it lays down the foundations for developing an entire R&D process, even for large-scale, long-term projects – which makes it incredibly useful to both design and business leaders.

Kalevi Ekman, Professor and Director: Aalto Design Factory, Aalto University

Designers aiming to change the world are always in pursuit of new approaches that can help them realize their potential, even if they are already strongly motivated creative people. This search is a driving force that leads them to become deeper thinkers, and this is also what drives them to learn new things. So far, they had to do with basic research in order to understand complex problems, namely looking within the field of design itself, while this book shows them how to find knowledge that lies outside the field. Wonderfully written, each well-structured chapter of the book encourages designers to develop their own knowledge from the ground up.

Yukari Nagai, Dean Professor: School of Knowledge Science, JAIST

Muratovski's clear, methodical coverage of the major approaches to research provides the succinct introduction and on-going practical resource that every undergraduate, graduate, or practicing designer might need to begin contributing, themselves, to the next stage of the field's development. Armed with the lessons contained in this practical guide, they will not only make further contributions to the marketing bonanza and paradigm shift in corporate leadership already underway, they will help move design from problem finding to problem predicting and also, it seems, teach us much about what it means to be human in a world of ever accelerating technological change.

Branden Thornhill-Miller, Director of Research, Preparing Global Leaders Foundation. Adjunct Professor: Economics & Psychology, University of Paris V (Sorbonne). Fellow: Harris Manchester College, University of Oxford

Research for Designers works well to illuminate for Master's and Doctoral level students how and why important shifts in design are taking place around the world from 'product creation' to 'process creation' and from 'a field of practice' to a 'field of thinking and research'. In course development and lecturing on design at universities such as Stanford, St. Petersburg Polytechnic, Borås, Aalto and Tongji, I have until now been searching for good new books of this kind. One down.

Antti Ainamo, Professor: Fashion Brand Management, University of Borås. Adjunct Professor: Management Studies, Aalto University School of Business. Adjunct Professor: Strategic Design, Aalto University School of Arts, Design and Architecture

FOREWORD

Imagine the world as it was two and a half million years ago. Everything you could have seen – everything in the environment – was natural, set in place by natural processes, modified only by weather, time, and possibly animals. No human beings existed to change or disturb the natural order. And then something quite unusual took place. *Homo habilis* made the first stone tools (Friedman, 1997: 54–5; Mithen, 1998: 105–128; Ochoa and Corey, 1995: 1–8; Watson, 2005: 23–5).

These were our ancestors – and making tools was one of the activities that made us human in the first place. *Homo habilis* was one of the advanced animals that made tools. Tools and our tool-making behaviour helped to make us human by helping to shape the modern brain, and with it, the mind that shapes our mental world. All this goes back two and a half million years to the unknown moment when the first of our remote ancestors manufactured the first stone tool.

Design, in the most generic sense of the word, began with those primitive tools. Our pre-human ancestors were designing well before they began to walk upright. Four hundred thousand years ago, we began to manufacture spears. By forty thousand years ago, we had moved up to specialized tools. Urban design and architecture came along ten thousand years ago in Mesopotamia. Interior architecture and furniture design probably emerged with them. It was another five thousand years before graphic design and typography got their start in Sumeria with the development of cuneiform. After that, things picked up speed.

As professions go, design is still young, but the practice of design predates professions. Today, we have replaced cuneiform with ASCII characters. Instead of chipping rock, we download rock music from the Apple Store. If we haven't completely replaced spears with pruning hooks or swords with plowshares, we do provide a far wider range of goods and services than the world has known before. All goods and services are designed. The urge to design – to consider a situation, imagine a better situation, and act to create that improved situation – goes back to our pre-human ancestors. The modern design profession is unlike anything we have known in the past.

Nobel Laureate Herbert Simon defined design in the broadest sense of human action. To design, he wrote, is to '[devise] courses of action aimed at changing existing situations into preferred ones' (Simon, 1982: 129). Design involves a wide range of processes that human beings use to plan the future. We design the artifacts and processes that move us from the present to the future. Design involves the strategic choice of goals, and planning the actions we take to reach those goals.

The word 'design' entered the English language in the 1390s. It began as a verb describing a process of intention and action. To design is 'to conceive and plan out in the mind [. . .] to have as a purpose: intend [. . .] to devise for a specific function or end', then later, 'to make a drawing, pattern or sketch of [. . .] to draw the plans for [. . .] to create, fashion, execute or construct according to plan: devise, contrive [. . .]' (Merriam-Webster, 1993: 343). Thought and intention come first.

In this sense, design is a universal human capacity. In fact, every creature able to plan future actions and carry them out can design. Anyone with a clever dog knows this. Famous accounts describe dogs and horses that plan and design. Design, learning, and judgement go together, and these inform the process by which we plan. Again, human beings are not alone in this capacity – for example, Mary Catherine Bateson (1972: 104–120) recounts the story of a horse learning to canter, apparently abstracting general principles as he did so. Gorillas, orangutans, chimpanzees, and other primates certainly design. Nevertheless, human design is different. Two specific facts distinguish human beings from other creatures.

The first of these is the human ability to represent our strategic intentions in diagrams, blueprints, drawings, models, and descriptions. These represent our intentions. They also serve as instructions that show others how to execute the plans we conceive.

The second of these is the fact that we do more than design to realize our own goals. We design on behalf of others, working to meet their goals and solve their problems. Design is a service, and we make the goals and needs of other human beings our own goals as designers. When human beings engage designers to work in this way, they become professional designers. They design for a living.

In the twentieth century, the design profession took shape in such fields as graphic design, information design, product design, industrial design, and design management. Some architects and engineers also began to think of their work as design.

Today, we see design in an even larger frame: 'Modern design has grown from a focus on products and services to a robust set of methods that is applicable to a wide range of societal issues. When combined with the knowledge and expertise of specialized disciplines, these design methods provide powerful ways to develop practical approaches to large, complex issues. [. . .] The major problems facing humanity today involve complex systems of stakeholders and issues. These challenges often involve large numbers of people and institutions intermingled with technologies, especially those of communication, computation, and transportation. Health, education, urbanization, and environmental issues have these characteristics, as do the issues of sustainability, energy, economics, politics, and overall wellbeing' (Friedman, Lou, Norman, Stappers, Voûte and Whitney, 2014: np).

For Herbert Simon, all professional practices involve design in the broad human sense. So it is that physicians, managers, engineers, and lawyers design, as do politicians seeking to pass laws and generals trying to win battles.

In the twenty-first century, design involves a wider range of challenges than typical of design in the twentieth century, and a wider range of goals. Design also involves a broader context and greater complexity.

Today, as always, designers act on the physical world, address human needs, and generate the built environment. These common attributes have typified design since the time of *homo habilis*. This was true of people who made clay pots in Mesopotamia, shaped wheels for Roman chariots, wove linen in medieval Lithuania, or prepared arrows in the Americas before Europeans came.

Contemporary technology and social systems add four substantive challenges. These have grown in scale since the industrial revolution of the 1700s. The substantive challenges are: increasingly ambiguous boundaries between artifact, structure, and process; increasingly large-scale social, economic, and industrial frames; an increasingly complex environment of needs, requirements, and constraints; information content that often exceeds the value of physical substance.

These changes gave rise to three important differences in the context of professional design. These are: a complex environment in which many projects or products cross the boundaries of several organizations and stakeholder, producer, and user groups; projects or products that must meet the expectations of many organizations, stakeholders, producers, and users; demands at every level of production, distribution, reception, and control (Friedman, 2012: 148–51). These challenges raise an important question. How can we know in a reasonable way that our work as designers offers responsible solutions to the problems of those who ask for professional help? The answer to this question is the starting point for Gjoko Muratovski's *Research for Designers: A Guide to Methods and Practice*.

The physicist and philosopher Mario Bunge (1999: 251) defines research as the 'methodical search for knowledge'. To say that we know something is to say that we understand it, and that we can apply what we know to the problems we face. For Bunge, 'Original research tackles new problems or checks previous findings. Rigorous research is the mark of science, technology, and the "living" branches of the humanities'. Synonyms for research include exploration, investigation, and inquiry.

Muratovski's book shows designers how to answer questions and solve problems in a methodical, systematic way. To say this is to say a great deal. We call on designers to solve many kinds of problems. Design is nearly always an interdisciplinary field, and sometimes a transdisciplinary field. The different kinds of problems we face for any given project may require us to use many different methods. We must therefore have a deep understanding of some research methods and an awareness of many more methods than we ourselves can master. We tie these understandings together with an understanding of research methodology. A research method is a way to solve a problem; research methodology is the comparative study of methods and the kinds of problems that any given method can help us to solve. *Research for Designers* offers a broad introduction to the issues involved in both.

Research for Designers is a valuable textbook for design students who want to understand the key issues in research they will need as professional designers. It offers a robust yet concise overview for research students earning a PhD. It is a useful resource for experienced researchers and for those who supervise and teach research students. While there have been short guidebooks to design research in the past, this is the largest and most comprehensive text available in English to date. It meets a real need in our field.

In his keynote speech for the 2007 congress of the International Association of Societies of Design Research, Kees Dorst (2008) described design research as a revolution waiting to happen. This revolution builds on earlier understandings of professional practice, but the revolution requires more. Today, the revolution is under way – earlier approaches are undergoing evaluation, new methods are emerging, skilled researchers are generating the methods of inquiry we require to solve the challenging problems we face.

A book such as Gjoko Muratovski's *Research for Designers* helps research students move from studying research skills and methods to practising effective research for advanced design practice.

For working researchers and teachers, *Research for Designers* offers a toolkit for better research, and with it, the improvements our field needs in projects and publications. While the design field has grown dramatically in the number of conferences and journals where researchers present their work, overall quality is not what it should be. The revolution we need requires the kind of progressive research programmes that typify mature disciplines. This phase of design research is in its early stages.

Tore Kristensen (1999: np) states that a progressive research programme involves 'building a body of generalized knowledge; improving problem solving capacity; generalizing knowledge into new areas; identifying value creation and cost effects; explaining differences in design strategies and their risks or benefits; learning on the individual level; collective learning; and meta-learning.' A great deal of design research involves useful individual learning to solve situated problems for specific clients – but this kind of research goes no further than professional practice does. The difference between practice and practice-based research requires building a body of generalized knowledge, then generalizing the knowledge into new areas while helping the field to learn as a community.

Designers often make a distinction between 'knowing that' and 'knowing how', as though design research involves knowing how to do something practical rather than describing something in the world as scientists do. One of the great problems in the field involves exactly this distinction. Designers already do know how to do something. The difference between design and design research is this. Showing a product shows us 'that' a designer knows 'how' to do something. Research shows us 'how' to do it ourselves. And Gjoko Muratovski's *Research for Designers* shows us the 'how' of how to do research.

Step by step, *Research for Designers* demonstrates the facets of a solid research project. Experienced researchers understand these issues as a form of tacit knowledge. Muratovski explains the details of each step: states the research problem; discusses the current knowledge of the field; examines past efforts to examine or solve the problem; describes the methods and approach used to solve the problem; compares these with alternative methods; discusses problems encountered in the research, and explains how the researcher addresses these problems; explicitly offers a result that contributes to the body of knowledge within the field; and states the implications for future research.

Research shows others how to do what the researcher has learned. This is as true for practice-based research as it is for scientific research. Chemists show others how they solved a chemistry problem. Mathematicians demonstrate every step in a proof. Engineers explain the problems they face in selecting a metal or a process for a specific application. Sociologists and anthropologists explain their ways of understanding how people behave. In design, we may need to examine or explain issues much like any of these – and we need to show others how we reach the results we finally present. Whether that result is a process, a product, or a system, research means offering an explanation as well as the final result. The explanation makes sense of the result, so that others can use the concepts and ideas, the methods, or the results to further their own work.

Research for Designers introduces readers to the 'how' of research.

For any serious researcher in any field, there is always more to learn. The great contribution of this book is that it offers the solid foundation that researchers need if they are to start well. With *Research for Designers*, Gjoko Muratovski makes a useful and timely contribution to a necessary revolution.

Ken Friedman
Chair Professor of Design Innovation Studies
College of Design and Innovation
Tongji University
Shanghai, China

University Distinguished Professor
Centre for Design Innovation
Swinburne University of Technology
Melbourne, Australia

PREFACE

Design is all around us; it influences how we live, what we wear, how we communicate, what we buy, and how we behave. Yet designers are rarely invited to participate in the planning of the strategies that determine what kind of design solutions should be developed, for whom, or why. Instead, most designers tend to focus on delivering outcomes without necessarily questioning whether the proposed outcomes are also the right solutions. The creative process of design, which is often based on tacit knowledge, intuition, assumptions and personal preferences, is often seen as a standard way of working in the field – and this is often what makes design alluring to people – but this process can be improved and enhanced. This book can show you how.

Let us begin by taking as an example Alessi's Juicy Salif (1990) designed by Philippe Starck and Apple iPhone (2007) designed by Jonathan Ive. Both of these beautiful products are considered as design icons today. Yet the thought process behind the design of both is very different. At one end we have a stunning looking but useless and overpriced lemon squeezer.

Image of Juicy Salif and Apple iPhone

Juicy Salif is neither practical, nor does it resolve any problems for the end user; in fact, it creates more problems if used as intended – which in itself is a paradox when it comes to product design. Rather than improving the original concept of the lemon squeezer, as would normally be expected from a product designer, we see the opposite here. Juicy Salif fails to hold back the lemon pits and the rind that one would normally expect from a lemon squeezer; there are ergonomical problems associated with the height of the lemon squeezer when placed on an average countertop; and the form itself is expensive and difficult to manufacture. Then again, the lack of all of these things adds to the beauty of the object itself. Its shape is instantly recognizable and iconic, and regardless of the high price tag for such an item, this product sells well. However, rather than using it, most owners simply choose to display it for decoration purposes. That is why this design can better be described as a sculpture than a product. On the other hand, the iPhone is equally beautiful in terms of design but also groundbreaking in terms of innovation. Its stylish look paired with a highly intuitive user interface system changed the whole mobile phone industry. The seamless user experience set a new standard in the industry almost overnight and changed the way people used their phones. The introduction of the App Store allowed for people to customize their phones and to use them in ways that they had never used them before – making the whole mobile phone experience a very personal one. The difference between the two objects is that the iPhone is a research-driven problem-solving exercise, designed with the end-user in mind, while Juicy Salif is simply a self-centred creative expression driven purely by aesthetics. What these two examples show is that design can be deceptively attractive, regardless of whether the end result is useful or useless.

The conflicts between 'beauty and function' and 'power and ideology' are constant in the culture of design, but finding the right balance can be very important (Bengtsson, 2012: 86–8). Yet not all designers are interested in pursuing such an ideal. Some designers want to focus on the process of 'making', others on the process of 'thinking'. As discussed above, in both cases the outcome can be aesthetically pleasing, but the impact that design has within the spheres of business and society can vary significantly. In line with this, I would like to quote a passage from Staffan Bengtsson's *IKEA the Book: Designers, Products and Other Stuff* (2013):

> Let us also say a word or two about us – about human beings in the midst of all these designed objects. Those of us who work with design and have voluntarily thrown ourselves into the lion's den of the design world know that the designer, when at his or her best, could also be called a 'behavioural scientist'. Some designers are content to create a chair; others who are more problem-oriented think more about our need to 'sit'. Some simply create a glass while others reflect upon the art of 'drinking' and come up with a drinking glass that really fulfils the desire to drink. We could identify two different schools of design: those who choose the noun 'glass' and those who prefer the verb 'to drink'. In the end, I'm convinced that the latter school is the one that wins our trust and our love. They focus on what is to be human. The things and objects that equip us for living. Chairs and glasses that work, that don't complicate

things for us. Yet still the marketplace is overflowing with products whose creators don't seem to have understood that without insight and empathy for human behaviour, there can be no truly heartfelt design. (Bengtsson, 2013: 89)

In order for designers to become leaders capable of defining strategies rather than just working on their implementation, they will first need to learn how to understand and solve complex, intricate and often unexpected problems. The solutions for these problems might not lie within the domain of design alone, and they may be found across a range of subjects and specialities. Therefore, designers will need to adapt themselves to unfamiliar situations and learn how to collaborate with non-designers, recognize patterns among different types of problems, draw on their knowledge and the knowledge of others, search for facts from diverse sources in order to prove or disprove their ideas, and make informed decisions in a systematic and insightful way.

The use of this type of research in design is important because this represents a willingness to look beyond the immediate concern of project execution, which means that new and unexpected solutions could emerge. In this context, research can be seen as a process of intelligence gathering, information analysis, and deductive reasoning that can lead to better and more effective design outcomes. Nevertheless, designers rarely operate in a strategic manner. Rather than conducting research, most designers usually focus on investigating form, style, and processes of making, without taking into consideration the broader context in which their designs will be used. However, if designers want to be recognized as thought leaders who can play a significant role in the development of new insights and solutions, they will need to learn how to conduct research and operate in a cross-disciplinary manner – and this inevitably becomes a question of design education. However, introducing these skills within the design curriculum can be a challenging process.

Design is taught in a variety of educational institutions – from technical institutes and art and design schools to art academies and universities. All of these education providers have different approaches to design education and subsequently different expectations from their students and graduates. A traditional design education typically revolves around a studio culture where the study environment is part classroom and part workshop where students study about design and practice their skills. However, a contemporary design education should be a cross between a studio and a laboratory – it should be a place of teaching, experimentation, and research.

In a typical design education model, it is not uncommon for students of design to study alongside artists and in the beginning of the studies even to share similar subjects such as drawing, painting, or sculpture. In such classes design students are often taught how to apply principles of fine and applied art into what eventually becomes a form of commercial art – or design. From drawing, prospective designers learn how to draft and sketch; from painting they learn how to use and mix colour; and from sculpture they learn how to create forms. These and other things that they learn usually revolve around the principles of aesthetics – which are essentially principles associated with beauty and good taste. For designers (and artists alike), this involves knowledge of the appropriate use of line, direction, size, texture, movement, space, light, contrast, tone, rhythm, balance, harmony, composition, proportion, and ratio. Along the way, students are also encouraged to develop their own personal styles and to enhance their skills and techniques through practice. With time, students begin to develop an intuitive understanding of what is 'good' or 'bad' design – first in terms of whether something is aesthetically pleasing while still being functional, and second, whether the design is innovative in terms of whether it has challenged some existing conventions in a new and unpredictable way. This way of learning is further supported by introducing students to exemplary design references from past or current design styles and design movements as seen from a historical perspective. Alongside this, and depending on the area of study, design students are also assigned to adjunct courses on anything from ergonomics and material properties to technologies of production, layout and typography in order to expand their knowledge in the field of their interest. This is a generalization, of course, but nevertheless, this is more or less how a structure of a typical design education looks like.

Then, in addition to this, there are two approaches that designers can follow. Design endeavours can be pursued either for oneself (design as an inward-looking practice) or for the benefit of others (design as an externally-driven process). When approached in an inward manner, design inevitably becomes a form of personal self-expression. Even though the design outcome may be intended for an audience, it is the artistic style of the designer that drives and inspires the design process. When approached in an external manner, design can be seen as a problem-solving process that places the needs of others at the forefront. Here, the designer works by identifying and defining the problem first and then seeks for creative solutions capable of resolving this problem. In this case, the design outcome is driven by research rather than style.

That is why this way of designing also requires an additional set of skills to those discussed above. Designers working in such environments have the ability to participate in the development of the design brief, rather than having the design brief delivered to them – as is often the case. In this way, they can become aware of possibilities that may not have been previously envisioned, or they can contribute by providing new and different perspectives to the client or the end user. This is how design becomes a critical element of the strategy formation process. Once established, the principles of this way of working can be almost universally applied, regardless of the nature of the project. For example, market leaders such as Apple, Nike, Harley Davidson, Dyson, IBM, BMW, IKEA, and Nintendo already use design in this way. Similar design thinking approaches have also received traction both in the public sector and in the non-government sector. Nowadays, many governments and various non-commercial organizations increasingly use the services of design consultants capable of developing creative solutions to new or existing problems, ranging from nation branding to healthcare.

The type of approach that design students choose to follow in their career often depends on the design philosophy of their education provider, or on the teaching preferences of their lecturers. Nevertheless, the type of education they gain can be instrumental to way they see the world around them. For most designers, the studio is a safe environment where they share the same 'language' and the same interests with like-minded individuals. The 'real world', on the other hand, tends to appear as new and often frustratingly unfamiliar territory. Yet this environment can become a natural habitat for designers trained to use research and to work in a cross-disciplinary manner.

Regardless of this, there is a still a need for studio designers to work alongside design researchers. Studio designers can contribute by developing conceptual designs that do not necessarily need to be constrained by the market demands or even by the actual needs of the potential end-users, while design researchers could work on developing implementation strategies. Experimenting with new concepts, new forms, and new applications can often lead to breakthrough ideas that can be further developed and adapted for mainstream use later on. This way of design experimentation is often done in design areas such as transportation design – with the development of concept cars, or in fashion design – with haute couture. While this way of working can also be described as a form of design research, I have to note that this is not the type of research that I will present to you in this book. The research that I will discuss in this book will focus on creating substance, rather than style.

Having good technical proficiencies or a strong design style is no longer enough for emerging designers to succeed in an already saturated profession. New designers will need to develop research skills in order to be competitive not only within their own field, but also outside of it. Research skills aligned with the ability to analyse new problems, question existing solutions, and think in an unconventional manner can increasingly outweigh the technical design skills in the long term – especially when it comes to developing a design career that can make meaningful contributions to business and society.

ACKNOWLEDGEMENTS

I would like to thank the team from SAGE Publications for their work on this publication. I would especially like to thank Mila Steele, the Senior Commissioning Editor, for initiating this project, and for her guidance and support in developing *Research for Designers*. Also, I would like to express my gratitude to all of the reviewers and experts who assessed this book for its applicability and impact to academia, industry and the public sector. Your support and feedback has been greatly appreciated.

INTRODUCTION 1

KEYWORDS   Aims   Delineation
                Objectives   Limitations
                Audience

The role that designers play within the business sector and in society is changing. In order to make meaningful contributions to both, designers will need to learn to ask the right questions in order to identify what the real problems are. They will also need to learn how to conduct research in order to resolve these problems. In the process, learning to navigate through a range of cross-disciplinary issues in order to understand the broader social, cultural or environmental impact of their work will also be necessary.

By working in increasingly complex environments, contemporary designers aspire to deliver new and innovative solutions to existing problems, or at least to transform less preferred solutions to more desirable ones. While some of the problems that designers try to address are evident, others still need to be detected. In either case, designers need to demonstrate new levels of understanding of what these problems are before they begin to develop solutions. This is a process that always begins with the question: What is it that we want to resolve?

The answer to this question is rarely straightforward and pursuing it can be best described as a journey through the field of knowledge. This investigative process leads designers not only through the creative industries – where they often look for inspiration – but also through other disciplines where they will need to look for existing knowledge in order to make informed decisions. Once the problem is identified and placed within a given context, the search for gaps in this knowledge and possible resolutions continues. Once this information is gathered, a process of analysis and interpretations begins – and only then should design solutions follow.

Large design projects often transcend disciplinary boundaries and require involvement of teams of diverse experts. In such cases, designers may be required to assemble and lead cross-disciplinary teams and develop briefs on behalf of their clients. Yet in order to do so, designers will need to demonstrate management and leadership skills that constantly challenge the limits of what design practice entails. This is a lengthy process that requires a cultural change for many designers used to operating within the constraints of their own discipline alone, but as the field of design evolves, this change is inevitable. This book is a step in that direction.

Below I will explain what are the aims and objectives of this book and the nature of the intended audience. In addition to this, I will delineate the content of the book – chapter by chapter – and outline the book's limitations.

1.1 WHAT IS THIS BOOK ABOUT?

As the title says, this book is a guide to research for designers. The purpose of the book is to introduce designers and emerging design researchers to some of the most commonly used research approaches. The book is written under the premise of cross-disciplinary design research and education, which means that I will introduce a range of perspectives on using research within this context. However, I make no attempt to provide an encyclopaedic or comprehensive collection of all available research methods and research practices out there. Instead, I will only give an introduction to some of the most commonly used research approaches in design. In return, I hope that this book will provide you with information on how to embark on a research path, how to develop a research question, how to select appropriate research methods, how to communicate your research to the relevant stakeholders, and how to convert your research into a professional design brief that will lead to an effective design solution.

1.2 WHO SHOULD READ THIS BOOK?

Due to its academic complexity and unfamiliar terminology, studying research methods and methodologies can be one of the most challenging areas for designers that embark on a research path. Most of the existing literature is aimed at senior academics, and students often find this type of literature perplexing or difficult to understand. Therefore, the content of this book and the writing style is not aimed at senior academics and experienced researchers. Instead, the most suitable audience for this book would be design students enrolled in undergraduate or postgraduate courses on research methods and methodologies; emerging researchers such as PhD students, early and mid-level career researchers; as well as design professionals interested in applying research into their practice.

1.3 WHY DO YOU NEED THIS BOOK?

The use of research is a major component in many university-based design programmes. In addition to teaching design methods, many design schools increasingly teach research methods that can help emerging designers make informed design decisions, or help them to understand their field better. The use of research, however, is not only limited to the constraints of the university. High-performing industries are also driven by research. However, it has to be noted that when it comes to design practice, research is not always used as a strategic resource. For example, studio-based designers rarely engage with research in a way in which this book will describe research, but many corporate-based designers and design consultants do – and the need for professional designers who understand how research is conducted and applied is becoming increasingly important. Then again, I have to stress that this book is not concerned with the process of making – which is often examined in the study of design methods. Rather, this book is concerned with the process of (design) thinking – a subject matter often represented in the study of research methods.

The relationship between design and research is a broad field of inquiry and there are many different ways in which one can examine this field. That being said, there are many divergent views on design and research, and these views may vary from school to school, between design areas, and between design academics and design professionals. Design research is also recognized as an area of it own and this covers everything from investigations into practical design applications to strategic planning and theoretical speculations. Academic design research differs markedly from research that is commonly found in design practice – even though this should not be the case. Unlike practice-based research, which is often self-reflective in nature and is aimed at improving the practice of the individual or the team, academic design research aims to advance, change or challenge the normative body of the design field and to gather a deeper understanding of the field itself. Overall, design research is informed as much by the theory and practice of design as it is by the repository of scholarly work that comes from other fields as well. As such, design research can be seen as creating a balance between academic inquiry and practical application, while negotiating a plethora of methods available to a design researcher in an increasingly cross-disciplinary field.

1.4 CONTENT

The content of this book is divided across nine key chapters. Each chapter, except the Conclusion, has its own subchapters whose purpose is to engage you further into the topic by following a step-by-step process. The first chapter, the Introduction, which you are currently reading, does not require a separate explanation. All books of this type begin with one and the purpose of the introduction is to explain what the book is about, who is it for, and to set the stage for what will follow. Therefore, here I will introduce the content of this book from Chapter 2.

In Chapter 2: Design and Research, I will touch upon some of the problems and the opportunities associated with the role that research plays in the field of design. In doing so, I will first begin by acknowledging that design is an evolving field that constantly shifts its focus and adapts to change. Through a brief historical overview, I will explain how research was introduced to design, and why. Then, I will discuss the complexities of design research and the divergent views on this issue within the design community. Further on, I will discuss the benefits of introducing cross-disciplinary education and research in design. First, I will introduce what this entails, and then I will present some discussions on this topic. Overall, here I will reflect on the opportunities and the challenges associated with such model of design education and research.

In Chapter 3: Research Essentials, I will outline some of the key things that you need to know and do before you begin your research. Here I will discuss how to frame a research problem and how to produce a statement about your research. Then, I will explain what a research question is and what a hypothesis is – two terms that you will come across frequently as a researcher. In addition to this, I will discuss what a review of the literature entails and why every research needs one. Furthermore, I will outline several different approaches to conducting a literature review; I will discuss what makes a literature review valid and reliable; and I will explain what is a saturation in literature reviews – or in other words, how do you know that you have gathered enough information about your topic of interest. Then, I will briefly discuss why you need to compile a glossary of key terms, and perhaps most importantly, I will explain what you need to take into consideration when writing a research proposal. Following this, I will explain what research methods and methodologies are and I will introduce you to four key research approaches: qualitative, quantitative, visual, and applied research. In addition to this, I will explain why cross-referencing your findings is important and how you can do that by triangulating your research. In line with this, I will also explain how you can combine different research approaches by conducting multi-method research.

In Chapter 4: Qualitative Research, I will discuss how this type of research is conducted, and why it is relevant to designers. This type of research can be quite detailed, but it is by no means prescriptive. There are no strict rules, formulas, or recipes that you should follow when conducting qualitative research. Therefore, I will only provide you with some general guidelines. In time, as you build up your experience, you will be able to develop and refine your own research techniques and strategies and go beyond those discussed in this book. Furthermore, I will introduce to you some of the most commonly used qualitative research approaches that you can use for data gathering and analysis: case studies, cultural probes, interviews, ethnographic observations, archival and documentary research, ethnography, phenomenology, historical research, and grounded theory. If you are a novice researcher, some of the research terms may appear quite confusing and intimidating, but as you will see, they all stand for rather simple things.

In Chapter 5: Quantitative Research, I will explain how this type of research is conducted and what kind of quantitative research is relevant to design. Unlike qualitative research, this type of research is quite structured and follows strict procedures. Here I will provide you with some general principles that you need to be aware of when conducting a quantitative research. A particular focus will be on surveys and experiments. In the section on surveys I will list a range of methods that you can use for data collection purposes, such as face-to-face interviews, telephone interviews, written questionnaires, and online questionnaires. Here I will introduce you to the complex world of asking the right questions and I will outline a range of formats that you can use when framing a questionnaire. In the section on experimental research I will introduce observation studies as a typical method for gathering and analyzing data – more specifically, User-Centred Design (UCD) Research.

In Chapter 6: Visual Research, I will discuss different types of research that can be described as visual. For example, some types of research that are often used in ethnographic studies use participatory visual research methods such as photography or video as ways of recording data or eliciting information from participants. Other types of visual research that will be specifically discussed in this chapter focus on the analysis of found images and objects. In line with this, I will introduce you to visual and material culture studies. These studies examine how images and objects provide information, meaning, function, or pleasure. Here I will present three research methods that you can use to conduct a systematic and empirical study of images and objects: compositional interpretation, content analysis, and semiotics. These research methods can be brought together in a sequential order, or can be used individually – depending on the nature of your research project.

In Chapter 7: Applied Research, I will discuss one of the most popular research approaches in design, and I will explain how this type of research is quite different from the previous research approaches. While the other types of research were focused on understanding the problem and identifying the solution, this research is focused on developing the solution and refining the result. In that sense, this is a practice-driven research rather then a theory-driven one. Here I will focus on two key aspects of applied research – practice-based research (where a creative artifact is the basis of the investigation) and practice-led research (that leads to the new understandings about the design practice itself). The main applied research method that I will discuss here is action research.

In Chapter 8: Research and Design, I will discuss how you can present your research in the form of a report and an executive summary, and how to use your research in preparing a design brief and design report. In addition to this, I will provide you with information on how to disseminate your research better by preparing a well-structured abstract accompanied by appropriate keywords.

Finally, in Chapter 9: Conclusion, I will reiterate the need for this book and I will highlight once again the importance of research in design. The conclusion will be followed by a list of references that I have used throughout the book, and an index.

1.5 DISCLAIMER

The review of the literature that I have conducted in the course of writing this book implies that there is no one definite position about what design research should include. Even in the field of research – in general terms – there are number of numerous positions for many of the things discussed in this book. Nonetheless, I have made an attempt to select an assortment of some of the most commonly used research approaches within the field of design, and I have tried to interpret them objectively by using a range of academic sources. Then again, as this is not a definite book on the topic but only a guide, not everything has been included. For example, I have not gone into the examination of design methods as I believe that this should be covered in a book on design practice, and not in a book on design research. Also, I have to stress again that both design and research are very broad topics. In an attempt to keep things as simple as possible, I have omitted certain things and I have not represented some aspects in sufficient depth. That is why I would like to encourage readers to use this book in conjunction with other books that deal with specific research approaches in greater depth. For a possible reading list on these topics, please look at the list of references at the end of the book.

1.6 CONCLUSION

The purpose of conducting research in the context of design is either to inform designers about their practice, or to help them make informed design decisions. *Research for Designers: A Guide to Methods and Practice* is a cross-disciplinary book that aims to introduce basic research practices to designers. The concepts presented in this book transcend the boundaries of the design field and I have looked at a range of other disciplines in order to bring some of the best research practices together within the context of design. However, it has to be clarified that this book is neither a definite work on the subject of research nor one on design, but only a guide that offers a 'how to' approach to research. The book can be useful to all designers who are engaged in research, whether that might be within a university framework or in professional practice. The book is also suitable for most university courses on research methods and methodologies taught to designers.

1.7 SUMMARY

In this chapter I have delivered an introduction to the book, listed the book's aims and objectives, and discussed why this book is necessary to emerging researchers. In addition to this I have explained the focus of the book, the audience for whom the book is intended, and the book's limitations. Finally, I have provided a brief outline of the book, chapter by chapter.

DESIGN AND RESEARCH

KEYWORDS   Design Research
Design Thinking
Design Education
Cross-Disciplinarity

Interdisciplinarity
Multidisciplinarity
Transdisciplinarity

In his book *Design Research*, Peter Downton makes a bold opening statement: 'Design is a way of inquiring, a way of producing knowing and knowledge; this means it is a way of researching' (2003: 1). This is a wonderful construct and this is how we should be looking at design. However, in reality the practice of design is rarely a research-driven process aimed at producing new knowledge. When it comes to professional practice, very few designers would have formal training in research, will know how to use research methods, or even understand what research entails.

The *Oxford Dictionary* describes research as a 'systematic investigation into and study of materials and sources in order to establish facts and reach new conclusions' (Oxford Dictionaries, 2013a). This implies working to a fixed plan and according to an established form of procedures. Then again, few designers feel the need to learn how to conduct research in this particular manner because many designs do not need rigorous research in order to be developed or produced. The methods of design vary greatly and they can range from being highly structured to interpretive and lateral. They can be investigative in nature, but this investigation is often self-exploratory and it is focused on the immediate processes of design. For many designers this way of working is sufficient and the story ends here. This way of working limits the potential contribution that designers can make to business and society. In order for designers to develop themselves as professionals of broader significance, they will need to learn how to incorporate scientific research in their practice. This is not an easy task. Unlike design, research is not an intuitive process. In fact, it is quite the opposite; it is a process that requires conscious reasoning and there are rigorous rules that need to be followed in order for the research to be verified and recognized as valid. All of this calls for a significant cultural change in the field of design.

The biggest challenge here is that design has been traditionally placed under the domain of applied arts, rather than science – where research dominates. Because of this, design is often perceived as an artistic practice that is often driven by intuition rather than research based on strict principles of validity. Then again, art and science do not necessarily need to be separated from each other. During the time of the Renaissance, merging both was a customary practice for the leading creatives of the period. A prime example of this can be seen in the life and work of Leonardo da Vinci (1452–1519). Da Vinci was equally comfortable in producing masterpiece artworks such as *The Last Supper* (1498) and the *Mona Lisa* (1504–1505), while studying subjects ranging from human anatomy, biology and hydraulics, to engineering bridges or developing plans for a helicopter, an airplane, and a submarine. While da Vinci may have been an extraordinary individual, many luminaries of this period shared similar interests in working across disciplines. Yet somehow, in modern times design has become an increasingly monodisciplinary, art-driven field. Then again, this comes as no surprise given that many formal design programmes have been developed and taught in art schools that were formed around the nineteenth-century principles of the Arts & Crafts Movement – a decorative arts movement that sought to revive the ideal of craftsmanship in an age of increasing mechanization and mass production. Even though the world has changed significantly since then, the legacy of this movement still prevails even today, in the twenty-first century, and this way of teaching, learning and practising design continues to serve as a dominant model across the world.

A common practice in the design industry today still entails that once designers become proficient in a range of technical and artistic skills like drawing, rendering, production, model making, printmaking, typography, or layout – or whatever skills are seen as necessary within the domain of their particular design area – it is considered that they have mastered the 'art' of design. Then, when designers develop their skills to a professionally acceptable level, it is expected that they will differentiate themselves by excelling in a certain technique or style of work. In return, they are often hired on the basis of their skills and creative abilities. If a client believes that the design style of a certain designer can be used as a 'profitable differentiator' for a business or product, then the designer can make a living on the basis of his or her skills and creative output (Muratovski, 2012a: 45). However, as I will discuss further on, things are changing and design has begun to move in another direction.

Nevertheless, I have to note that some might argue that the process of experimentation that allows designers to develop unique sets of skills or creative outputs is a form of research. As both design academic and professional designer, I see the process of experimentation with style and technique as being a part of the design practice and not as a form of research. Any designer, just like an artist or a craftsperson, can enhance his or her skills through continuous and dedicated practice. This process is not always systematic, nor does it necessarily lead to establishing facts or new solutions. Instead, this process helps designers develop a particular style of work. In some cases this process can follow research criteria and then this can be described as an elementary form of design research – in a sense that this is research which is focused on only one particular area: the methods of conducting design practice. But, as I will discuss further, there is much more to design research than this.

2.1 NEW LEARNING

The need for design experts who can bring different disciplines together in new ways is increasingly recognized on a global level. According to the Design Council's 2010 report on design education in the UK, businesses, policy makers, and academics are increasingly making the case for the importance of design as a tool for innovation, productivity, and economic growth. This is dynamically linked to the design skills supply in two ways: the appearance of new technologies, new industries, and new services; and a supply of differently skilled people who can drive innovation.

As industries change and converge, traditional education systems are becoming less capable of supplying industry with people who have an appropriate and useful mix of skills and experience. While this might be a challenge, it is also an opportunity – especially for designers

(Design Council, 2010). In addition to this, the Design Council also points out that the skills that are increasingly valued by companies in all sectors include Creativity, Flexibility, Adaptability, Communication Skills, Negotiation Skills, and Management and Leadership Skills (Figure 2.1). As there is no one particular mix of skills that can guarantee good innovation performance in all circumstances, broadening the mix of skills with teams and individuals from other fields is one way to help innovation happen (Design Council, 2010).

From a design perspective, this means that the way designers are trained and educated will need to be changed, or at least adjusted, so that designers can learn to work in a cross-disciplinary fashion. This, in a way, supports Richard Buchanan's (1999) argument that design should adopt a *neoteric* model of education – a form of 'new learning' based on novel problems encountered in practical life and in serious theoretical reflection. This comes in contrast to the *paleoteric* model that can be found today throughout many universities – a form of 'old learning' that

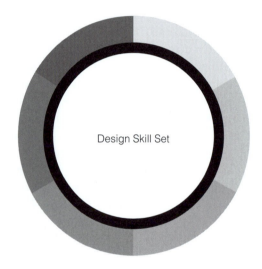

Creativity

Flexibility

Adaptability

Communication Skills

Negotiation Skills

Management and Leadership Skills

Figure 2.1 Design skill set

focuses on expanding the knowledge of a particular subject matter, often in greater and greater detail, but rarely contributing substantially to the field of knowledge (Buchanan, 1999, 2001). Ken Friedman (2003) shares a similar view. According to him, in the evolution of every discipline there comes a time when the foundations of the discipline need to shift from 'a rough, ambiguous territory to an arena of reasoned inquiry', with things such as research methods, methodology, and philosophy emerging forward (Friedman, 2003: 507).

2.2 DESIGN EVOLUTION

A fundamental problem in the designers' world today – particularly when designers want to make a genuine difference with their work – is that in most cases they are perceived as decorators, artisans, or stylists (Muratovski, 2012a: 45). As design continues to evolve and to mature as a profession, the definition of design constantly changes and expands. As the world changes, problems that businesses and society are facing, are becoming more and more complex. Designers are adapting to the new challenges, but new problems require new knowledge – and that is why the need for introduction of cross-disciplinary research in the field of design is becoming increasingly important.

The main reason why designers are still not broadly recognized as critical thinkers can be found in the origin of the profession itself. Early designers came from many backgrounds and they were introduced to the profession because of their ability to contribute artistically, decoratively, or constructively to the industry's growing needs for the development of new or improved products and mass communications (Owen, 1989: 4). Since then, the notion of design itself, and what designers can do, began to change significantly, but many of the original perceptions of the design profession remained.

Designers, unlike architects and engineers, do not necessarily work with a set of principles and rules that prescribe the scope of their work – as Victor Margolin points out (1992: 113). Rather, they invent the subject matter of the profession as they go along. If we look at the history of twentieth-century design, we will see that this has often been the case with many leading designers. Take for example Raymond Loewy (1893–1986) – the iconic American designer/stylist who began his career as an illustrator for Macy's department store and *Harper's Bazaar* and went on to work on an extraordinary range of design projects. From the toothbrush to the locomotive, the lipstick and the ocean liner, he shaped the culture of everyday life in America between 1925 and 1980. With clients ranging from Coca-Cola, Lucky Strike, Greyhound, Shell, and even US President Kennedy, Loewy placed himself in a unique position to produce highly memorable icons of consumption that in a way defined the myth of the American dream. In his illustrious career, Loewy exhibited strong interdisciplinary spirit and took on projects that many of his contemporaries would never even consider. For example, at the height of his popularity he was even involved in the development of NASA's Skylab – the first US space station (Schönberger, 1990: 7). Other prominent designers of that era such as Norman Bel Geddes, Henry Dreyfuss, and Walter Dorwin Teague shared similar experiences and challenged the conventions of their own profession. Dreyfuss and Geddes, for example, moved on from designing products to creating model cities of the future for the New York World's Fair in 1939, with Loewy designing a future rocketport for the same Fair. In the post-war years, creative pioneers such as Franco Albini, Charles and Ray Eames, Mario Bellini, and Richard Rogers continued to break design 'taboos', experimented with new design methods, forms, and materials, and inspired a new generation of designers to follow suit (Margolin, 1992: 113).

The idea of change is constant in the annals of design history – especially when it comes to redefining what design is and what design does. Design is no longer used only within the context of objects, visuals, or spaces, or even for resolving specific problems. As the trends in the field indicate, design is now becoming more about listening, asking, understanding, and drafting new possibilities and alternative realities. For example, many designers currently engage in facilitating positive futures such as developing energy-saving products and processes, creating human-friendly environments, encouraging political participation, and even reducing crime. As a result, design as a way of thinking is increasingly being sought in situations where in the past it has not been expected to be part of the solution (Muratovski, 2006: 82–3). However, the road to this point was long.

The design work that was carried out in Europe and in the US from the middle of the nineteenth century through to the first half of the twentieth century began as a trade activity (Swann, 2002: 49). The demands of the industry were introduced into art and craft studios, and early designs began to be treated as applied or commercial art. In time, design programmes were introduced in art schools, and as a result many principles of art became embedded in the design process (Muratovski, 2010a, 2011a). Another big change in the field of design occurred during the Second World War (WW II) when the military started commissioning the corporate sector to help them produce more efficient war machines. As the industries changed their focus, designers followed suit and began to investigate ergonomics, mass production techniques, performance, and efficiency. When the war ended, all these new ways of working continued to be used by the corporate sector and this continued to influence the way designers work (Bayazit, 2004: 17–23).

As the field of design grew in size and artistic expressions were increasingly combined with social and business acumen, design was no longer seen merely as a craft but as an emerging profession. As any other profession, design was also characterized by a tradition of practice and conscious recognition of a distinct type of working and thinking. With time, things in the field of design began to change and the field continued to evolve. Even though the original purpose of design was to follow the needs of the industrial economy, certain design schools and some design professionals continued to challenge industry practices and to introduce new currents of thinking and working (Swann, 2002: 49). For example, in the 1960s, the design focus shifted from developments in technology and form to consideration of human needs and behaviour. This was also a time when designers increasingly became interested in defining their role in society (Bayazit, 2004: 18–19). In other words, the world of design evolved from studying things to studying humanity (Almquist and Lupton, 2010: 3).

The ever-evolving nature of the field has helped design to go beyond the definition of a trade and to be recognized as a rigorous area of study; from a technical profession, design evolved to become an academic discipline in its own right. In the US, between the 1980s and the 1990s, due to encouragement and demand of the industry, the American government funded the development of new academic research units in a range of design schools across the country. In the 1990s, design research began to gain momentum and this resulted in an increase of doctoral programmes in design in the US and across the world (Bayazit, 2004: 27). Nevertheless, as with any other legitimate disciplinary field, design still needs to fulfil several criteria in order to maintain its status. As a discipline, design needs to demonstrate 'presence of a community of scholars; a tradition or history of inquiry; a mode of inquiry that defines how data is collected and interpreted; [...] requirements for what constitutes new knowledge; and existence of a communication network' (Del Favero, 2014: para. 2). Therefore, the field of design has an increasing need to produce its own base of knowledge, better expertise, and new skills. For that reason, training in design needs to follow a 'system of orderly behaviour' that is manifested in scholarly approaches to understanding and investigating new knowledge, ways of working, and philosophies of thinking – all of which require research (see Del Favero, 2014: para 1). Then again, both 'research' and 'design research' are not straightforward terms and they warrant further discussion.

2.3 RESEARCH REVOLUTION

To many people, the word 'research' connotes some kind of mystique and it suggests an activity that is somehow exclusive and removed from everyday life and from practice. Most people are unsure what researchers do, why they conduct research, what is the purpose and the benefit of their research, and how research contributes to people's overall quality of life and general welfare, let alone design. To add to this confusion, 'research' is a commonly misused word that bears many meanings in everyday life. We hear the word used in a context of various activities. For example, people often use research to describe the process of looking for an item or information, or when reading about something they are unfamiliar with. Businesses often mention research in their sales pitches when they want to promote some kind of innovative product, even when they have slightly modified an existing product to which they might have added some new features. Many of these activities use the word 'research' incorrectly. The correct ways to describe such activities include terms such as 'information gathering', 'documentation', 'self-enlightenment', or 'product development' – and none of these are equal in meaning to research (Leedy and Ormrod, 2010: 1).

Defining research in a context of design is also problematic. A young discipline such as design is inevitably faced with many conflicting ideas and philosophies, and general understanding of what design research entails is often a cause of debate (Buchanan, 2001: 17). For example, as mentioned above, design education – except for engineering design and architecture to some extent – has had the tradition of the fine and applied arts as its model. In this model, personal exploration is often seen as a sufficient substitute for research (see Owen, 1989: 8). For some designers, design practice itself is perceived as a research process and design methods are sometimes equalled to research methods (see Downton, 2003: 1–12; for an alternative view see Friedman, 2003: 519). For others, doing research into design processes is synonymous to doing design research (for comment on this, see Dorst, 2008: 6). However, the position I will take for the purpose of this book is that design practice is not the same as doing design research, but that the study of design practice can be considered as design research (see Bayazit, 2004: 16). Even so, I have to add that studying design practice alone is a limited way of looking at design research (see Buchanan, 2001: 17; also Dorst, 2008: 6).

In general, designers rarely participate in research that determines what kind of designs should be produced, and for whom – or why. Most designers choose to focus on investigating design methods that can deliver better form, style, function, and ways of working, and tend to present these activities as research (Laurel, 2003: 16–19). However, many of these activities are not always recognized as research by many universities, or by various corporate or government bodies that fund research activities. Therefore, most of the design research that is currently undertaken is not considered to be of the standard of a scientific discipline (Buchanan, 2001: 19).

Nevertheless, issues such as this have prompted Kees Dorst (2008) to call for a design research 'revolution' – a fundamental revision of how research is used in design, and for what. According to Dorst, in order for design to become a scientific discipline aimed at studying design, which he defines as 'a complex area of human activity', design researchers will need to follow four key steps. First, the researchers will need to have the tools to conduct 'observations' of complex human activities, then they will need to be able to 'describe' their observations, 'explain' what has been observed and described, and finally 'prescribe' possible solutions that could improve these activities (2008: 4–5).

This, however, is not a new and radical way of approaching design. Some design-driven companies, such as IKEA, already operate in this way. For example, according to IKEA's 2004 catalogue, we can see that at least their children's department has operated in this way since 1979:

> In order to understand children and how their world is different from ours, we at Children's IKEA bring in renowned professors who know about childhood development, child safety, human behaviour, and psychology. Then we test every child's toy and piece of furniture we sell, run risk analysis, and document the results – all against the world's toughest safety standards. (Cited in Bengtsson, 2013: 299)

Unfortunately, as Dorst points out, design researchers frequently ignore most parts of this research process and choose to focus on the efficiency and effectiveness of the design process instead – often at the cost of excluding everything else (2008: 4–5).

Then again, it has to be acknowledged that not all designers want to adopt such a scientific model. Many still prefer to hold on to the 'traditional' model of design education and practice. In design environments that foster this model, whether this might be design schools or design studios, designers are trained to imitate the works of others and tend to focus on the development of technical skills above anything else. This is also known as the 'apprenticeship' model of study and work. In this model the students and the junior designers assume the roles of 'apprentices' and the lecturers and senior designers assume the role of 'masters' of the trade (Muratovski, 2011a).

Even though this classical way of studying and working is still very popular in the field of design, some progressive design schools such as the Institute of Design in Chicago (originally founded as the New Bauhaus) at the Illinois Institute of Technology are opposed to this model.

According to Charles L. Owen, who is a key figure at the Institute, this model is holding back the field of design from introducing new insights into the industry. As he points out, many students choosing design programmes often exhibit a dislike of or an inability to deal with the content of other fields outside their core profession. In the learning process, their reservations, prejudices, and knowledge gaps usually go unattended because their lecturers – most of them with industry experience – are products of the same process and hold similar viewpoints. This in return creates a vicious cycle that withholds the progress of both design and industry. Upon graduation, students go into industry to design departments or consultancies staffed by graduates like them who hold similar views. They then influence the schools from their professional positions to ensure that the schools continue to prepare students as they were prepared, so that design graduates/future employees will have the same skills and attitudes as they have – which they perceive as necessary for employment in the industry. Since in most cases design schools employ lecturers with industry experience, design professionals inevitably return to the schools to complete the loop and train more students to work just like them. Therefore, in order for the field of design to evolve beyond this level, this 'incestuous loop', as Owen puts it, must be broken (1989: 7–8).

Owen is not the only one who has noticed this anomaly. David Durling and Brian Griffiths also point out that design schools often attract students of a particular kind whose tendency is to shun theory in favour of 'making'. These students usually take a narrowly focused view of the subject of their interest, to the point of exclusion of external influences. According to them, new possibilities in design education will arise if different types of students are attracted to design education – students who are more accepting of theorized grounding of design together with interests in the foundations of other disciplines (Durling and Griffiths, 2001).

Bruce M. Hanington also recognizes the value that research adds to both design practice and industry and concurs with both Owen (1989) and Durling and Griffiths (2001) when he says that that the introduction of scientific research methods in design practice depends significantly on the type of education emerging designers have (Hanington, 2005). Then again, the introduction of traditional art and crafts fundamentals in design education can be beneficial on a foundational level as it helps students develop a new set of skills and explore new ways of looking at the world around them. Lecturers with industry experience can provide valuable insights into the mechanics of the 'real world' and can advise students on what to expect upon their graduation. Nevertheless, design education will need to go beyond this in order to enable students to create breakthrough innovations, and that is why we also need research in the field of design. Then again, it has to be noted that some designers do exhibit concerns that formal research might compromise their creative output, but as I will argue below, this is far from being the case.

2.4 DESIGN THINKING

Increased introduction of integrated cross-disciplinary research and critical thinking in the field of design is creating new opportunities for the new generation of designers. Rather than presenting themselves as creative, artistic service providers who operate on the surface of the problem, many designers have already begun to redefine themselves as strategic planners capable of understanding complex issues. A number of global trend indicators have already identified the potential of design to act as a major force that can improve local economies, environments, and human life by integrating design in fields such as finance, construction, sustainability, health, housing, and public organizations. These new trends indicate that designers' tasks have begun to shift from 'product creation' to 'process creation' and that research is becoming increasingly important – especially since new design knowledge is being appropriated from the fields of social sciences, environmental studies, business management, and beyond (Muratovski, 2012a: 46).

If we look at the scope of the projects that contemporary designers already work on, we can see that many already act as social scientists and business strategists – even though they may be unaware of this and are often undereducated for such tasks. Yet, on day-to-day basis designers identify problems, select appropriate goals, plan, and deliver solutions to problems that involve complex social, political, and economic issues (Friedman, 2012; 144–6; Norman, 2010). The inclusion of formal research in the process of design is helping designers to understand their tasks better and to make informed decisions that can lead to more effective design solutions (Muratovski, 2006: 259, 2012a: 46–7). This way of working has lead to the idea of 'design thinking'.

'Design thinking' is a relatively new term to which different meanings are often assigned. In order to simplify things, I will use the framework of the term as outlined by Dan Formosa, a PhD scholar, award-winning designer, and founding member of the New York-based consultancy Smart Design. According to him, design thinking is a new approach to problem solving that relies on innovation and research when it comes to the development of new products and services (Formosa, 2012). Then again, as Formosa points out, innovation does not necessarily mean invention. Rather, innovation means a new and unique way of thinking, even when it comes to existing problems. For many companies design thinking grounded in design research has become a key to achieving a competitive advantage in a rapidly changing technological world. As evidence of this, Formosa points to Smart Design's impressive list of clients who adhere to this principle: Coca-Cola, Ford, General Motors, Hewlett Packard, Intel, Johnson & Johnson, Kellogg's, LG Electronics, McDonald's, Microsoft, Nike, Samsung, Shell, Toshiba, Toyota, and Yahoo (Formosa, 2012).

In time, the ability of design to deliver innovation and act as a driver of commercial success or social change is likely to increase further. But in the meantime, as members of a relatively new discipline, many designers still need to establish themselves as thinkers and consultants capable of addressing contemporary multifaceted problems. This, however, is not an easy task. On the one hand, the field is being shunned by other disciplines that claim to be better equipped to deal with complex business and social problems than designers. This argument is mostly based on the fact that many designers do not have the same investigative and analytical skills that other, more established disciplines have. On the other hand, traditional designers question whether this disciplinary evolution is necessary or even desirable, especially since many design programmes are still based in art schools. However, what many fail to understand is that design is an ever-evolving field that ultimately acts as a reflection of society. As the fabric of society changes, so does design. Therefore, in order for design not to be marginalized or left behind as a discipline, designers will need to find a way to remain relevant and collaborate with other fields. For many, this will mean stepping outside their comfort zone. But in return, this way of thinking has the potential to change the traditional design outputs and to produce outcomes that are no longer mere artistic refinements, but meaningful contributions to society, the environment, and the economy (Muratovski, 2012a).

2.5 CROSS-DISCIPLINARY DESIGN RESEARCH

The world is becoming an increasingly complex place. Negative trends like unsustainable population growth, ageing, global terrorism, and increased stress between people and technology are taking their toll on society. Other critical uncertainties like globalization, natural disasters, environmental depletion, and global epidemics are still present and will continue to be relevant problems in the years to come (Muratovski, 2012a: 46). Such multifaceted problems – often referred to as 'wicked problems' in the design community (see Rittel and Webber, 1973) – demand new solutions and unconventional approaches in order for us, as a global society, to improve or even maintain our quality of life as it is.

All of this impacts the field of design in a profound way, in terms of both practice and education. While the demand for designers with technical skills is still constant within the industry, society today demands a new generation of designers who can design not only products and communications, but systems for living as well. For many designers, this means a shift from providing artistic services to becoming strategic planners and professional 'thinkers' who can work across disciplines. However, in order for designers to rise to the challenge they will need to become capable of understanding human needs and behaviour, and they will need to develop new problem-solving skills (Muratovski, 2012a: 46–7). This leads us to consider a cross-disciplinary model of design education and research. This model is driven by two key motives: pursuit of results that can be applied in practice; and the search for inspiration that can lead to new, overarching research questions and exchange of methods and conceptual frameworks (Aagaard-Hansen, 2007). In line with this, I have summed up cross-disciplinary design research as an amalgamation of interdisciplinary, multidisciplinary, and transdisciplinary ways of working and associated research practices:

- **Interdisciplinary Design**: Interdisciplinary ways of working call for a collaboration between different areas of knowledge within the same discipline. For instance, two or more mono-disciplinary design teams working alongside each other on the same project. An example of such collaboration can be seen with Apple's iPhone, where product designers have worked alongside user experience/user interface (UX/UI) designers on the development of an innovative new product. One team has designed the form of the phone, and the other has designed the interface of the phone. Both designs, in this case, are meant to support each other.

- **Multidisciplinary Design**: Multidisciplinary ways of working call for a collaboration between two or more different disciplines when working together on the same project.

This might include a team of designers working with a team of medical practitioners on the development of a new line of hospital furniture and appliances. In such a case, both teams share the knowledge and experience from the viewpoint of their own disciplines, and the result is a co-designed outcome. For example, medical practitioners can help designers to establish the parameters of the problem and may work closely with them through all stages of the design process by providing the necessary feedback.

- **Transdisciplinary Design**: Transdisciplinary ways of working call for a 'fusion of disciplines' – a way of working in which designers have 'transgressed' or 'transcended' their own disciplinary norms and have adapted ways of working from other disciplines (see Lawrence and Després, 2004). This is a case when designers have achieved a sufficient level of knowledge to enable them to work across disciplines in new and innovative ways. This approach is most suitable for working on complex problems for which no single discipline possesses the necessary methods on its own to frame or resolve them. Working in this way requires an extensive amount of knowledge of research methods and methodologies and many years of experience. Designers capable of working in a transdisciplinary mode will be able not only to work in cross-disciplinary teams, but also to lead them (Muratovski, 2011b).

The benefits of transdiciplinarity are already recognized within the field of design (see Cutler, 2009). For example, this approach can provide a systematic and comprehensive theoretical framework for the definition and analysis of various social, economic, political, environmental, and institutional factors influencing design. Nevertheless, a working model of how transdisciplinary design can be framed within design practice and design education is still not fully developed (Muratovski, 2011a). As the complexity of this research model requires a high level of academic proficiency and institutional support, the only place where it can be nurtured further, at least at this stage, is within design education – specifically, doctoral education in design. However, even in this case, there are several steps that need to be followed first.

2.6 CROSS-DISCIPLINARY DESIGN EDUCATION

Design is changing from a craft-oriented profession whose emphasis is on individual creativity and commerce, into a discipline that is robust and committed to conceptualization, configuration, and the implementation of new ideas. Integration of knowledge from other disciplines is particularly important in this process. This, however, does not mean that design should abandon its heritage. Successful design – as Friedman (2002) argues – is a merger between crafts-oriented and interpretative ways of working with scientific knowledge about people, information, and society. That is why he encourages designers to form partnerships with other disciplines. According to Friedman (2002), designers working with social scientists will renew the idea that design is a process that serves both clients and end-users. Margolin provides a similar argument by stating that design is a part of 'a large social process' and that the study of design is a study of 'human action that arises from a social situation' (2010: 71).

Nevertheless, for a cross-disciplinary partnership to work, other disciplines will have to become more familiar with the principles that guide design, while by the same token designers will have to become more familiar with the principles of other disciplines – not necessarily as scholars in the field, but as professionals whose work is essentially informed by a wide range of factors (Friedman, 2002). What is more, Friedman (2002) also believes that in the future the distinction between 'analysers and creators', or between 'designers and researchers', will fade substantially, as everyone engaged in the process of defining, planning, and configuring artifacts and systems will be considered as 'designers' and 'researchers'. In line with this, Friedman also argues that design is an integrative discipline that already sits at the intersection of several large fields:

> In one dimension, design is a field of thinking and pure research. In another, it is a field of practice and applied research. When applications are used to solve specific problems in a specific setting, it is a field of clinical research. (2003: 508)

Furthermore, Friedman also argues that design can be placed within six general domains: Natural Sciences; Humanities and Liberal Arts; Social and Behavioural Sciences; Human Professions and Services; Creative and Applied Arts; and Technology and Engineering (see Figure 2.2).

Design can incorporate some or all of these domains in various capacities depending on the needs of the project. For example, from one perspective, design can be seen as a field of practice and applied research; from another, it can be seen as a field of thinking and scientific research – and often, these two perspectives cross over (Friedman, 2003: 508). Then again, Buchanan (1999) argues that the right approach is finding a balance between research and practice as the strength of design research is not in developing theory alone, but in developing the proper relationship between theory and practice.

Given the complexity of the above-mentioned issues, Friedman (2002) also argues that we need a new paradigm for design education. As the transition of design from an arts and crafts practice to a discipline driven by theory and research is becoming increasingly visible, so is the need to introduce different models of design education. As many design tasks involve dealing with 'complex adaptive systems', a 'design science' approach to design education will be able to address those developments in the field. By design science, Friedman (2002) refers to a model of technical or social science that focuses on how to do things and accomplish goals. As such, sciences of this nature emerge when skills-based professions move from traditional 'rules of thumb' or 'trial-and-error' methods to the use of theory and scientific method (Friedman, 2002).

Terence Love (2001) also argues that educating designers to be able to address 'non-routine situations' implies more than teaching creative thinking. Designing across disciplines requires skills and cognitive attributes that will enable the individual to draw on material developed in other disciplines at a professional level. In addition to this, he proposes that the very nature of cross-disciplinary design requires designers to have a high level of commercially-based professional skills and cognitive understanding across a wide area of disciplines. This cannot be

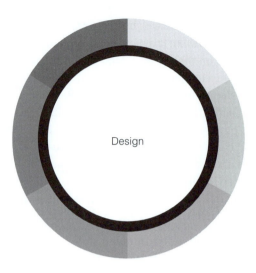

Design

Natural Sciences

Humanities and Liberal Arts

Social and Behavioural Sciences

Human Professions and Services

Creative and Applied Arts

Technology and Engineering

Figure 2.2 Illustration of Friedman's model of design

taught within the 'traditional' model of design education, as cross-disciplinarity requires an advanced theoretical and cognitive model of education that brings together research methods and methodologies, theories, and findings of a wide range of disciplines (Love, 2001).

Considering that the field of design does not have a formally established cross-disciplinary model of education and research, for a similar model we can look to the health sector. The health sector covers a broad range of different areas of knowledge and successfully brings together diverse types of professional practitioners with equally diverse types of researchers. A cross-disciplinary model of working there has been introduced on a sequential level – beginning from an inter-disciplinary point of view and then moving on to a transdisciplinary model in a step-by-step process. In this model researchers gradually move in the direction of integration and practical application (Aagaard-Hansen and Ouma, 2002; Rosenfield, 1992). If design students follow this model of education from an undergraduate level to a postgraduate level, then by the time of doctoral graduation they will have developed a high level of cross-disciplinary skills that can enable them to generate new knowledge within the field of design and even lead diverse research teams (Muratovski, 2011a, 2011b).

2.7 THE CHALLENGES OF CROSS-DISCIPLINARY PRACTICE

Regardless of the benefits of cross-disciplinary research, implementing this in practice can be challenging. In the process, designers may encounter problems establishing collaboration with other researchers due to lack of knowledge of other disciplines, divergent standards, different methodological approaches, or simply due to negative attitudes and prejudices (Muratovski, 2011a, 2011b). As these issues are general in nature, the same problems can be found among other disciplines (see Aagaard-Hansen, 2007). Some of these issues include the following: Quantitative vs. Qualitative Methods; Closed vs. Open Research Approach; Objectivity vs. Subjectivity; and Causality vs. Description, as described below.

- **Quantitative vs. Qualitative Methods**: For researchers accustomed to working within particular discourses, it can be difficult to come to terms with alternative research approaches. For example, difference in data collection methods is usually the first and the most obvious issue that is raised. Each research group may consider 'their' method to be the only appropriate way of gathering data in a particular situation. Therefore a cross-disciplinary team will first need to reach an initial, common understanding that the data collection methods need to derive from the character of the research questions, and not by personal preferences.

- **Closed vs. Open Research Approach**: The choice of data collection methods is directly linked to the degree of openness of the research itself. If the aim of the research is to end up with a concise figure describing a certain occurrence (e.g. a combination of variables), then a closed approach is needed. If the aim is obtaining a balanced picture of a phenomenon, then a more open approach is suitable. Both approaches are appropriate under certain circumstances – the first when exploring tangible, quantified correlations between different variables, and the second when the main aim is the provision of a multi-faceted and overarching description of the new field. The closed approach is necessarily based on the researchers' preconceived categorization, while the open approach is trying to avoid exactly that, and to allow the categories to emerge from the data. Both approaches are valid, depending on the circumstances. The challenge here is agreeing on what research approach is the right approach for a particular research problem.

- **Objectivity vs. Subjectivity**: The open approach can also be described as a subjective approach. Designers, similarly to anthropologists, function as their own data collection instruments and they allow themselves a greater degree of freedom when it comes to introducing changes in the research process, or interpreting the data. From the perspective of researchers who apply controlled, quantifiable research methods, this often causes distrust in the objectivity of the data produced, as they find it difficult to draw a line between the scientific findings and the researcher's personal opinions. In return, this position causes scepticism in the eyes of qualitative researchers, as their scientific position acknowledges subjectivity as a basic precondition for research. The challenge in the cross-disciplinary collaboration will be in finding the right balance between the subjectivity and objectivity in research.

- **Causality vs. Description**: Descriptive research, on one hand, is aimed at describing phenomena 'as they are'. For example, this includes studies that document behavioural patterns in a certain population, or studies of cultural practices of certain ethnic groups. On the other hand, causal research tries to illuminate specific relationships or clusters of interactions that activate particular behaviours or elicit such practices. Notwithstanding the importance of both ventures, this is an area where the two scientific discourses often differ (Muratovski, 2012a, 2012b).

These are only some of the challenges of cross-disciplinary research. Other issues can range from problems of terminology, conflicting evaluation procedures, and different ways of reporting research (Aagaard-Hansen, 2007; Muratovski, 2011b). Then again, many potential challenges can be addressed by applying several practical solutions. As an obvious first step, cross-disciplinary teams first need to obtain 'mutual knowledge' about their own disciplines. Insight into the basics of discipline-specific methodologies, theoretical and historical aspects of the various disciplinary discourses can be helpful in the process of understanding and respecting the position of other disciplines (Aagaard-Hansen, 2007).

Due to its complex nature, the management of cross-disciplinary research poses another challenge. Like many things in life, research is influenced by power and status. Research projects can be seen as 'battlefields' of individuals as well as disciplines. Historically, some disciplines have been perceived as being more 'powerful' than others – either because of access to funds or by virtue of status. In return, disciplinary boundaries are often propped up by attitudes rather than reason. The question of 'who decides what to study' within a cross-disciplinary research team is often one of power balance. Negotiating this balance is perhaps the main objective of research managers or principal investigators, followed by their ability to create and maintain a working environment in which synergism between the disciplines can blossom (Aagaard-Hansen, 2007; Muratovski, 2011a, 2011b).

2.8 CONCLUSION

In the nineteenth and early twentieth centuries, design was meant to be used as a tool to make products and communications more appealing to the masses, either through beautification or by improved functionality. Things are somewhat different today, and design is increasingly being seen as a strategic resource of broader significance. This has happened due to the introduction of research within the field of design and the willingness of some to look beyond the constraints of their own profession and challenge existing conventions. Nevertheless, for many others, design is still perceived as a kind of 'mythical gift' that allows designers to provide creative solutions in a consumer-driven marketplace. While some might find this appealing, the mystique that surrounds the notion of how design works puts into question the accountability, responsibility, and validity of the profession (Swann, 2002: 49; see also Buchanan, 1998: 63–6).

Given that design is an interdisciplinary profession aimed at serving different needs, designers are now expected to work in multi-disciplinary teams whose nature and consistency changes according to the nature of the projects. Also, in order to progress higher within their profession, or within other corporate echelons, designers will need to demonstrate higher integrative skills. This means that they will need to learn more things than they once had to in order to remain competitive and in demand (Friedman, 2012: 144).

The difference between design education today and design education over the past century is that now, in a post-industrial economy, designers are expected to replace the old ways of working based on common sense, trial-and-error, and personal experience, with new ones based on strategy modelling, simulations, decision theory, and systems thinking (Friedman, 2012: 149). Therefore, in order for designers to work successfully in increasingly complex environments and contemporary economies, in addition to their general technical skills they will also need to gain a range of new research skills – hence the need for new knowledge that can transcend disciplines.

Cross-disciplinary research comes in many forms, ranging from quantitative market research to personal interviews, experimental design analysis, and qualitative research. The great benefit of cross-disciplinary research is that it can help designers to gain a keen understanding of various phenomena, people, cultures, and belief systems – and this kind of knowledge can be indispensable in the real world. As such, cross-disciplinary research represents a willingness to look beyond the immediate concern of crafting a project, as well as openness towards integrating new insights to both design and industry (see Ireland, 2003; Zimmerman, 2003). For example, cross-disciplinary research can challenge existing assumptions and provide a sound and up-to-date overview of potential business development opportunities. This type of research can provide business entrepreneurs with directions that are often new and important – directions that may not be identified within mono-disciplinary environments (Cooper and Press, 2006).

The need for more designers with cross-disciplinary research skills is even more evident if we take into account that a great deal of the corporate research that can be classified as design research is already carried out by experts who were not trained as designers. Google, Microsoft, IBM, Hewlett-Packard, Intel, and many other large corporations already hire doctoral graduates coming from fields ranging from electrical and software engineering to anthropology and psychology to conduct their research on future products and systems development, and this research is then used in the development of design briefs. This is obviously a downfall for the field of design as designers should be a part of this research and development process (Margolin, 2010).

In order for things to change, designers will need explicit, quality education, and experience in research methods. This, however, raises the need for qualified design educators who can teach research methods and guide integrated design projects and strategies, as well as integrate such specialized courses within university design curricula (Hanington, 2010). Currently, there are not many design academics that have such skills, but with universities increasingly demanding that their teaching staff obtain doctoral degrees, things will most certainly begin to change in the near future. As a result, making research an integral component of design education can help create a new generation of designers capable of introducing changes to the practice of design as well. This process is unlikely to happen overnight as the changes within the design curricula will need to be introduced gradually, but evolution of design practice through design education is inevitable (Muratovski, 2011a).

In spite of the complexity associated with this type of research, there can be many opportunities for generating new knowledge when researchers with diverse backgrounds begin working in a cross-disciplinary fashion (Aagaard-Hansen, 2007). The challenges and opportunities that I have presented here, albeit in simplified and polarized form, do highlight the need for relevant and innovative cross-disciplinary research within the field of design. Designers who pursue a cross-disciplinary model in their own education will be better equipped to work in complex environments, and in time they can even lead cross-disciplinary teams towards the pursuit of new knowledge (Muratovski, 2011b). Overcoming these challenges is certainly not an easy task, but it is not an impossible one. This book will hopefully introduce you to a number of techniques that can help you to achieve this.

2.9 SUMMARY

In this chapter I have examined design research and its role in the field of design. Here I have touched upon some of the different ways of seeing research within the design context and I have explained the need for adopting a scientific approach to design research. Furthermore, I have considered the potential for developing a model of cross-disciplinary research that can transcend the disciplinary bounds that are inherent in the typical monodisciplinary design practice and research. A review of the literature shows that such a model can be placed within a broader educational framework by bringing interdisciplinary, multidisciplinary, and transdisciplinary ways of working together. The proposed taxonomy highlights the benefits of this model for the advancement of the field of design and suggests the introduction of cross-disciplinary ways of working in design education and research.

RESEARCH ESSENTIALS

KEYWORDS

Research Problem
Research Statement
Research Question
Hypothesis
Literature Review
Glossary of Key Terms
Research Methods
Research Methodology

Qualitative Research
Quantitative Research
Visual Research
Applied Research
Triangulation
Multimethod Research
Ethics
Research Proposal

Learning about research and doing research is important in both an educational context and in practice. Considering that research plays an important role in the resolution of real-world problems, these are skills that will serve you for the rest of your life (Leedy and Ormrod, 2010: xvi). Learning technical skills such as drawing, modelling, or design software is also important, but developing critical thinking skills can be far more valuable in the long term.

Paul D. Leedy and Jeanne E. Ormrod provide a simple explanation of the value of research: the purpose of research 'is to learn what has never been known before; to ask a significant question for which no conclusive answer has previously been found; and, by collecting and interpreting relevant data, to find an answer to that question' (2010: xvi). I believe that, as a designer, the ability to answer such questions is far more important than the ability to make beautiful, yet meaningless things.

3.1 DEFINING A RESEARCH PROBLEM

At the heart of every design project lays a problem. The ability to understand this problem is paramount to the success of the design outcome. If you do not understand exactly what this problem is, then you will not be able to design a solution that can address this problem. Therefore, a clear definition of the design problem is the first requirement in the design process. The design problem is also a research problem, and what follows next is as much a research process as it is a design process.

As you begin the process of identifying a research problem, you will need to keep two things in mind: your problem should address a question that can 'make a difference' in some way; and the research should lead towards new knowledge in your field by finding new ways of thinking, suggesting new applications, or paving the way for further research in the field (Leedy and Ormrod, 2010: 45). When considering a problem for research purposes, there are several situations that you should avoid. For example:

- Research projects should not be used for achieving 'self-enlightenment'. Gathering information in order to learn something about a certain area of knowledge is different from looking at a body of data that can contribute to a solution of a problem. For example, learning about how something works or how something was built is not a research problem.

- A problem whose purpose is comparing two sets of existing data or calculating their correlation to show a relationship between them is not a suitable research problem. These are undemanding issues that do not require critical thinking. There is no 'why' question in these kinds of problems. Absence of an identification of a 'cause' frames these issues as statistical operational activities and not as research problems.

- A problem that leads to a 'yes' or 'no' question is not a suitable problem for research. Such situations merely skim the surface of the issue and they do not provide the call for a deep investigation that a real research requires (Leedy and Ormrod, 2010: 45).

In order for you to be able to identify appropriate research problems, you must already be sufficiently knowledgeable about your topic of interest. If you are not already familiar with the area that you intend to study, then you will not know what are the limitations of this area and what kind of problems need to be addressed. That is why, in an educational environment, large-scale design research projects are normally conducted at a postgraduate level when it is accepted that the students have already obtained sufficient knowledge of the field and are now able to engage in research to further the knowledge in the field. Even so, emerging researchers still need to demonstrate an awareness of the trends and best practices in their industry, read literature in their field of interest, attend professional seminars and conferences, and seek the advice of experts in their field (see Leedy and Ormrod, 2010: 47).

In addition to this, you will need to consider the following. If you are selecting a research problem for a postgraduate thesis, chose a topic that intrigues you and motivates you. The topic of your research should be based on something that you are genuinely interested to work on. Postgraduate research problems take a long time to complete, so work on something that you are passionate about and that you believe is worthy of your time and effort. However, you also need to consider whether others will find this topic interesting and worthy of attention. Your research should have a broader appeal or application and should not be based solely on your own personal interests (see Leedy and Ormrod, 2010: 47–8).

3.2 FORMULATING A RESEARCH STATEMENT

Once you have identified what the research problem is, you will also need to articulate this problem in a way that is 'carefully phrased and represents the single goal of the total research effort' (Leedy and Ormrod, 2010: 48). This will help you form your research statement where you can also explain your research aims and objectives. This statement should be clear and understandable to everyone, regardless of whether they are experts in the field or not. If you cannot explain in simple terms what the problem is that you are trying to address, the chances are that you still do not have a good understanding of what the problem is. Therefore, make sure that everyone can understand exactly what you mean. If necessary, provide additional clarification of your research problem (2010: 49).

To exemplify this, I will refer to John S. Stevens's dissertation *Design as a Strategic Resource: Design's Contributions to Competitive Advantage Aligned with Strategy Models* (2009), which was submitted to the University of Cambridge, UK for a Doctor of Philosophy degree. As it can be seen from the thesis title, his research problem is focused on investigation of design's contribution to competitive business advantage.

This is enough to give the reader an indication of what the problem is in an instant, but nevertheless, this is a rather broad statement when presented on its own. Therefore, when formulating a research statement you also need to think about the feasibility of the research project. At times some ideas cannot be followed through simply because they are too ambitious or impractical. That is why when you are formulating your research problem you will need to develop an understanding of what the limitations of the problem are. For example, some research problems might be overly ambitious or may require unreasonable resources for them to be investigated in terms of time, funding, logistics, or equipment (Leedy and Ormrod, 2010: 49). You can overcome this by delimiting your research and by producing a follow-up statement that explains how will you do this. What you can do here is reduce the problem to a point when the problem becomes feasible simply by setting the limits of the problem; or you can choose to focus on a part of the problem instead. For example, in Stevens's dissertation, under the section 'Aim of the Study' you can find the following statement:

> There is already much empirical work that describes the valuable contributions design can make to a firm, and the many challenges of managing design as a resource. Similarly, there are many theories and models of corporate strategy in empirical and industry literature. This study does not seek to challenge or add to these. The aim of this research is to consolidate and align these two fields. A clearer and more complete understanding of the relationship of design to strategy is valuable both in industry and to the body of empirical knowledge. (2009: 1–2)

This statement makes it clear what he intends to do with this study. Nevertheless, some research problems might be too large or too complex to be solved as stated. In such cases, it is quite acceptable for a problem to be broken down into several smaller sub-problems. There are several things that you need to keep in mind when doing this: for example, each sub-problem should be able to be completely resolved within its own framework. Even though each sub-problem is a part of a larger problem, you should be able to address them independently from each other. However, all sub-problems together must add to the totality of the main problem, without producing unnecessary information. You can include anywhere from two to six sub-problems (Leedy and Ormrod, 2010: 52–4). Following this principle, Stevens further elaborates on his research statement:

> This study seeks to align the many views on the strategic benefits of design capability for a firm, and to clarify the practical and conceptual relationships of these benefits: what does it mean for design to be strategic?

> To achieve this, the study will first refer to empirical and industry literature of both design management and business strategy to synthesize a consolidated view of the conceptual overlap between them both; that is, a set of design capabilities that reflect i) what contributions design is capable of, and ii) what is strategically beneficial to a firm.

Second, the research will attempt to validate this set in industry by answering: Are these phenomena observed in practice? Are they recognised as strategically important by providers and users of design expertise?

Thirdly, the research aims to demonstrate how this consolidated conceptual view can provide a rich description of design practice in a firm. (2009: 1–2)

3.3 FRAMING A RESEARCH QUESTION OR A HYPOTHESIS

Once you have identified a research problem and you have provided a clear statement of that problem, you should proceed by forming a research question or a hypothesis. According to Leedy and Ormrod, a hypothesis is 'a logical supposition, a reasonable guess, an educated conjecture' to the research problem (2010: 4). On the other hand, a research question is quite different from this in terms that the question does not offers a speculative answer to the research problem. The main research problem can be followed up by a key research question or a hypothesis, and each sub-problem can be accompanied with additional questions or hypotheses (Leedy and Ormrod, 2010: 56).

The hypothesis provides a tentative answer to the research problem. As such, the hypothesis directs your thinking to possible sources of information that will aid you in resolving the research problem. The research process that will follow from there is meant to establish whether your hypothesis is correct or not. In research, hypotheses are rarely proven or disproven. Instead, they are either supported or not supported by the research data. If the initial hypothesis is rejected by the data, a new hypothesis can be introduced. When a hypothesis is supported by the data, the hypothesis can evolve into a theory. A theory, according to Leedy and Ormrod, 'is an organized body of concepts and principles intended to explain a particular phenomenon' (2010: 4). Nevertheless, theories can still be challenged if they are contradicted by new data.

Also, it is worth mentioning that it is not uncommon for researchers to begin with a question and then to follow up with a hypothesis, or the other way around. In any case, hypotheses are more relevant to experimental research and research questions are more common in qualitative research. The purpose of both, in essence, is to provide the researcher with a position from which the research can begin. In the end, the findings of the research should be able to answer the research questions, or support or not support the hypotheses (Leedy and Ormrod, 2010: 56). Then, once you conduct a review of the literature in your field, you can further refine your research question or hypothesis.

3.4 REVIEW OF THE LITERATURE

Typically, research proposals and research reports have a section titled 'Review of the Literature' (or 'Literature Review'). The review is meant to describe the theoretical perspectives in the field of your interest and to help you familiarize yourself with previous research findings that may be of relevance to your research problem (Leedy and Ormrod, 2010: 66).

By reviewing the relevant literature in your field you will become well-informed about the state of the knowledge in your area of interest. Depending on the scope of your review, you can even become an expert in the field (Bell, 2005: 99). However, what this means is that you are not gathering or creating your own data but you are using existing data that someone else has collected, recorded, and analysed. In order to do so, you need to thoroughly study what is already known in your field, identify an area that needs further research, and then make claims based on your findings. This includes reading related journal articles, books, newspaper or magazine articles, and official websites, and then writing your own comments, reflections, and analysis of what you have read. Your claims should be reasonable and based on the available evidence. This is commonly known as identifying the 'gap' in the knowledge.

The scope of your research will determine how much you will need to read on a particular topic. There is obviously a significant difference in the amount of reading required when working on a PhD thesis, compared to that for a minor research project (Bell, 2005: 99). The most important thing about literature reviews is that they are meant to provide yourself, and the reader, with a picture of the state of knowledge in the field – even though this is only a temporary picture as the state of knowledge changes continuously. However, review of the literature is more than simply gathering facts about your topic of interest. First of all, a researcher needs to demonstrate that he or she has studied the work in the field with insight. A critical review, as Judith Bell explains, involves 'questioning assumptions, querying claims made for which no evidence has been provided, considering the findings of one researcher compared to those of others and evaluating' (2005: 100). Then, once all the facts are gathered, the researcher must select, organize, and classify the findings into a coherent pattern (2005:100).

3.4.1 TYPES OF LITERATURE REVIEW

Depending on the type of research that you are interested in pursuing there are several approaches to literature review that you can consider: Chronological, Historical, Thematic, Methodological, Theoretical, and Meta-Analysis.

- **Chronologically Organized Literature Reviews**: Chronological reviews present the findings in a sequential order. This means that the researchers review works based on the publication date, in which case the data is presented from the most recent to least recent. The purpose of these types of reviews is to show the progress in the development of the literature on a particular issue.

- **Historical Literature Reviews**: Historical reviews show an analysis of how theories and ideas in relation to a particular issue have developed over time. Although these types of reviews are similar to the chronological reviews, in terms that they too present the data in a sequential order, the focus is on the developments of historical trends and not on the publication date of the data.

- **Thematic Literature Reviews**: Thematic reviews present various themes or topics that are common across the literature. The purpose of the thematic reviews is to help the researchers examine various perspectives in relation to the phenomenon in question – whether this might be converging research approaches, methodologies, or findings.

- **Methodological Literature Reviews**: Methodological reviews examine various methodologies by which a particular issue can be studied. These types of reviews look at processes of, procedures in, or approaches to conducting studies in relation to the topic of interest, for the purpose of assessing their effectiveness and finding ways for improvement.

- **Theoretical Literature Reviews**: Theoretical reviews are reviews that are based on particular theories or reasoning. As such, these types of reviews provide an analysis of how various theories have examined or framed particular issues. Theoretical reviews are best used when the literature comes from a broad range of theoretical perspectives, or when the researchers want to criticize particular theoretical constructs.

- **Meta-Analysis**: Meta-analysis is used for conducting a quantitative review of the literature. These types of reviews are used for statistically summarizing results from other studies based on the same research question. Meta-analysis provides a useful technique for gathering information from a range of smaller studies over a period of time. However, these types of reviews are rarely used for purposes of design research (McAllister and Furlong, 2009: 22–4).

3.4.2 VALIDITY AND RELIABILITY OF THE LITERATURE REVIEW

Literature reviews can vary in the level of rigour that has been used in setting the parameters for inclusion of the material. The stricter the parameters, the more valid are the reviews and especially the conclusions and the recommendations that come as a result. Ultimately, a good literature review search should be replicable by others. Therefore, researchers should clearly outline the processes that they used to identify and collect the data. This, in return, will increase the reliability of the review (McAllister and Furlong, 2009: 24–5).

3.4.3 SATURATION

A common problem for novice researchers is knowing when to stop reviewing the literature. In theory, the answer would be never – as Leedy and Ormrod (2010: 77) point out – but from a practical perspective, the review has to be completed eventually. A good time to stop reviewing is when you come across repetitive patterns of information. For example, when you continually come across familiar arguments, methodologies, and findings, this means that you have reached a level of saturation and you can stop with your review of the literature (2010: 77).

Finally, at the end of your review make sure that you reference everything correctly and cite every source that you have used in a reference list or a bibliography. Once you have done this, the next step is to describe how you will conduct the research. I will reflect more on this further on in the book.

3.5 GLOSSARY OF KEY TERMS

In addition to the literature review, I also need to stress the importance of providing a glossary of the key terms that you will be using in your research. Often, terms can have multiple meanings and it may not be quite clear what exactly you mean by some terms. For example, even the use of the word 'design' can be quite problematic, simply because 'design' means different things to different people. In any case, people may not necessarily need to agree with your definition of the terms, but as long as everyone is clear as to what exactly you mean by the terms that you use, your research can be understood better and assessed appropriately (Leedy and Ormrod, 2010: 58).

The glossary of terms is something that you will need to include in your research proposal, and subsequently in your research report. When providing a definition of the terms that you will be using, you can use the following statement: 'For the purpose of this research, [the term] will be defined as [provide definition here].' Here you can use definitions provided by dictionaries, encyclopaedias, or by other researchers in the field. In any case, you will always need to cite your sources. You can include the glossary of terms either at the beginning of your research proposal and report, or as an appendix.

3.6 UNDERSTANDING RESEARCH METHODS AND METHODOLOGIES

For novice design researchers, and students especially, one of the most daunting questions is: What are your methods and methodology? When it comes to preparing a research proposal, this is the part that often presents people with most difficulties. This is also the part that reviewers most rigorously review. In order for you to establish your credibility as a researcher, you will need to be able to describe with confidence what kind of research you propose to do, and how you plan to do it (Moore, 2000: 39).

According to the *Oxford Dictionary*, method is 'a particular procedure for accomplishing or approaching something'; in the case of research this stands for conducting a systematic investigation of some kind. Methodology, according to the same dictionary, is 'a system of methods used in a particular area of study or activity' (Oxford Dictionaries, 2013b).

A simple way of looking at this is to think of the methods as 'tools' and methodology as a 'toolkit'. These tools (the methods) are various techniques of investigation such as interviews, questionnaires, video documentation, participant observation, or user testing. The toolkit (the methodology) provides an explanation to why out of all the tools out there you have selected this particular set, and what it is that you are trying to do with them (Madden, 2010: 24–5).

Here is an example. Imagine for a moment that you are good at fixing things around the house. In your shed or garage you may have a wall on which you hang all your tools. On this wall you have all kinds of tools for all kinds of jobs that might come about, from screwdrivers to wrenches and drills; you have everything you need to fix things around the house. Some of these tools you can use for most of the work that needs to be done on a regular basis, and others you can only use for specific things. For example, when you need to fix an electricity problem, you take a toolbox and you put in that toolbox all the tools that you may need to resolve that particular problem. If, let's say, you have a carpentry problem or a plumbing problem, then you will do the same, except that this time you will pick some other tools that are more appropriate for these types of jobs. In most cases you will probably carry around a screwdriver or a hammer, but not always. And in some cases you may need to use a tool that is only good for one kind of job.

As most things in life, learning how to do research will take time and you will need some guidance along the way. Therefore, think of this book as an instruction manual that can give you directions on what kind of tools you need to have in order to deal with some of the most common problems around the 'house'. Also, bear in mind that you may not have many tools at the beginning of your career, but as you become more experienced in doing this kind of work, and as you learn how to deal with more problems, you will add more and more tools to your collection.

3.6.1 WHY IS THIS IMPORTANT?

Often, when working on a design project or when conducting research, many of the things you do may appear to be self-evident and hence require no explanation, yet this is rarely the case. When you are conducting research at a university or at work, you may be discussing your ideas with your lecturers, supervisors, or colleagues in great detail and they will probably have a good idea what it is that you are trying to do and achieve, and why. Nevertheless, at any point you should be able to present your research proposal or research report to other people who do not necessarily understand the details of your work, or do not have a chance to talk to you in person about what it is that you are doing and why. These people might be external reviewers, members of committees that need to approve your funding, give you ethics approval, or permission to carry on your research, or they might be your clients. For example, you may need to present your research proposal or report to people who may not be research proficient, such as prospective investors or business managers who may not understand exactly what it is that you are doing, but the future of the project may depend on them. Imagine the situation in which the CEO of a major corporation needs to make a decision on whether to invest in a project based on your recommendations: How will you convince the CEO and the board of directors that you know what are you doing, and that this is exactly what their company needs? As Raymond Madden argues, an important part of getting beyond the anxiety of justifying your research is to explain clearly what you plan to do, and why. Accordingly, well-selected methods supported by a clear methodology can fortify your research and will put debates about your objectivity and subjectivity aside (Madden, 2010: 26).

3.6.2 HOW DOES THIS LOOK IN PRACTICE?

Let us say that you are a communication designer working on a brand development of a new energy drink. How will you approach this problem? While the primary consumers of energy drinks used to be athletes, a simple observation of the world around you and a basic literature review will tell you that the market has changed. Today, the primary consumers of energy drinks are teenagers and young adults aged 18 to 34. Further investigation into this area will inform you that 34 per cent of 18- to 24-year-olds are regular energy drink users, and about one-half of university students consume at least one energy drink per month in the hope of increasing their energy levels to compensate for a lack of sleep, or to mix with alcohol – at least that is the case in the US (Heckman et al., 2010: 304). So, in order for you to understand this market you may need to spend a certain amount of time conducting a fieldwork observation at various university environments, night clubs, various gathering places, shops where energy drinks are being sold, and so on. Also, you may need to conduct a number of informal interviews or distribute questionnaires, and take hundreds of photographs, or hours of video footage. In addition to this, you will probably need to identify what the leading energy drink brands in the market are and analyse their branding strategies, advertisements, and marketing strategies before you start making assumptions about how the brand you are working on should look and communicate its message. The choices that you will make at this stage will be your research methods.

Before you choose your data gathering approaches, however, you will need to be clear about what it is that you are trying to learn here. For example, how much time do you need to spend conducting participant observations? Do you need to spend one week, three months, or one year conducting fieldwork? Perhaps you need to commit yourself to one year of observations of youth activities in order for you to identify whether there are any changes in the consumption patterns during different seasons (summer break vs. winter break). Then again, it is very unlikely that in a corporate environment you will have the time to conduct such a lengthy study; if so, how will you conduct a shorter, yet reliable study, and how will you choose the locations for your observations? You cannot be everywhere, so how will you decide where you need to be? Also, since you know who your target audience is, would you choose informal interviews over formal questionnaires, or would you use both – and why? What kind of social, cultural, or local customs and values do you need to be aware of before deciding on what is the best way for you to interact with the target audience? How would you go about gathering data about the competitor brands? What is it that you hope to learn from them, and why? If you are choosing more than one research method, as will very likely be the case, can you explain how the methods that you have chosen relate to each other?

Having so many questions might be overwhelming in the first instance, but the more answers you have at the beginning of your research, the better. At this stage it is very important to know where you want the research to take you. The set of methods that you have chosen can help you get there, and the reasons behind them will define your methodology. Think of this part of your research as preparing 'a map for the research journey' (Crouch and Pearce, 2012: 53).

3.7 CHOOSING A RESEARCH APPROACH

In an ideal world, a perfect researcher will be familiar with the widest possible range of methods and will use them selectively and accordingly to different situations. In the real world, most researchers are likely to be familiar only with a limited range of methods (Moore, 2000: 101). What you need to be aware of is that there are many different ways of approaching a problem and collecting data. In this book I will introduce you to four types of research that are commonly used by designers who conduct research within a university environment or in professional practice: Qualitative Research, Quantitative Research, Visual Research, and Applied Research.

There are more research approaches out there, but here I will only focus on these four. In doing so, I will also highlight their characteristics and will give you suggestions on when and for what purpose you can use them. The main differences between these research approaches lie in their aims and objectives, and this can be seen in the way the data are collected and analysed. However, it has to be noted that even though these approaches may be ideologically different and will use different methodologies, they often share the same or similar methods of investigation.

- **Qualitative Research**: Qualitative research examines how individuals see and experience the world. This type of research can explore a range of social phenomena and capture people's thoughts, feelings, or interpretations of various meanings and processes (Given, 2008). The research focuses on situations that occur in the 'real world' (in natural settings), and these situations are studied in all their complexity. As such, qualitative research is rarely about simplifying things. Instead, this type of research recognizes that the problem in question has many dimensions and layers (Leedy and Ormrod, 2010: 135). Therefore, as a designer you should use qualitative research when you need to gain new or an in-depth understanding of a particular problem. This approach is most beneficial when you are dealing with unfamiliar situations or issues.

- **Quantitative Research**: Quantitative research, on the other hand, is primarily used for describing, simplifying, and generalizing things. A designer can use quantitative research in order to draw conclusions about a particular population of interest (or in other words, a target group of prospective users or consumers), or test various design features. Because it is not possible to collect data on the entire population, quantitative research is used for testing random samples from the population of interest. Once the testing is completed, the results are assessed and a conclusion is drawn in a statistical manner (Lewis-Beck et al., 2004: 896). Unlike with qualitative research, this approach is not meant for developing a new theory, but for testing or verifying an existing one, or for measuring specific attributes or characteristics, also known as variables (Creswell, 2003: 125–6).

To give you a simple example, quantitative research can tell you the proportion of people in a given population who prefer the colour red when used in a certain design, while qualitative research can tell you why. Or, if you approach this in another way, you can use qualitative research to understand the underlying psychological meaning behind various colours, while you can use quantitative research to identify what colour might be most suitable for a particular packaging or a product that you might be working on. By combining both methods you can often enhance your understanding of the problem that you are dealing with. Then again, depending on the situation, you may need to use only one of these approaches.

- **Visual Research**: The visual research to which I will refer in this book tries to analyse 'found' images and objects – things that already exist and have been gathered. I use the term 'visual research' for studying images, forms, and objects because they can all be studied based on their look or appearance. That is why I have grouped both visual and material culture studies under the banner of visual research. Therefore, for the purposes of this book, I will define visual research as a type of research that enables designers to look for patterns and meanings in all forms of media – both visual and material – and to critically examine images, forms, and objects ranging from illustration, photography, film, and advertising, to products, fashion, and architecture. Visual research of this kind can be used in conjunction with qualitative or quantitative methodologies, or with a combination of both. Material research, which can be used for studying the properties of the materials, will not be covered in this book as this is a type of research most suited to the field of engineering.

- **Applied Research**: Applied research is a type of research that enables practitioners to investigate and evaluate their own work (McNiff and Whitehead, 2012: 7). This type of research approach can be found in a number of different disciplines, including design. In the case of design, this type of research has been primarily adopted from the field of art and it is often used in a similar manner. This is the case because the design profession originally grew out of an applied arts tradition that used to bring artistic skills and commercial practices together (Swann, 2002: 50).

When it comes to design, there are two main areas of investigation: practice-based, where a creative artifact is the basis of the investigation; and practice-led, where the research leads primarily to the new understandings about the design practice itself (Candy, 2006a). Even though there can be some overlaps in the methods that can be found in other research approaches, applied research is significantly different when it comes to purpose. While the other three approaches are outer-directed, in that you can use them to gain an understanding of the external factors associated with the problem that you are trying to resolve, applied research is inner-directed. Its purpose is to help you improve your own creative work and/or design practice. The most popular type of applied research is action research.

3.8 RESEARCH TRIANGULATION

There is always a benefit in using multiple sources of evidence when conducting research. This process of cross-referencing your research is called 'triangulation'. This way of working can help you establish credible, valid, and reliable research practice. According to Robert K. Yin (1994: 92), there are four ways by which you can triangulate your research (see Figure 3.1). For example, you can do the following:

- **Data Triangulation**: You can bring together various data sources.
- **Investigator Triangulation**: You can engage different researchers to work on the same problem.
- **Theory Triangulation**: You can exam.ine different perspectives on the same data set.
- **Methodological Triangulation**: You can bring a range of different methods together.

Data Triangulation ——————————————————————————————— ▲

Investigation Triangulation ——————————————————————————— ▲

Theory Triangulation ———————————————————————————————— ▲

Methodological Triangulation ——————————————————————————— ▲

Figure 3.1 Models of data triangulation

In this book I will mainly focus on methodological triangulation – a research approach also known as 'multimethod research'. In the literature, this approach has also been referred to as 'multi-strategy research', 'mixed methodology', or 'mixed method research' (Bryman, 2006: 97–8).

3.8.1 MULTIMETHOD RESEARCH

Multimethod research is based on the idea that using more than one method during the data collection or analysis phases of a study can be more useful than using a single method (Schutz et al., 2009: 244). This kind of research approach can enable you to explore new theories or to test or generate new hypotheses by combining data in new and unique ways. The way this works is by using qualitative information to identify certain issues or phenomena, and then using quantitative research as a follow up, or vice versa – as it is often the case with visual research or applied research. The main benefit of using multiple methods is that this research approach allows for greater flexibility in exploring new ways of thinking about people, constructs, and events. Also, the use of multiple methods can enable you to simultaneously answer confirmatory and explanatory questions, which in return can allow you to generate and verify a theory in the same study (2009: 247–8). Regardless of this, in many cases you could still only use qualitative or quantitative research if you believe that this is sufficient for your research project.

3.9 ETHICAL RESEARCH

Ethical conduct in research is an important part of research both in professional practice and in academic life. Ethical standards are set in place to act as guidelines that are there to provide researchers with a direction during their decision-making process in all stages of the research process, whether that might be planning, conducting research, or publishing. Good understanding of these standards is particularly important in a university environment where prior to your research you are required to submit an ethical application for any research involving participants, and where you will need to adhere to strict codes of academic publishing when it comes to dissemination of your research.

The need for the introduction of ethical standards related to research participants was introduced and broadly accepted after WWII in response to the biomedical experiments that were conducted on prisoners of war. Over the course of time, these standards have been constantly revised and updated to ensure that the research participants are protected from adverse consequences. These ethical standards do not only take into consideration the wellbeing of the research participants, but also – where applicable – the rights of the parents, the agenda of the teacher, the vulnerability of the students, the political context of the school, and the privacy of the family (Larson, 2009: 3). The following list drafted by Kristen Larson, even though not exhaustive, provides a range of potential risks for a research participant:

- A sense of obligation to participate in the project (for example, students in classes, children, employees in their work setting).

- Deception that leaves out information that may impact the participants' choice to participate.

- Physical discomfort.

- Situations resulting in stress.

- A change in emotional state or mood.

- A change in physiological functioning.

- Potential loss of privacy, reputation, or dignity.

- Distress from being induced into uncharacteristic or unexpected behaviour.

- Being a member of a vulnerable population, including children, the elderly, people with mental illness, people with a history of abuse, people with chronic or terminal medical illnesses, people who are incarcerated, and the homeless. (2009: 6)

As a researcher, you must take measures to address these risks in your research proposal. You can do this by including procedures that offset the effects of the risk; provide a convincing argument that the perceived risk is not greater than that which the participant might experience in daily living; or provide a convincing argument that the benefit of the knowledge obtained will justify the risk (Larson, 2009: 6; see also Aguinis and Henle, 2004: 38).

In addition to taking ethics into consideration as to how research participants are treated, we need to consider how the research is being conducted and published (see Larson, 2009: 13–14; see also Aguinis and Henle, 2004: 44–6). For example, there are four common ethical mistakes in analysing and publishing data:

- **Data Fabrication**: Researchers should not be making any adjustments to the data without documenting this in their report, or filling in missing data with fabricated information in order to support their hypothesis.

- **Elimination of Data**: Researchers should not try to censor or eliminate data that differs remarkably from the rest of the sample. When such data is deemed as non-representative of the general population and maintaining this data in the sample may lead to incorrect conclusions, the removal of this data needs to be documented and justified in the publication.

- **Exploitation of Data**: Researchers should not make any undue claims or overstate the significance of their findings. While the media often makes sensationalistic claims, academic integrity requires that researchers accurately state their findings.

- **Plagiarism**: Researchers should not represent another person's work or data as their own, and they should always indicate direct quotes and cite their sources.

Academic research is generally undertaken with the hope that new discoveries will contribute to new knowledge in the field of interest, or contribute to the human condition and benefit humanity in some way. All academic research, regardless of its nature, must be driven by ethical considerations. This also takes into consideration the whole spectrum of what research involves – from the researcher's motivations for conducting studies, to the wellbeing, freedom of choice, and dignity of the participants, to the dissemination of the research through publishing (Larson, 2009: 2). The impact of unethical research can be damaging not only to the research participants, but also to the reputation of the researcher, to the institution behind the research, and to the academic field as well. Unfortunately, as Larson (2009: 14) points out, few unethical studies tend to become more widely known and better remembered than the multitude of quality, ethical studies. That is why credible research institutions, and universities especially, apply rigorous procedures to ensure that the research they produce and disseminate is of the highest ethical standard.

3.10 WRITING A RESEARCH PROPOSAL

In a university setting, and often in the real world, every research project starts with a research proposal that needs to be approved by someone – by supervisors, clients, or by a commissioning body. Often, many students and emerging researchers embarking for the first time on a research path see the research proposal as an 'inconvenience' that stands between them and the funding or approval to proceed with the research. Nevertheless, research proposals are a necessary component of any research endeavour, and they can serve as a useful tool for managing the research process (Moore, 2000: 29).

The approval of the research proposal is a confirmation that the researcher understands the problem and the needs of the project, and that the researcher has demonstrated a clear plan on how to proceed from here. Basically, a research proposal is an outline of what you propose to do. First, you need to think about what you intend to do research on. The next step is to explain why you would want to do this research: Why is this research necessary? To whom it is important? What do you hope to achieve with this?

Even though this might be obvious to you, you will still need to make an explicit statement for others. For example, for academic research projects you may first need to present a basic research proposal to the university in order to obtain an acceptance to a postgraduate programme, and then you will probably need to present a more detailed proposal to your supervisor in order to get an approval to proceed with the research. There are several reasons for this. Both the university and the supervisor will need to make sure that your research project will be appropriate for the degree that you have applied for; they will need to establish whether they can provide the resources that you may need; and they will need to be reassured that you have the skills required to undertake the project that you are proposing to work on (Moore, 2000: 30).

Obtaining funds from a sponsor is not that different from obtaining an approval from a supervisor. If you would like an organization to commit funds to your project, first you will need to convince them of the value of your research to them – or even better, provide them with evidence of this. Such evidence can come from prior research, from review of the relevant literature in the field, from official reports, from interviews with practitioners in the field, or from the results of a small pilot study. All evidence must be well documented and cited in full. Then, you will need to argue that you will make good use of the funds when you get them. In some cases, the funding body might consult external referees to review your proposal and to judge the need for this research, the validity of your aims and objectives, the methodology, and the required resources. Organizations do not like to take risks with their money; therefore, you will need to use the proposal to demonstrate that you are an expert in the field and that you have a clear plan for what you are proposing to do (Moore, 2000: 30–31).

Regardless of who you are preparing your proposal for, you need to keep in mind that this is neither an autobiographical nor literary work – the writing needs to be direct and to the point, and the language should be clear, sharp, and precise. Therefore, avoid providing any unnecessary and irrelevant detail. Also, do not make any personal or anecdotic statements. Basically, do not include anything that is not directly related to the research problem and its solution (Leedy and Ormrod, 2010: 117–18).

Whether your research proposal is meant to lead you to an academic degree or to some kind of funding, it first must demonstrate that you are capable of doing the work satisfactorily. This is your opportunity to show your knowledge of the subject, express your understanding of any related issues, and demonstrate your familiarity with the necessary research techniques. At the very least, writing a proposal forces you to think about important details of your research before you embark on a research path. The proposal helps you to put your work in perspective and acts as a framework for your research (Moore, 2000: 33–4).

3.10.1 CONTENT OF A RESEARCH PROPOSAL

There is no one set way on how to prepare a proposal, and some institutions and organizations have their own guidelines or templates that you should follow when submitting proposals to them. In principle, research proposals should be simple, clear, and logical. Here is a basic content structure that you may use when preparing a research proposal:

1. Title and Subtitle

2. Research Problem

3. Research Question

4. Knowledge Gap

5. Stakeholders

6. Research Implications

7. Research Methods and Methodologies

8. Ethical Considerations

9. Resources

10. Appendix 1: Glossary of Key Terms

11. Appendix 2: Budget

12. Appendix 3: Timetable

A research proposal begins with a title and subtitle. This is the first information that the readers see. Therefore, use a clear title that sets the theme of your study and a subtitle that is descriptive in nature. Then, begin by providing a brief summary of your research problem. This should be followed by a research question: What are you going to research? Be as specific as possible when answering this question. Then, provide some information on the gap in the current knowledge: Why are you going to research this particular issue? If your research is meant to have a practical application, then you will also need to discuss about your stakeholders: Who will benefit from or be affected by this research? Then, you should reflect on the research implications: What is the significance of researching this area and what are the potential social, cultural, environmental, or economic benefits? Once this is clarified, you should give details on how you will carry out your research by describing your proposed research methods and methodology.

When you are asked to give details on your research methods and methodology, what this means is that you are asked to explain what kind of research you will be conducting, and why. Methods are techniques that you use to conduct your investigation such as interviews, questionnaires, video documentation, participant observation, or user testing. The set of methods that you have chosen, and the reasons behind them, are a part of your methodology. Methodology is the idea behind the system of methods that you are using. Well-selected methods and clear methodology will make your research stronger and more credible. Then, once you have addressed these points, you will need to provide an ethics statement: Are there any ethical issues that need to be taken into consideration? If there are, you will need to apply for ethics approval prior to conducting the research. Following this, you will need to reflect on some practical aspects of your research: What kind of resources do you need in order to conduct your studies?

Finally, you can include three appendixes: one that provides a glossary of the key terms that you have used in the proposal; one that includes a budget line that lists what kind of funding you need, how much, and what for; and another that provides a timeline that shows how long it will take you to complete the research and what your key milestones are in the process (see Figure 3.2).

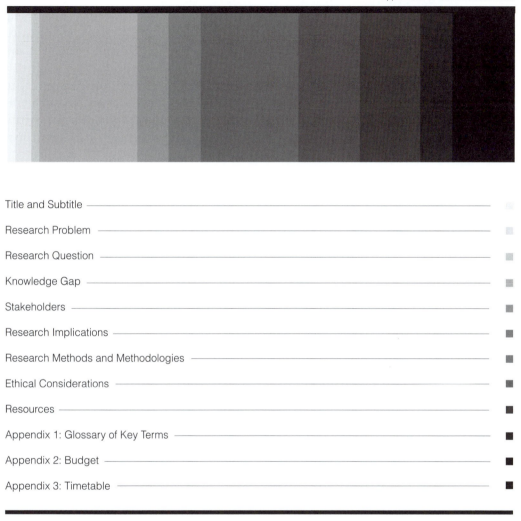

Approximate Content Distribution Ratio

Title and Subtitle ————————————————————————————————————

Research Problem ————————————————————————————————————

Research Question ————————————————————————————————————

Knowledge Gap ————————————————————————————————————

Stakeholders ————————————————————————————————————

Research Implications ————————————————————————————————————

Research Methods and Methodologies ————————————————————————

Ethical Considerations ————————————————————————————————

Resources ——

Appendix 1: Glossary of Key Terms ————————————————————————

Appendix 2: Budget ————————————————————————————————————

Appendix 3: Timetable ————————————————————————————————

Figure 3.2 Content of a research proposal

3.11 CONCLUSION

In every subject area – including design – there is a constant need for new knowledge and there are problems that wait to be resolved. We can contribute to the field of knowledge and we can begin to solve these problems only by asking the right questions and by seeking answers through systematic research (Leedy and Ormrod, 2010: 1). At one end, the pursuit of new knowledge characterized by building theories and conceptual frameworks is usually found within academia, while at the other end, the pursuit of practical solutions to pressing problems falls in the domain of industry consultants and professionals. Whether your research is theoretical or it calls for a practical application, you can still use the same techniques and manage your work in a similar way (Moore, 2000: vi–xi). This, however, does not imply that universities and industry work in isolation from each other. Universities increasingly try to produce industry-relevant research, and industry continues to fund 'blue sky' research projects that can deliver new knowledge that may eventually lead to new products or services. Design, as a discipline, is ideally positioned to produce research that can be relevant to both academia and industry.

3.12 SUMMARY

In this chapter I have discussed the importance of research in design and what you need to know before embarking on a research path. Here, I have discussed issues related to framing research problems, problem statements, research questions, hypotheses, literature reviews, research methods and methodologies, ethics, and research proposals. Yet this is only the beginning and there is much more that you will need to learn before you begin your research. Next, I will introduce you to various approaches to research and research reporting. In addition to this, I will also discuss how to apply research to practice, and how to use research for preparing more effective design briefs and design reports.

QUALITATIVE RESEARCH

KEYWORDS
Qualitative Research
Case Study
Ethnography

Phenomenology
Historical Research
Grounded Theory

As the field of design becomes increasingly complex and far reaching, the need for generating a deeper understanding of everyday problems is forcing designers to look beyond their profession and into other fields in their pursuit for answers (Muratovski, 2006: 24–5). The lack of qualitative research skills represents a fundamental problem in the designer's world today, particularly when designers want to make a genuine difference with their work. While the demand for traditional designers with 'old school' technical and artistic skills (enhanced with proficiency in design software) is constant within the industry, society today demands a new generation of designers that can design not only products, but systems for living as well. For example, modern-day concerns associated with global issues such as economic crises, globalization, terrorism, overpopulation, environmentalism, and multiculturalism cannot be addressed through conventional design practices alone. These problems demand new solutions, innovative concepts, and unconventional approaches based on new theories (Muratovski, 2012a: 45–6). For this reason, qualitative research can become particularly useful when used within a contemporary design practice that deals with complex problems.

4.1 WHAT IS QUALITATIVE RESEARCH?

Qualitative research is best described as an in-depth research. This is the type of research that you can use when there is a little information on your topic of interest, when the variables are unknown, or when the relevant theory base is inadequate or missing. In most cases, qualitative research is used for formulating general research problems, and for asking general questions about the phenomena that are being studied. Qualitative researchers collect numerous forms of data from a wide range of sources and examine this data from many angles. Therefore, it can be said that the purpose of qualitative research is the construction of a rich and meaningful picture of a complex and multifaceted situation.

According to Leedy and Ormrod (2010: 136–7), qualitative research should be used when you need to describe, interpret, verify, or evaluate something. For instance, you can use qualitative research if you want to understand the nature of certain situations, settings, processes, relationships, systems, or people. You can use it to gain new insights about a particular phenomenon, for developing new concepts or theoretical perspectives, or to discover what kind of problems exist within certain areas of interest. You can use qualitative research if you want to investigate the validity of any assumptions, claims, theories, or generalizations within a real-world context, or if you want to judge the effectiveness of particular policies, practices, or innovations. Examples might include some of the following questions:

- What are the problems that elderly people encounter in their everyday lives?

- How can we reduce the levels of waste in the metropolitan areas?

- How can we design a better healthcare system?

- How can we design better working environments?

- How can we create better recycling processes?

- What are the most effective ways for promoting healthy lifestyles?

While these research questions are loosely defined in the beginning of your study, as your work develops, the questions will become more specific and will formulate more concrete hypotheses. This is a normal part of the research process. As the study progresses you will gain an increasing understanding of the question that you are investigating and your perceptions of the problem will change accordingly. Since qualitative research is based on open-ended questions it is not always easy to identify the exact methods needed for each particular study ahead of time. Therefore, as the question shapes over time, so will the methodology. In addition to this, you need to be aware that qualitative research requires considerable preparation and planning. This type of research also calls for a solid understanding of any previous research related to the problem in question. You should be able to gain this knowledge by conducting a literature review (Leedy and Ormrod, 2010: 136). As you will see below, qualitative research can be used within a number of research frameworks that are in some respects quite different from each other. Yet they all have two things in common: they focus on phenomena that occur in natural, everyday settings; and they investigate them in all their complexity (2010: 135).

There are many qualitative research approaches, and as a researcher you should be able to select those that are most relevant to your research. In this chapter, I will introduce to you some of the most commonly used qualitative research frameworks in design: case studies, ethnographic research, phenomenology, historical research, and grounded theory. In most cases, these research approaches will be sufficient, but you can always explore other qualitative research approaches by reading further on the subject.

4.2 CASE STUDIES

A case study is a qualitative research framework that provides the tools for researchers to study a complex phenomenon by using a variety of data (Baxter and Jack, 2008: 544). This phenomenon can be any situation, occurrence, or a fact that is observed to happen. The phenomenon is studied in-depth for a defined period of time and within a set context. A case study can be beneficial if you need to learn more about a little known or poorly understood issue or situation – especially how it has changed or developed over time (Leedy and Ormrod, 2010: 137).

4.2.1 CONDUCTING A CASE STUDY

In order for you to develop a case study, you will need to use various forms of data collection to inform your work. While you are gathering information about the phenomenon in question, you also need to record details about the context that surrounds the case, including information about the physical environment, as well as any historical, economic, cultural, and social factors that may be of some relevance. By defining the context, you will be able to determine the broader relevance of your case study (Leedy and Ormrod, 2010: 137–18).

After you have identified the topic of your research, you will need to say how you will study this topic. This also means identifying what things you will not be covering in your research. This is important because a common problem when working on case studies for many researchers is their tendency to investigate a topic that has too many objectives, or that is too broad (in other words, lacking a focus). In order for you to avoid this problem, you should set clear parameters for your case study. There are three ways in which you can do this. You can set parameters in terms of time and place, time and activity, or by definition and context. This will ensure that your study remains focused and reasonable in scope (Baxter and Jack, 2008: 546–7).

Also, in your research proposal you will need to identify what your reasons are for choosing to conduct a case study research. Depending on what you are trying to achieve, you may choose to focus on a single case if you need to investigate its unique or exceptional qualities for the sake of promoting understanding or informing practice for similar situations, or you may choose to conduct a 'multiple' or 'collective' case study where you bring together two or more cases that are different from each other in some ways. This is beneficial for the purpose of making comparisons, building a theory, or proposing a generalization of some kind (Leedy and Ormrod, 2010: 137).

4.2.2 DATA COLLECTION

Data collection for case studies may come from various archival or documentary sources (relevant documents, newspaper articles, official records, physical artifacts, and/or various audio-visual materials), as well as from ethnographic research such as direct observations (observing people without interfering), participant observations (observing people while being a part of the group you are observing), or from conducting interviews (Yin, 1994: 78–80).

A very common research method in case studies research includes gathering information based on archival records and on documentary information. The use of archival records can be broadly defined as a 'source-oriented' research, and documentary information as a 'problem-oriented' research. A source-oriented approach is undertaken when the investigation of the source materials motivates the research. This type of research requires access to archival records of a particular organization that is the subject of the investigation, or a collection of documentation or artifacts about that organization which might be stored elsewhere. The problem-oriented approach takes into account an issue that has been examined by other sources and does not represent a first-hand record of the issue in question. Here, the research question is formulated on the basis of reading secondary sources. Often, this is a good way of establishing the focus of the study before going to the relevant primary sources, such as archival research (Stokes, 2011: 108–9). However, what you need to be aware of is that unlike documentary evidence, archival records can vary in terms of their usefulness from case to case.

ARCHIVAL RECORDS

The use of archival records is a method that can be used in many methodologies of research. This method is especially useful when it is used in case studies (Yin, 1994: 83), or in historical research (Stokes, 2011: 110). Examples of archival records may include:

- **Service Records**: Lists of clients served over a given period of time.
- **Organizational Records**: Organizational charts and budgets over a period of time.
- **Maps and Charts**: Geographic characteristics, such as borders, toponyms, or geodesy of a place at a certain period.
- **Registers**: Past records of names or commodities.
- **Surveys**: Census records or previously collected survey data.
- **Personal Records**: Diaries, calendars, telephone listings.

Archival research requires careful planning and you need to make sure that you know what you are going to look for, and why. This is a process that usually follows nine steps:

Step 1: Define your research topic

Step 2: Define your research question

Step 3: Identify the archival sources

Step 4: Define the range of your study

Step 5: Gather your data

Step 6: Collate the information

Step 7: Refer back to theory

Step 8: Write up the findings

Step 9: Provide a summary and conclusion

To begin with, first you will need to define the object of your analysis and make sure that you can access the records that you would like to analyse. Then, you will need to ensure that your question relates to the literature in the area. A clear and concise research question will help you to define the scope of your research better. Also, you will need to visit the archive early in your research project and find out how much material is available on your topic. Then, think about whether this material is manageable. If too little material is available, or too much to handle, then you will probably need to rephrase your research question. Be flexible with your expectations when you are conducting archival research. The material that you are looking for may not always be what you are expecting to find. Once you have a clear idea of what material you have available, redefine the range of your study. Make sure that you have the necessary permissions and that you will have enough time to study the material. Once you have surveyed the whole range of the material that is available to you, begin looking at the content in greater detail. Take careful notes of the items that you are investigating. Once this is done, you will need to gather your notes and any information that you have collected together. Then you will need to start categorizing your material. Compare your findings with those that are available in this area. Consider the following questions when doing this:

- Does the evidence that you have gathered support your initial hypothesis?

- Is there anything you have discovered that has changed your mind in regards to some initial theories that you have read?

- Have there been any surprise findings?

- Have there been any false paths that you have followed?

Organize your ideas around themes and relate what you have found to your initial research question. Provide a summary and conclusion, including any recommendations for further research (Stokes, 2011: 113–14).

DOCUMENTATION

Information based on documentary evidence can be used in any research methodology. This type of information can take many forms. For example, when conducting a documentary research, you can consider a variety of documents:

- **Corporate Communications**: Letters, memorandums, and communiqués.

- **Organizational Documents**: Agendas, announcements, minutes of meetings, and other written reports of events.

- **Administrative Documents**: Proposals, progress reports, annual reports, and other internal documents.

- **Formal Studies**: Other formal research conducted on the same topic.

- **Media Reports**: Newspaper and magazine articles, as well as other reports in the mass media.

You have to be aware that these documents are not always accurate or unbiased. Therefore, you should be careful to accept documents not as literal recordings of events and situations, but as points of view. For example, few people know that even the official transcripts of the US congressional hearings are often deliberately edited by the congressional staff and by those who may have testified prior to them being printed in their final form (Yin, 1994: 81). In most cases, the final transcripts include what someone believed that needed to be said, rather than what has actually been said – and this is a common practice in many places. Therefore, savvy researchers listen to audio recordings of such hearings or interviews and cross-reference them with the transcripts in order to identify any crucial information that might have been deliberately left out. At the very least, the benefit of having official transcripts is that you can verify the correct spellings of people's names and organizations.

As with any research, documentary research is an investigative process. Documentary evidence should always be used in context with evidence from other sources. You should avoid basing your conclusions on information that comes from one source alone. Once you have gathered information from a variety of documents, you will need to identify whether this evidence is corroboratory or contradictory. If the evidence is contradictory, then you need to examine things further and try to present an unbiased perspective of the situation by including additional evidence. At times, you can also learn new things not only from the content of the document, but also, for example, from for whom was this document meant, or who was on the distribution list. This can give you some insight into the audience for this document, or the communications and networking practices of a particular organization. And again, because things can sometimes appear to be misleading, this information should only be taken as a clue and not as a definite fact (Yin, 1994: 81).

Further on in the book I will introduce you to more data collection methods. At this stage, you need to be aware that each of these sources has its strengths and weaknesses, and that no single source has a complete advantage over the others. In addition to this, you need to be aware of three basic principles of organizing your data collection for case studies. These principles include:

- **Collection of Multiple Sources of Evidence**: Evidence that comes from two or more sources.

- **Formation of a Database**: Formal assembly of evidence that is distinct from the final report.

- **Chain of Evidence**: Outline of the explicit links between the questions asked, the data collected, and the conclusions drawn.

The incorporation of these principles will significantly increase the quality of your case study (Yin, 1994: 78–80).

4.2.3 DATA ANALYSIS

Once you have gathered and organized the data, you can begin with the data analysis process. There are five steps that you can follow in this process:

Step 1: Organize the details surrounding the case

Step 2: Categorize the data

Step 3: Interpret all single instances

Step 4: Identify any patterns

Step 5: Synthesize and generalize

The first step means that you should organize the 'facts' about your case in a logical order of some kind (e.g. in chronological order, or by topics). Then you need to identify categories that can help you cluster the data into some kind of meaningful groups. They can be based on anything really, as long as these clusters support your research question in some way. Then, you need to examine specific documents, occurrences, or other data for any specific meanings that they might have in relation to the case. Once you have done that, the data and their interpretations need to be examined for any underlying themes and other patterns that may characterize the case in broader terms. Finally, you need to construct an overall 'portrait' of the case, and this may include a list of conclusions and recommendations that go beyond the case itself. It is important to be aware that when only a single case is studied, any generalizations are tentative and must await further support from other studies such as additional case studies, other kinds of qualitative studies, or experimental research (Leedy and Ormrod, 2010: 138).

4.2.4 PREPARING A REPORT

A case study is an excellent opportunity for gaining a significant insight into a particular issue by gathering data from a variety of sources. This research approach allows you to answer 'how' and 'why' types of questions, while taking into consideration how a particular phenomenon is influenced by the context in which it can be found. Nevertheless, this is a complex form of investigation and it is not so easy to report the findings in a concise manner. Also, there is no one definite way to report a case study. You can either tell a story, provide a chronological report, or you can systematically address each proposition – it all depends on what do you have to say, to whom you are reporting, and what would they expect to receive from you (Baxter and Jack, 2008: 555–6). In any case, you can use the following structure to frame your report (see Figure 4.1):

1. Introduction

2. Data Gathering

3. Data Analysis

4. Discussion

5. Conclusion

In the introduction you should provide a rationale for the research project by explaining why this case study was worthy of in-depth study. In other words, you need to be clear on what the reader can learn from this study. Then you should describe the phenomenon that you have studied, as well as the setting and any other relevant details about the case. You should be as thorough and objective as possible. Following this, you also need to tell the reader about the information that you gathered:

- What have you found?

- Did you conduct interviews (and if so, with whom)?

- Have you examined any documentation?

- Did you use any media reports or official statements?

You will need to make sure that you have listed all your data collection methods. Then you should analyse the data and describe what the data suggest. This could include a description of any relevant trends, themes, personality characteristics (if applicable), and so on. In the discussion section you will need to provide your own interpretation of the 'facts'. Here you need to support any patterns that you have identified with sufficient evidence to convince the reader that this pattern does, in fact, exist. If some data contradicts the pattern you propose, you should report that. Your report should represent a complete and unbiased account of the case. Finally, in your conclusion, you need to answer the question: So what? In other words, you will need to explain:

- How does this study contribute to the broader field of knowledge?

- What can we learn from this study and what is its connection to the larger scheme of things?

Approximate Content Distribution Ratio

Introduction

Data Gathering

Data Analysis

Discussion

Conclusion

Figure 4.1 Structure of a report on case study research

Here you can compare your case with other cases and note similarities and dissimilarities. You can argue that your case either supports or disconfirms a particular theory or hypothesis. Also, you can use your case study to support a particular intervention or action, or to oppose one (Leedy and Ormrod, 2010: 138).

4.3 ETHNOGRAPHIC RESEARCH

Ethnography is a type of study that involves an in-depth, systematic study about groups of people by observing or participating in the lives of the people who are being studied (Madden, 2010). As such, ethnography studies social interactions, behaviours, beliefs, and perceptions that occur within groups, teams, organizations, and communities. The main aim of ethnography is to provide rich, holistic insight into various cultures and sub-cultures (people's views and actions), and the environments that surround them (sounds, sights, spaces, locations, etc.). This is usually done through fieldwork research based on detailed observations, participation, and interviews (Reeves et al., 2008: 512). While there are some similarities with case study research, the research approach here is somewhat different.

The roots of ethnography can be traced back to anthropological studies of small rural or tribal societies, often located in remote parts of the world. Early ethnographers would visit these societies, participate in their daily activities, and document their social arrangements and belief systems. Later on, this approach was applied to a variety of urban settings and contemporary social sub-groups that we may encounter in our everyday lives (Reeves et al., 2008: 512); it also applies to social interactions that occur in quite familiar settings such as workplaces, hospitals, and schools (Crouch and Pearce, 2012: 85). Some new developments in ethnographic research include 'auto-ethnography', in which researchers' own thoughts and perspectives from the social interaction form the central element of the study (Reeves et al., 2008: 512), and 'cyber-ethnography', in which the researcher can look at a range of social relations that take place in online networks and communities on the Internet (Madden, 2010: 175–6).

Ethnography can be a valuable research approach for designers. From a designer's point of view, we can study either various cultural practices that occur in particular societies that are of interest to us, or we can study the objects that are integral to those practices. For many centuries designed objects have been seen as important devices for understanding a particular culture and its practices, and this continues to be the case today as well (Crouch and Pearce, 2012: 84).

Let us have a look at the mobile phone as an example. The mobile phone was developed partly in response to particular cultural practices such as intensification of work and the increased use of the car. For many people it became important to be able to contact their work colleagues when they were out of the office, or they themselves needed to be available when they did not have access to a fixed phone. This triggered the idea of the mobile phone. First mobile phones were designed for use in cars. As the use of mobile phones became more popular and demand for them grew, smaller and lighter carry-on mobile phones were developed. As other technological developments such as wireless broadband and digital cameras became increasingly popular, they were also added as additional features to the mobile phone. Mobile phones have been designed in response to our changing cultural practices. With the help of ethnographic observations, mobile phones will continue to be redesigned to reflect any new developments in our lifestyles or personal preferences (Crouch and Pearce, 2012: 84).

4.3.1 CONDUCTING ETHNOGRAPHIC RESEARCH

Ethnography is a research practice that seeks to understand human groups (societies, cultures, or institutions) by placing the researcher in the same social space as the participants in the study. This is face-to-face, direct research that values the idea that to know others, one must do what the others do – or at least be present in the same environment. In many cases, this includes living with the participants, eating with them, working with them, and in general, experiencing the same daily patterns as them. That is why if you are conducting an ethnographic research, you will need to study people in their typical environment where they interact with each other in routine or even ritualized ways. In doing so, you should not try to distort or manage the natural setting of your research, or ask people to do things that they would not normally do. This is also the key distinction between fieldwork and a laboratory. Unlike experimental research, which will be discussed later in the book, ethnographers cannot and should not try to control what happens in their field situation (Madden, 2010: 16–17). There are many things that you will need to take into account when it comes to planning and conducting an ethnographic study, but I will highlight three key things that you should pay particular attention to: be aware of what type of communication you will have with people; be aware of the level of integration you have within the community; and be mindful of the duration of your study.

TYPE OF COMMUNICATION

In ethnography, talking to people is crucial. On many occasions you will need to explain your intellectual motivations for conducting research to lay audiences in order for your project to proceed. That is why you will need to be aware of any social, cultural, or historical politics at play that may be of relevance to your initial contacts. In some cases even issues of age or gender might pose a problem in establishing proper communication. Every part of this process includes a great deal of persuasion, negotiation, and pleading. And in order for you to be able to deal with any such issues, you also need to pay close attention to the way you communicate with others.

To work in diverse settings also means that you will come across a range of language and communication issues. When I refer to 'languages' here, I do not necessarily mean foreign languages. Sometimes language problems can occur due to the use of unfamiliar idioms or dialects, and sometimes because of jargon or slang. Some examples of this include Cockney vs. Scouse or Jamaican English, New Yorker vs. Texan, or Metropolitan Australian English vs. Rural Australian English. Many people can experience language differences even in their own households; for example, a generational difference in vocabulary often occurs between teenagers and their parents. These are just very basic examples, but when you are conducting fieldwork, you may encounter much more complex situations where you will not be able to fit in because of language differences. Therefore, as part of your fieldwork preparation, you also need to look into the language issue.

Regardless of this, even if you are familiar with the language you will need to be cautious about how you use it. While it is essential to know the language of the community that you will be investigating, it is not always advisable to use it. In some communities you may be commended for your ability to speak the correct language, or at least for your attempt to do so, but in other communities you may experience a resistance because you might be seen as using a language that does not belong to you. One simple example of this, to go back to the teenagers–parents situation, is that no matter how modern the parents think they are, they will always appear to be using outmoded or ill-fitting teen vocabulary in communication with their teenage children. And even if they do know the latest teen slang, it will appear inappropriate for them to use it simply because of their age and appearance. Therefore, what you need to be aware of is that sometimes the difference in language is there to mark the difference between cultures on purpose. Even if you do understand the language of your group of interest, this does not mean that you are expected to use it to its full extent – or at least not in the early stages of your fieldwork when the participants do not know you well enough. In any case, once you are out there, you will learn soon enough what is the appropriate thing to do (Madden, 2010: 59–62).

LEVEL OF INTEGRATION

When it comes to fieldwork observations, in some cases you will be an 'outsider' – a careful observer, interviewer, and listener. In other cases, you will be an 'insider' – actively engaging in the daily activities of the group that is being observed. In any case, you will need to take extensive field notes, audio/video recordings, and photographs, and collect artifacts (objects of relevance to the group). The benefit of engaging in participant observation is that you can gain insights into the group and their behaviour that could not be obtained in any other way. But be aware that there is always the risk that if you spend a long time conducting fieldwork, you can become too emotionally involved and risk losing the ability to assess the situation accurately. This means that you have become over-integrated in the culture that you have been studying. This is a real problem if it happens. In the literature there are many cases where the researchers became so emerged in the culture they were studying that eventually they went 'native' (a term used by ethnographers) and became actual members of that group, for better or worse. For a researcher, this is a highly undesirable outcome. Even if the study is eventually completed, under such circumstances it may be rendered as subjective and biased (Leedy and Ormrod, 2010: 139).

DURATION OF STUDY

Another thing that you need to take into consideration is the length of your study. While ethnography was once seen as a long-term research commitment where researchers could spend many months and even years living with communities (with 12–18 months being a typical stay), nowadays ethnographic studies are conducted over much shorter periods of time. These changes have been brought about because of funding constraints and time pressures in both university environments and within the corporate sector. In some cases, especially when it comes to conducting ethnographic research for corporate clients, you can even spend only portions of the day during a one-week period or within one month conducting an ethnographic study.

This so-called 'step-in-step-out' ethnographic research is usually conducted in a familiar setting, and that is why it can be done in a much shorter timeframe than usual (Madden, 2010: 80). Conducting this type of ethnographic research is normal in industry as companies often find it unfeasible to engage in lengthy ethnographic studies in the same way as academia does. Companies known for using this type of ethnographic research include IBM, Apple, IDEO, Design Continuum, Cheskin, Intel, Xerox, Herman Miller, and Microsoft (Plowman, 2003: 35).

Another element of this type of research is that these studies can be multi-sited, they can focus on a particular aspect or element of a society or culture, and they do not necessarily need to be as holistic as in the past. Nevertheless, they still share the same goal, and that is to build theories of culture and society; build theories of human behaviour and attitudes; and appreciate what it means to be human in particular social and cultural contexts (Madden, 2010: 16–17). Finally, the main aim of the ethnographer is to conduct 'cultural interpretation'. This should not include insiders' meanings, but concepts that are comprehensible to individuals outside that society. These concepts should be presented without prejudice and with an open mind (Riemer, 2009: 205–6).

4.3.2 DATA COLLECTION

As mentioned above, ethnographers gather information by direct engagement and involvement with the culture that they are studying. During their observations, ethnographers use field notes, informal or conversational interviews, cultural probes, and various types of visual research such as video recordings and photo-documentation, photo-elicitation, or photo-essays (Reeves et al., 2008: 513; Rose, 2012: 297–327). There are six steps that you should follow prior to gathering data:

Step 1: Select a community to study

Step 2: Identify a site where you can study the community

Step 3: Identify the community leaders

Step 4: Gain access to the site

Step 5: Establish rapport with the community

Step 6: Identify the key informants

The first step in conducting ethnographic research is for you to identify a community that you would like to study and to gain access to a site that will help you to gather data about the culture that you are trying to investigate. Ideally, this will be an environment in which you will be a 'stranger'. You can, of course, conduct ethnographic research in an environment that you are familiar with, or where you already know some of the participants, but you might find it hard to maintain your objectivity because of that. By being so close to the situation you may have difficulty in maintaining a sufficient detachment, or you may project a biased perspective on the cultural process that you are observing (Leedy and Ormrod, 2010: 139).

When you are dealing with a new environment, the best way for you to gain access is through a 'gatekeeper' – a person who can provide you with an entrance to the site and introduce you to the community. Ideally, this would be a person who has significant influence, or at least respectable and positive social standing within that group. This might be a person who acts as a group leader (official or unofficial), or comes from a position of social authority within that group. Then, after gaining entry to the site, you will need to establish a rapport with the people you are studying and gain their trust – but you must be open about your reasons for being there. At this stage, you need to use a so-called 'big net' approach, which means intermingling with everyone and getting an overall sense of the social and cultural context of the site. In time, you will identify 'key informants' who can provide you with relevant information and insights, and can facilitate contacts with other helpful individuals (Leedy and Ormrod, 2010: 139).

Furthermore, as a researcher conducting an ethnographic study, there are several ways by which you could gather data. For example, you could talk to people, observe people, spend time with people, or conduct cultural probes.

TALKING TO PEOPLE

Talking to people, in the context of ethnographic research, means conducting interviews. There are many forms of interviews. Some, which are less formal, are part of our popular culture and occur on television shows such as news reports, current affairs, celebrity 'chat' shows, documentaries, and so on. Other, more formal interviews are used in courtrooms and police stations for oral history collection or for gathering facts and evidence. And there are many other occasions where various forms of interviews are used. Ethnographers use both formal and informal interview styles to gather data: from casual conversations and structured interviews that follow a series of questions, to face-to-face questioners and surveys (Madden, 2010: 67–8). In either case, the way the questions are asked can be crucial. For example, in some cultures, direct questions can be considered rude and discomforting. In other cases, if the question is not direct enough, you may receive an ambiguous answer. Conducting an ethnographic interview is a balancing act. Often, you will need to ask open-ended questions and request clarification as the interview goes, but you also need to be aware that the conversation can easily get sidetracked. Then again, leaving the conversation to get sidetracked may sometimes inform you about certain issues that you were not aware of previously. As Madden (2010: 69) puts it, ethnographic interview is a complicated exchange that relies on many conversational norms and patterns in order to be productive.

The interview is a method that you can use to find out about people's ideas, opinions, and attitudes. There are different types of interviews, but for research purposes, 'interview' can be defined as a form of conversation between a researcher and a participant that is usually guided by a session of formal questions. There are two main reasons why you need to conduct an interview, or a series of interviews: you can either use interviews as a primary research method, or in conjunction with other research methods as a way to gather additional information about a person or some issue. In some cases, you will need to conduct an interview with only one person who is perhaps an expert in the area that you are examining. In other cases, you may need to interview several people, as a way of ensuring that the information that you have gathered is valid and representative of a broader group of people (Stokes, 2011: 114).

As a designer, you may need to conduct interviews for several reasons – from interviewing your client for the purpose of defining what your brief will be, to conducting interviews with participants in regards to the project you are working on. What you need to be aware of is that interviews can be very time-consuming, so only conduct interviews if they are absolutely necessary. For example, do not use interviews as a way of gathering background material on a company. This information might be readily available in some form on the company's website, or can be requested from the company's public relations or marketing department. Interviews should be conducted only for eliciting personal attitudes and opinions (Stokes, 2011: 117–18).

There are at least five types of interviews that you can conduct: structured interviews, semi-structured interviews, in-depth interviews, focus groups, or oral histories:

- **Structured Interviews**: These interviews call for an almost instant response on the part of the participant, and once a question is answered, the next one follows. The answers are normally spontaneous and require little probing. This is a rigid form of interviewing where you control the circumstances of the interview so that the data are collected in as consistent a manner as possible. Unlike other types of interviews, structured interviews exclude the possibility of further clarification and discussion (Moore, 2000: 121).

- **Semi-structured Interviews**: These interviews provide an opportunity for an extended response, but they are also limited by their format and scope.

- **In-depth Interviews**: These interviews offer a thorough examination of what the participants might feel about certain issues. These types of interviews are open-ended and assume a conversational manner.

- **Focus Groups**: Focus group interviews are similar to in-depth interviews in that they both engage the participants in detailed discussions about their feelings towards a particular issue or a set of issues. The main difference is that focus group interviews take into consideration how people feel about these issues in the light of other people's feelings.

- **Oral History**: Oral history interviews are used when you want to interview people about their past memories and experiences.

Different types of interviews should be used for different types of research. For example, structured interviews are most suitable for conducting a survey as part of a quantitative study. In-depth interviews, focus groups, and oral histories are best suited for a phenomenological study.

In terms of an ethnographic interview, I will focus on semi-structured interviews, as they are often the first step towards gathering qualitative data from your participants. This type of research can be seen as being 'half-way' between the rigidness of the structured interviews and the flexibility and responsiveness of the in-depth interviews. Semi-structured interviews are developed in a similar way as structured interviews, in that many of the questions are close-ended, which means that the participants have limited options for response. However, some questions can be left 'open-ended' in order to allow for further discussion. Similarly to the structured interview, the questions here are also asked in a predetermined sequence (Moore, 2000: 121–2).

You also need to be aware that open-ended questions work well only with participants who are happy to express themselves in writing, and are able to do that succinctly. These types of questions are also difficult to process, because you will have to establish some kind of system of ordering the results. Nick Moore (2000: 111) suggests setting up a coding frame that you can use for compiling the answers. According to him, you should look at the first 20 or 30 responses and list the answers. This will provide you with a sufficient range of responses on which you can set up the coding frame. Then you need to take out the duplicate answers or those that are essentially similar and refine the range of responses. Give each of them a code or a number, and then work through all of the answers, coding them accordingly. In this way, you will be able to reflect on the answers in a qualitative manner.

Finally, there are five basic steps that you need to follow when using interviews as your research method:

Step 1: Carry out preliminary preparations

Step 2: Plan the interview process

Step 3: Prepare your questions

Step 4: Plan the documentation process

Step 5: Reflect on the interview once you are done

Do your background research first. Find out as much as you can about the structure of the industry, or the company, or the problem that you are interested in addressing. This will help you to target the right people for the interview and to formulate your questions better. If you are conducting group interviews, make sure that you have participants who are representative of the group and can provide you with typical perceptions and perspectives for that group. Ask for permission to conduct interviews early in the project. Do not assume that everyone you ask for an interview will agree to be interviewed. It is a good idea first to write to your potential participants informing them about your project and asking for their permission to be interviewed. If you are conducting an interview as a part of your studies, you will also need to apply for ethics approval from your university.

Interviews can be conducted face-to-face, by telephone or Skype, via email, through letters, or by a survey. Think about what would be the best way for you to conduct your interview. Will you be able to attend the interview in person, or will you need to conduct the interview from a distance? Think about what might be the most convenient for your participants as well. Ask your participants about what are their preferred dates and times (and location, if face-to-face interview) for the interview to take place.

Prepare your questions in advance and practice them so that you do not need to read them, or at least so you can be prepared to ask questions on the basis of a bullet points list. Be friendly and courteous with your participants. Thank them for agreeing to talk to you. Do not use academic jargon in an interview. If the participants use a term that you do not understand, apologise and ask them to explain the term to you. Listen carefully to the responses and be flexible with your questions. Consider whether there are any cultural issues that you need to be aware of when you are asking the questions. People may perceive and answer questions differently depending on their cultural background. Begin with small talk and try to conduct a natural conversation – this may bring out more interesting and spontaneous conversation from your participants. Avoid asking leading questions – questions that may imply that you expect a specific answer. Listen more than you talk.

Record the interview. Test your equipment prior to the interview and make sure that you have spare batteries and extra tapes (for analogue recorders) or extra memory (for digital recorders). Before you switch on the recorder, make sure that your participants are aware that you are recording them and that you have their permission to do so. Even if you are recording the interview, you will still need to take notes. This will help you to tick off the topic areas as they are covered, or you can write down additional questions that come to your mind while the person is talking so you do not interrupt the interview flow. Use the recording to transcribe the interview. This will help you to analyse the interview in detail and to extract direct quotes. This can be a very time-consuming process if you are typing up the entire interview. You can also consider employing an administrator who can do that on your behalf, or you can use transcribing software. The transcript of the interview should be included as an appendix to your research project.

Once the interview transcription is complete, you will need to reflect on the information that you have gathered. It is important that you compare what you were expecting to hear with what was actually said. Has your research question been supported or refuted by the interview? Have you heard anything that you find to be surprising or unexpected? Does the interview endorse what you were thinking, or has it given you some new ideas? If you have conducted several interviews on one topic, compare the interviews with one another. Are participants in agreement with each other, or do they differ in their responses – and if so, in what way? What might be causing these similarities and differences?

While the interview can be a valuable method for generating primary research, you also need to be aware that in an interview you will only hear what your participants want to tell you. This is the main weakness of this method, because your participants may not necessarily tell you the truth or disclose all details, for whatever reasons, and you may not have any ways to verify their statements. In some cases, a good way for you to figure out whether your participants are doing what they are saying is for you to directly observe the people you study, or to interact with them by participating in their day-to-day activates (Leedy and Ormrod, 2010: 149–52; Stokes, 2011: 117–20).

OBSERVING PEOPLE

Observing people is a way of gathering data by conducting a form of visual research. There are two main domains that you should be observing: structures and settings, and behaviours and interactions. The first thing that you should do is to look at the place where you are conducting the research. Places often have the power to influence people's behaviour. Sometimes they do this in a subtle way, and sometimes in more obvious ways. For example, structures like corridors, tunnels, bridges, or laneways can channel people, while plazas and halls can disperse them. Elements such as light, shade, colour, texture, material, closure, or openness can also influence behaviour. From a point of spatial design, ethnographic observation of places can be especially important. In any case, this kind of observation can tell you many things about the people that inhabit the place. You can begin your study by answering the following questions:

- What are your surroundings?
- How is this place alike or different from other similar locations?
- How would you describe the appearance of this place?
- What kind of place is this?
- Are there any special features?
- What are the social aspects of this place?
- Are there any elements or settings in this place that can affect social behaviour?

Once you have defined the physical characteristics of the place, then you can focus on the human activity within the settings (Madden, 2010: 101–4). Here is a list of potential things that you can reflect on:

- How will you define the activities that you are seeing?
- Are people standing, walking, running, sitting, or lying down?
- How will you describe their behaviour?
- Are they still or demonstrative, noisy or quiet?
- Do they behave in a friendly manner, or are they hostile?
- Are they engaged in some kind of routine, or are they passive?

- Is it a socially intense or socially diffused environment?
- How will you describe their communications?
- Are they using gestures when they are talking, and how loud do they speak?
- Are they standing close to each other, or are they maintaining a distance?
- Do they use mobile phones frequently?
- Can you notice any patterns of behaviour?
- Are there any social divisions that you can notice, whether by class, in appearance, setting, by gender, or age?
- If so, how do these groups interact with each other?
- Is there anything that particularly stands out to you, and why?
- Can you identify any specific codes of conduct?
- Can you sense any kind of normative framework that shapes their behaviour?
- Have you noticed any events occurring?
- Can you observe any unusual collective behaviour that could be read as a special event?
- What, on the basis of your observations, makes this a special event?

As a designer, you can also observe how people engage with particular environments, artifacts, or designed objects, and how they use them in their daily lives. You can look for ways on how you can optimize or enhance a particular design, or offer an alternative (Crouch and Pearce, 2012: 101). Often the answers are already there, it is just that someone needs to notice them and apply them.

BEING WITH PEOPLE

When you are conducting a direct observation, you assume the role of an eyewitness and you are recording what you are observing in a systematic fashion (Madden, 2010: 96–7). Participant observation, on the other hand, requires you to engage with normal activities and routines of the people that you are observing (2010: 77).

Being with people in an ethnographic context means to be immersed in the culture that you are investigating. Yet this means a partial immersion, because you need to maintain your objectivity and impartiality throughout your study as much as possible. The key to a good ethnographic study is for the researcher to find a way to be close enough to the group and the culture in order to learn from it, but not too close because sometimes it can be difficult to step back and look at things objectively. Participant observation as a research method can be used when you need to learn more about the inner workings and the internal culture of a particular group or an organization. This method brings direct observations and interviews together, and may even include your participation in some activities as a 'member' of that group. Yet, regardless of your level of engagement, you will need to maintain your critical position as a researcher and provide an independent reflection on your observations. Becoming a member of the group is not an ethnographic study (Madden, 2010: 77–80).

For example, you may want to gain insights into the corporate culture of a particular company, the attitudes of their employees, and their practices. The best method for doing this would be participant observation – by spending some time in the company and interacting with the employees. By using this method you can examine their decision-making processes, their professional norms and values, and how their corporate ideology gets translated into their design and branding solutions.. The advantage of this method over the interview is that with this method you can observe the situation first-hand, rather than relying on your participants' reports, which may or may not be biased in some ways (Stokes, 2011: 120–21).

The main obstacle in undertaking this kind of research is access. Often, in order for you to obtain access to conduct such a research, you may be asked to sign a non-disclosure agreement that is meant to prevent you from discussing certain details of the work they do in public. This is understandable because companies normally do not like their competitors or the public to know confidential details about their strategies, or what kind of products or campaigns they might have under development. If you do manage to attain access to conduct participant observation in such a setting, then it is very likely that all the data that you have gathered will be reviewed and even edited by the company before you could publish or present your research.

Participant observation of this kind requires a high level of commitment on the part of the company that is the subject of your study. Access for you to do this can only be granted at the highest level of the organization. If you do receive access to the company, take care and show respect for everyone because it can be very obtrusive to interrupt people with questions while they are working. Also, you will need to be well prepared before you begin your study. Try to find out as much as you can about the company and the industry in which the company operates, including the status of the company within that industry. A good practice is to write a description of the industry and show how this particular company fits in. This is something that you can also use in your research report later on. Another thing that you can do is to draw an organizational plan of the company and think about whether you will study the whole company, or a section of it. Prepare a detailed plan and a schedule, and make sure that your research questions can be appropriately answered by this fieldwork. Then, you should allocate times to conduct background interviews with key personnel so you can ask them about their roles and activities (Stokes, 2011: 122–3).

During your fieldwork, you will need to take cues from your surroundings on how to dress and behave. You should not cause more distraction than necessary, and that is why it is important that you blend in as much as possible. On the first day, you should try to introduce yourself to everyone and schedule time to meet with your participants individually, at their convenience, and talk about their work. Be sensitive about people's work and ask them questions only during quiet periods and away from their typical work environment (a talk during a coffee break is usually a good thing), or in the office at times when they are not particularly busy. Take notes as often as you can, but do that in an unobtrusive way – after the conversation. At the end of the day, sum up your notes and think about how they relate to your research questions. Think about any gaps that you can fill in the next day. Repeat this process every day for the duration of your fieldwork, which in most cases can last up to 10 days. If necessary, redefine your research questions as you go along. After the fieldwork, spend some time reading and organizing your notes. Reflect on your experience and begin writing your findings. While it is important for you to write what you have found out, it is equally important to write what you expected to find, but did not. Go back to the literature that helped you frame your research questions and see if your fieldwork confirms the theory or presents new ideas. Discuss your method and the steps that you have taken and reflect on whether you could have found out more if you had used a different approach. At the end of your report include a diary or a log of your visits and meetings as an appendix. Remember, the report should be based on your interpretations and analysis of what was going on, and it should not be a simple chronology of what happened. You should reference relevant theories and other writings that have informed your original research questions while writing the report (Stokes, 2011: 123–4).

CULTURAL PROBES

Cultural probes can be seen as a collection of 'evocative tasks' that are used for obtaining inspirational responses from people. Cultural probes cannot provide you with comprehensive information about people, but they can give you fragmentary clues about people's lives and thoughts (Gaver et al., 2004: 53).

As such, they can be seen as a series of tasks that can be used for obtaining inspirational responses from people. Sometimes people cannot express what exactly they are feeling about something, or they cannot describe something particularly well; but they can show you, or sketch out something instead. This way of gathering information can be quite effective when it comes to generating a deeper understanding of any social, psychological, organizational, and ergonomic factors that might affect your participants, or others like them, in their daily lives. This method is particularly useful for conducting rapid ethnography when time and funding is limited.

In the field of design, cultural probes are often used for gaining 'contextually sensitive' information that is then used to inform and inspire the development of designs that are influenced by the users themselves (Wyeth and Diercke, 2006: 385). This design process is also known as 'user-centred design (UCD)' (Norman, 2013), or 'empathic design' (Leonard and Rayport, 1997). UCD research can also be conducted as a part of a quantitative research, and this will be discussed later on in the book.

This type of design revolves around the idea that users should inadvertently guide the design process, while the designers act as facilitators and interpreters of this process.

A simple way to explain this is by saying that empathic design understands the unspoken needs of the users and gives people what they need, without them asking for it specifically. By developing deep and empathetic understanding of users' unarticulated needs, designers can challenge industry assumptions or existing corporate strategies and offer new design proposals. This way of working can also help designers to move away from their own conception of what might be the ideal design solution, to a design solution that is grounded in the reality of the situation. As such, this is a paradigm shift – a move from individualistic notions of creativity towards an understanding of creativity as a social process (Muratovski, 2006: 87). The major strength of this design process is that it allows for a deeper understanding of the social, psychological, organizational, and ergonomic factors that can affect the end users. This process can lead to development of designs that are more effective, more efficient, or safer (Abras et al., 2004: 767). However, unlike user-testing research methods that are conducted in controlled environments and whose aim is to develop 'design for utility', cultural probes are conducted in natural settings and their aim is to inspire 'design for pleasure' (Gaver et al., 2004: 53).

There are many ways in which you can conduct cultural probes. Perhaps the most popular technique of engaging your participants with your research activities is by using participatory visual research (Mitchell, 2012). This way of conducting research calls for the participants to create or provide you with images. You can ask for the images to be accompanied by captions and descriptions; or even better, you can ask the participants to discuss the images with you in an interview (see Mitchell, 2012: 4–5; also Rose, 2012: 298).

In other words, this type of research is based on the idea of inserting images into what is essentially a research interview. However, unlike using images that have been produced by the researcher, or by using already existing images, this type of study asks the participants to produce their own images (Rose, 2012: 304). Images in this case may include participant-made drawings, point-and-shoot photographs, and video recordings, video narratives, collages, family albums, or personal albums. The mass use of smart phones with built-in cameras and the proliferation of the use of social media channels such as YouTube, Facebook, Flickr, and Instagram have made it even easier for researchers to conduct this type of research.

Participatory visual research has a number of benefits. Images often carry a great deal of information. While interviews can explore many issues, an image can often prompt a conversation about other things, in different ways. For example, one research that explored the importance of consumption to youth identity in the UK found that young people were more willing to discuss issues related to race, ethnicity, and religion when they were asked to discuss the photographs that they themselves had taken as a part of the research process. Also, this type of research can be particularly helpful in exploring everyday things from people's lives that are often taken for granted (Rose, 2012: 305–6).

Should you choose to use participatory visual research, you will need to provide clear explanations to two key stakeholders. First, in your research proposal you will need to explain why you want to use this particular approach for generating data. Second – if you have received an approval to proceed with this – you will need to reassure your participants that any kind of image, no matter how unprofessionally produced, is perfectly acceptable and useful. Also, you will need to ask them not to try to produce images that 'they think' are more interesting to you (Rose, 2012: 307).

There are many other things that you can consider when conducting cultural probes. To give you a better understanding of what to expect, I will introduce two examples here: cultural probe for children; and cultural probe for the elderly.

CULTURAL PROBE FOR CHILDREN

In the first example, Peta Wyeth and Carla Diercke from the University of Queensland (Australia) used cultural probes with children to discover insights into their interests and ideas within an educational context (Wyeth and Diercke, 2006). Their probe included the following activities:

- **Fun Technology Collage**: Asking children to collect and present pictures of 'technology that look fun' from the Internet, magazines, newspapers or other media.

- **Subject Ratings**: Asking children to rate subject areas such as reading, mathematics, art, and music on two scales: enjoyment and ease.

- **Classroom Architect**: Asking children to draw a picture of their current classroom and a picture of a classroom of the future.

- **Technology Gadget**: Asking children to 'design' and describe a gadget that they think can assist them with learning at school.

- **Brainstorming**: Asking questions such as: What makes science interesting? What makes science boring? How could I make science more interesting?

- **Excursion Day Plan**: Asking children to plan a study trip as an alternative to their next mathematics lesson.

- **Science Toy**: Asking children to create a new toy that would help them to understand their science homework.

- **When I Grow Up**: Asking children to describe the work they would like to do when they grew up.

- **My Journal**: Asking children to record their thoughts, ideas, and memories from school in text and in pictures.

The cultural probes took the form of an activity pack and were distributed to children aged between 11 and 13 at a local primary school. The children were asked to return the completed probes in a sealed envelope to their teachers the following week (Wyeth and Diercke, 2006: 386).

The cultural probes demonstrated that children were best able to provide insights when the activities provided opportunities to be creative and appealed to their sense of fun. The evidence from the retrieved cultural probes suggested that children were prepared to spend a significant amount of time engaged in the completion of such activities. The results provided glimpses into the mental models of the participants, including their mindset when it comes to the concept of learning, popular culture, and technology, as well as future career aspirations. Then again, some activities generated significantly more responses than others. Based on the responses, it became clear that children prefer to engage more in activities that require them to be creative and constructive. A particularly popular activity was the gadget design exercise. Here, a number of children showed an interest in 'high-tech' features such as fingerprint recognition, solar power, voice recognition, wireless communication, and artificial intelligence. Also, most of the participants expressed an interest in all-knowing machines that could answer any question posed – preferably a robot that 'has two antennae as ears so it can catch signals in the air', 'walks normally', and 'has artificial intelligence but it can talk and think for itself' (Wyeth and Diercke, 2006: 386). In terms of excursion planning, children expressed their interest in escaping from the typical educational environment – the classroom. In their probes children responded that they would rather go to a theme park, the beach, ice skating rink, and even to the Moon, than spend time studying in the classroom. This response, however, does not mean that children do not like to study. What this means is that they recognize that studying can also be fun and that learning can occur outside the classroom too. The classrooms of the future, on the other hand, included balloons, balls, beanbags, pizzas, a cosy fireplace, group reading areas, a trampoline, a farmyard, and a swimming pool. A distinctive element here was that children perceived classrooms of the future to be more social in nature than current classrooms. When it came to technology, children expected their classrooms to have desktop computers, laptops, and wall-sized interactive screens. Children also enjoyed thinking about life when they grow up. This probe demonstrated that there is also a large diversity of individual preferences: engineer, paediatrician, computer game designer, physician, journalist, marine biologist, and fighter pilot were included in the list. A particularly popular activity was the one that required children to rate subjects. Responses to this activity showed that children carefully considered the extent to which they enjoyed particular subjects and how difficult they found them. Their responses appeared thoughtful and in most cases there was a strong correlation between perceived ability level and enjoyment. The results were in line with their individual preferences, meaning that there were no subjects that were favourites for all. In contrast, the study also recorded that children had a limited interest in completing a journal and a collage, and that they did not like to answer brainstorming questions (Wyeth and Diercke, 2006: 386–7).

What this study found is that children see futuristic explorations and activities where they could work outside traditional perceived educational boundaries as appealing and engaging. At the same time, they appeared unwilling to engage in activities that have been proven to work in traditional participatory design groups, such as keeping journals, engaging in brainstorming exercises, and making collages. What became apparent is that children are dependent on support from others and that activities need to be self-contained. For example, children were not prepared to complete activities that required material from outside the cultural probe pack to be used (Wyeth and Diercke, 2006: 387).

In this case, the use of cultural probes as a 'minimally-intrusive' research method has delivered a useful contextual insight in the lives of children. The findings, according to the researchers, will be used to inform the design of educational technology for children (Wyeth and Diercke, 2006: 388).

CULTURAL PROBE FOR THE ELDERLY

While working on a project funded by the European Union, Bill Gaver and Tony Dunne from the Royal College of Art (UK), together with Elena Pacenti from the Domus Academy (Italy), have used cultural probes to study interaction technologies that could increase the presence of the elderly in their local communities (Gaver et al., 1999). They conducted research in three communities: an affluent district near Oslo (Norway), a large planned community near Amsterdam (the Netherlands), and a small village near Pisa (Italy). In Norway, they were working with a group of elderly who have been learning how to use the Internet; in the Netherlands, with elderly that live in a neighbourhood with a poor reputation; and in Italy, they worked with the local government that was planning to build a centre for the elderly. For these designers, the choice of cultural probes as a research method was a preferred method for investigating a common problem in developing projects for unfamiliar groups from different cultures (1999: 22).

Geographic distances and cultural differences were taken into consideration when preparing the cultural probes and their dissemination. Originally, the probes were to be delivered via mail to the participants, but the researchers made a decision to deliver them personally and to use this opportunity to introduce themselves to their participants in person and to explain the purpose of their project. By doing so, they were able to see first-hand where and how their participants lived, and to engage in informal interviews. Finally, the cultural probes were distributed and correspondence addresses were exchanged (Gaver et al., 1999: 26). The probes contained several materials: postcards, maps, a disposable camera, a photo album, and a media diary:

- **Postcards**: In each probe there are 8–10 postcards. The postcards had images on the front and questions on the back. The questions were framed in such a way as to provide a better understanding of the participants' attitudes towards their lives, cultural environments, and technology, and they were juxtaposed with evocative images on the front of the postcards. The reason why the questions were placed on the back of the postcards rather than delivered on formal questionnaires was because the researcher's believed that postcards, as an informal and friendly mode of communication, could encourage more casual responses from the participants.

- **Maps**: Each probe contained several maps, ranging from a map of the world to a map of their neighbourhood. Each map came with its own questions and small 'dot' stickers for marking locations. The questions included: Where have you been in the world? Where do you go to meet people? Where do you go to be alone? Where would you like to go in your town, but you cannot?

- **Disposable Camera**: Alongside the camera, the designers listed several requests. They asked the participants to take a photo of their home, of the clothes that they wear each day of the week, of the first person they see on each of the days, a photo of something desirable, and of something boring. They also asked participants to take photos of whatever else they felt like sharing.

- **Photo Album**: Elders were also asked to create a photo album that would tell their story by using 6–10 pictures. Participants were encouraged to use photos from their own albums, of their families, their current lives, and from anything that was meaningful to them.

- **Media Diary**: Each probe contained a media diary in which the participants were asked to record their television and radio use. They were asked to be as detailed as possible and to provide information on what they watched or listened to, with whom, and when. They were also asked to note incoming and outgoing calls, and to note their relationship with the caller and the subject of the call. The entries were supposed to be made daily, for the duration of one week (Gaver et al., 1999: 22–4).

Unlike typical designs, the focus of this particular project was not on the development of new commercial products, but on new understandings of how technology can be used to assist the elderly. This type of project calls for an exploration into functions, experiences, and cultural phenomena that sometimes appear to be outside the norm. Gaver and colleagues' main worry was that their designs would seem irrelevant or arrogant without having the insider view of the communities for whom they were designing (1999: 22). Therefore, rather than designing generic solutions that could suit the needs of an average user, the designers here were seeking to discover new forms of pleasures, sociability, and culture based on their participant's beliefs, desires, aesthetic preferences, and cultural contexts. Their final goal was to offer these communities the opportunity to appreciate their social, urban, and natural environments in new and intriguing ways (1999: 25). At the end of the study, a range of recommendations were provided, tailored to each community individually. According to the designers, the communities accepted the solutions and became readily involved with them, making further suggestions on how things could be improved even more. Their additional engagement and enthusiasm in the project came to the fore because they could recognize themselves in the proposals (1999: 28).

Cultural probes can be seen as a collection of 'evocative tasks' that are used for obtaining inspirational responses from people. As such, they are often used for gaining 'contextually sensitive' information that is then used to inform and inspire the development of designs that are influenced by the users themselves. What you also need to remember is that cultural probes can be quite flexible in terms of how they are constructed. As you could see from the examples above, there is no recipe on how these probes should look. It is up to you to choose what form they will take, or what function they will have – as long as they can give you some insight into the problems that you are interested in studying. Ideally, you will frame the cultural probes in such a way that the participants will find them relevant, engaging, and easy to use. Bear in mind that you should not overwhelm your participants with requests, as they might reject your probes if it looks like too much work is required on their behalf or if they feel that they are too time consuming. Therefore, limit the tasks to a reasonable amount.

4.3.3 ETHICS AND RESEARCH PARTICIPANTS

Please note that students and academic researchers alike are advised to seek the advice of their university's research office on ethical guidance. It is an academic principle that all research must be conducted with ethical considerations in mind. In the process of your research you also need to make sure that you have offset any potential risk to you research participants. Here I will outline some of the key things that you need to consider when conducting research with human participants. This includes informed consent, deception in research, debriefing, confidentiality, and anonymity.

INFORMED CONSENT

Every time when you are planning to conduct research that involves human participants, you will need to prepare an 'informed consent' form. This is a document that notifies the prospective participant about the nature of your study, the risks involved, and about the participant's right to quit the study at any time. If the prospective participant signs the form, this means that the participant understands the requirements of the study and your research can commence (Aguinis and Henle, 2004: 39–40).

The need for informed consent varies from institution to institution, and some institutions may not require you to provide informed consent forms to your participants if your research will not cause any anticipated distress. This type of research often falls under the categories of observation of public behaviour, such as surveys that do not require any identification from the participants, research that uses archival or previously collected data, or activities that would normally take place in an educational or work setting (Larson, 2009: 6–7). When an informed consent form is needed, you should provide the following information:

1. Names and Institutions
2. Brief Introduction
3. Study Requirements
4. Withdrawal Statement
5. Risk Statement
6. Benefits Statement
7. Confidentiality/Anonymity Statement
8. Incentives
9. Contact Details

First you should start by including the names of everyone conducting the research and their institution(s). Then you should provide brief information about the study and its purpose. You should also indicate what is the expected length of participation in the research project and what are the procedures that the participant(s) will encounter. Here you should also include a statement that the participant(s) can decline participation or withdraw from the study at any time and without any prejudice or consequence. Following this, you should outline any factors that may influence their willingness to participate in the study (e.g. whether the study is likely to cause any discomfort or any adverse effects). You should also outline if there are any potential benefits from this research. In addition to this, you should explain the status of confidentiality of the research or the anonymity of the participant(s). If deemed appropriate, you could provide an incentive for participation. In some cases this may include money, a gift or a voucher of some kind. If this is the case, you should highlight this information as well. Finally, you should provide the contact details of a person that the prospective participant(s) may contact if they have any questions or concerns (Aguinis and Henle, 2004: 39–40; Larson, 2009: 7).

Once the consent is granted, you should document it with at least two or three copies. You should keep one signed copy of the form for your records and you can deposit another signed copy at your institution if you are required to do so. You should also give one copy to the participant. In some cases, consent might be given verbally – as in the case of a telephone survey, for example. Questionnaires delivered via mail should contain a statement saying that the participant gives their consent by completing and returning the questionnaire. In case your research includes audio and/or video recordings of the participant, you also need to ask for consent to record the participant's voice or image – unless these are being recorded during ethnographic observations when a researcher unobtrusively observes the behaviour that naturally occurs in public and the individual cannot be directly identified or harmed by the recording (Larson, 2009: 7–8).

When preparing a consent form, you need to take into consideration the comprehensive ability of your prospective participants and you must write the form in a language that can be clearly understood by them. This means that certain terms may need to be clarified or simplified. For example, you may need to explain what you mean by confidentiality or anonymity, or you may need to use plain language to explain the purpose of your study. In some cases, you may need to conduct research with participants who are unable to give valid consent by themselves, such as children under the age of 18 or developmentally disabled adults. In such cases, you are required to ask for consent from parents or legal guardians on behalf of your participants. Similarly, in an educational setting such as within a school, the right of providing consent does not lie with the teacher or the administrators, but with the parents of the child (Larson, 2009: 8).

Then again, there are certain cases when the researcher wants to investigate issues related to parent–child relations, parenting practices, family conflict, or abuse. These are complex issues for which gaining consent can be very difficult or the consent process can bias the results (Larson, 2009: 9). In such cases, it is best to consult your institution on how to proceed.

DECEPTION IN RESEARCH

In some cases, you may choose to engage in a deception due to practical reasons related to your research. For example, you may need to intentionally conceal or withhold some aspects of your study to the participant; lie in order to manipulate their behaviour; observe their behaviour without their knowledge; or engage members of your research team to pose as fellow participants to help elicit specific actions in order for you to obtain candid behaviour. The use of deception in research is commonly used in fields such as social psychology, personality psychology, and memory studies for the purpose of obtaining valid results. In such cases, you can include a statement in the informed consent form stipulating that some parts of your research may or may not include a form of deception or that the nature of the study might be withheld; or you can ask for permission to use the participant's data or recording during debriefing (Larson, 2009: 8–9).

However, it must be noted that the use of deception in research is not without controversy. There are two philosophical positions on this issue: utilitarian (driven by practical reasons), and deontological (driven by reasons of duty and obligation). The proponents of the utilitarian position believe that actions are ethical if they can provide a greater good for the greatest number of individuals. The proponents of the deontological position hold to strict universal codes of moral behaviour regardless of the consequences of the actions. According to them, any attempt at deception, regardless of how noble the reasons for that might be and what kind of benefits may result from this, is by default unethical and should not be practised (Aguinis and Henle, 2004: 35).

Nevertheless, the use of deception has the potential to reveal to the participants some unpleasant aspects of themselves and what they are capable of doing. In some cases, the participants might behave in a way that they may not have previously thought themselves capable of – in a negative way – and such realization may be potentially very distressing. Therefore, as Larson points out, according to the American Psychological Association, deception should only be used when the following criteria are met:

- The deception is justified by the significant potential value of the research.

- The deception does not involve aspects of the study that would affect the participants' willingness to participate.

- Alternative methods that do not involve deception are not available.

- The researcher has made arrangements to debrief the participant(s) immediately after the study, and once they have been made aware of the deception participants should be given the option to withdraw the data. (Larson, 2009: 10)

DEBRIEFING

In many cases, debriefing the participants after the data gathering stage is important. A researcher needs to consider that sometimes the experience of participating in a study can impact a participant's life. Sometimes, people's lives might be minimally changed if they learn something new, moderately if they change their self-perception, or substantially if they are manipulated into unexpected behaviour. The debriefing process gives the participants an opportunity to learn the true purpose of the research, to be made aware of the results and the conclusions of the study, and to ask any questions they may have. Therefore, the main purpose of the debriefing session is to minimize the impact of participating in the study and remedy any possible misconceptions that the participant might have as a result of the study (Larson, 2009: 11; Aguinis and Henle, 2004: 42–3).

CONFIDENTIALITY

When dealing with research participants, it is also important for you to explain how you will be handling and storing their data. In some cases it is important that you keep participant's data or any identifying information secure from exposure. This means that you will provide a safe and secure system for storing the data, which will prevent inappropriate access by unauthorized people. This also means that you will not be discussing the participant's data in public. However, you can share the data with other qualified researchers who are trying to verify your findings and who intend to use the data for that purpose alone. In this case, you will need to keep any identifiable information separate from the data itself. Some institutions have a policy of storing the data securely for a period of five to seven years, after which the data is professionally disposed of (Larson, 2009: 12).

ANONYMITY

Anonymity is somewhat different from confidentiality. While in the case of confidentiality you will know the names and any other personal details of your participants (but will not disclose this information to others), in the case of anonymity neither you nor anyone else will be able to identify the participants. This means that the participants are invited to participate in the study without being asked to reveal their identity. This is particularly necessary when dealing with sensitive issues where the participant's fear of disclosure is high and could affect the honesty of their responses. However, in cases of concern for the welfare of the participants, confidentiality and anonymity can be legally challenged and the information may be sought and disclosed to other parties. For example, research with children and adolescents has the potential of discovering mental health issues, self-harm, family problems, illegal activity, or behaviours that might compromise children's health. Such information, for legal reasons, cannot be held secret and the researcher has a responsibility to report this. Furthermore, as Larson also points out, research has indicated that adolescents often expect help or assistance in getting help when such issues are revealed during the study. Therefore, before gathering data from a vulnerable population, researchers will need to determine what their ethical and legal responsibilities are and how any disclosures of this kind will be handled (Larson, 2009: 12). The informed consent form should also include a statement outlining what steps will be taken if abuse, self-harm, or harm to others is revealed (2009: 12–13).

Please note that ethics in research calls for a much broader discussion than the one I have presented here. If you are conducting research in a university environment, your university will have its own ethics policies that you will have to adhere to. This means that every time you would like to conduct research that involves research participants, you will be asked to complete an ethics application that will first need to be approved by the ethics committee of your university in order for you to proceed. This is a 'safety mechanism' put in place by the universities that ensures that your research and its dissemination will not cause any damage, harm, or distress to your participants.

4.3.4 DATA ANALYSIS

Data collection and data analysis in an ethnographic study often occur simultaneously. Timely write-up of field notes and fieldwork documentation is essential. The more information you can include in your field notes, the better. But be aware that this often involves estimation. It can be quite difficult for you to quantify the number of people that you have observed in a crowd, or to identify their exact behaviour, but you must do so to the best of your judgement. Therefore, in addition to taking field notes, you should also consider making visual documentation by producing drawings or taking photographs and video recordings. This is also known as 'visual ethnography'. But remember, images, videos, and even audio recordings and transcripts should not be used instead of detailed field notes; they should complement them. Without the context that is documented in your field notes, recordings on their own will be of little value to you, or to anyone else who will try to make sense of your study (Madden, 2010: 103–109). Furthermore, because the analysis of the data happens almost simultaneously with the process of data collection, you will need to bear in mind the following three steps:

Step 1: Describe the data

Step 2: Categorize the data

Step 3: Interpret the data

First, the gathered data is organized into a logical structure. You can use a variety of strategies to do that. For example, you can:

- Describe events in a chronological order.
- Describe a typical day in the life of the group, or in the life of an individual within the group.
- Focus on a critical event for the group.
- Develop a story, complete with plot and characters.

Once you have organized your data, you will need to identify the meanings and categorize them accordingly. This could be based on patterns of behaviour, regulations, and critical events. The final step is your interpretation – what is the general nature of the group and its practices? You can use an existing theoretical framework for structure and support during the interpretation process (Leedy and Ormrod, 2010: 140).

4.3.5 PREPARING A REPORT

Unlike most research reports that are written in an impersonal manner, an ethnographic report is often a personal, literary narrative designed to engage the reader's attention and interest. With this in mind, your ethnographic report will need to include the following information (see Figure 4.2):

1. Introduction

2. Rationale

3. Context

4. Description of the Setting

5. Description of the Research Methods

6. Analysis of the Group

7. Conclusion

First, you need to begin your report by stating your research question. Then you need to describe the nature of your study and explain how the study relates to your question. You can include here any theoretical frameworks on which you have built your study. Then, you can point out why this study is important to the field of knowledge. This should cover your introduction, rationale, and context. Proceed by describing the group you studied and the methods that you have used to conduct your research. Provide detailed information on what people do and say, how they interact with each other, what systems and rituals they have in place, and so on.

The purpose of the report is to place the reader figuratively in the setting, and to help the reader experience the situation as vividly as possible. In addition to this, you will need to highlight any patterns of behaviour or occurring themes that you have noticed. Also, present evidence to support your claims. This could include description of artifacts, conversations with group members, and visual documentation. Sometimes, for the sake of an accurate representation you will need to use the actual language that the participants were using when describing something. Documentation of culturally specific terms, dialects, and idioms can prove to be very useful knowledge. Finally, you will need to conclude by explaining how your findings relate to your research question, as well as to concepts and theories in your discipline (Leedy and Ormrod, 2010: 140–41).

In addition to this, I would like to point out that you can choose to support your written report with audio-visual material or a photographic essay – a curated series of images and/or sounds accompanied with some text that can help you to better present your findings. This type of material can produce two effects: analytical and evocative. To achieve either, or both, you will need to consider the relationship between the text and the recorded material (Rose, 2012: 317–27).

Approximate Content Distribution Ratio

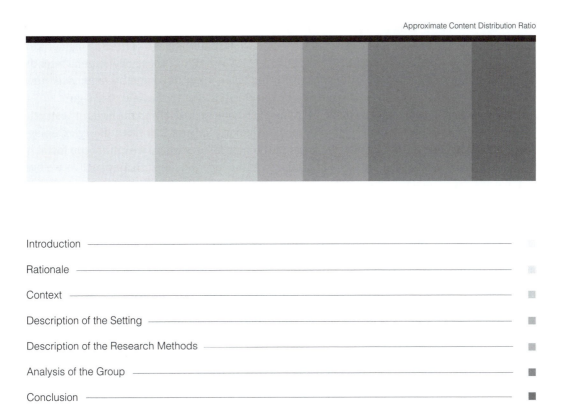

Introduction ⸺

Rationale ⸺

Context ⸺

Description of the Setting ⸺

Description of the Research Methods ⸺

Analysis of the Group ⸺

Conclusion ⸺

Figure 4.2 Structure of a report on ethnographic research

4.4 PHENOMENOLOGY

Phenomenological research is a type of research that attempts to understand participants' perspectives and views of various social realities (Leedy and Ormrod, 2010: 108). Explained in simple terms, you can use phenomenological research if you want to understand how people experience things and events. While phenomenological research is similar to ethnographic research in terms that they both gather information about other people's lives, the main difference is that this type of research focuses on individuals rather than groups. Here, the scope of the research is limited to experiences related to specific situations or events, with the main focus being the study of people's points of view about certain phenomena. The main question in this kind of study is: What is it like to do or experience [something]?

This could include myriad things. For example, in this way you can study the experiences of people caring for the elderly, living in social housing, managing a hotel, working at a

McDonald's restaurant, using an iPad – anything really. By looking at multiple perspectives on the same situation, you can make generalizations on what something is like from an insider's or a user's point of view (Leedy and Ormrod, 2010: 141). The study of these phenomena intends to examine experiences and situations that are often taken for granted and try to uncover new or forgotten meanings (Laverty, 2003: 4). So how is this relevant to the field of design?

In many cases, people today no longer purchase products exclusively on the basis of aesthetic qualities or physical performance; instead, they are looking for new identities, lifestyles, enjoyment, entertainment, or amusement. We are at the point in history where we cannot comfortably define ourselves without the presence of products. In the individualized society such as we live in today we use products and experiences to 'design' our own identity. We believe, consciously or unconsciously, that a certain combination of a car, watch, jeans, sunglasses, shoes, jewellery, mobile phone, or laptop defines our personality and even our individuality. We often use products that can help us express ourselves, define who we are, who we would like to be, and who we would like other people to think we are. In line with this, new consumer trends have followed as well. Now we, as consumers, even prefer to 'design' our own products and interfaces. That is why the industry today is readapting its delivery methods from mass-production and standardization to so-called 'mass-customization'. This new trend takes into consideration the consumers' desire to own and operate seemingly individual and customized products (Muratovski, 2006: 98–101). In return, whole new categories of products have appeared as a result of this re-energized material sense of wellbeing. Products are increasingly becoming 'dematerialized' as their value is being determined by the experience they deliver and by the story they tell. These new consumer demands have created a society in which the experience and the narrative behind the product are seen as more important than the product itself. As a result, products have become containers for stories, and designers have become storytellers (Holt, 2000).

If you are interested in working within this new and emerging concept of 'experience design', phenomenological research can serve you as a useful platform for conducting your research. While phenomenological research can be conducted as a separate study, it can also be used in conjunction with ethnographic research if more information is needed about a particular user base or a consumer experience.

4.4.1 CONDUCTING PHENOMENOLOGICAL RESEARCH

There are several research methods that can be used in phenomenological research, such as participant observation or focus groups, but the main method is the in-depth interview (Lester, 1999). This is a lengthy interview and can normally last between one and two hours. Participants are carefully selected and the sample size can range from 5 to 25 individuals, all of whom have direct experience with the object of your study, whatever that may be. In the case where the researcher himself or herself has personal experience with the phenomenon in question, every attempt must be made by the researcher to suspend any preconceived notions of those experiences. This can prove to be extremely difficult, but it is essential for the researcher to gain an understanding of the typical experience that others have had with the phenomenon without the risk of introducing any biased perspectives. A common problem here is that the researcher may interpret something in a way that he or she would expect to hear it, or may ignore some subtle cues that may lead the discussion in another direction (Leedy and Ormrod, 2010: 141).

Conducting phenomenological research on behalf of a commercial organization can often bring to the surface some deep issues, and can allow for voices to be heard that are normally ignored or rarely taken into consideration. But this is not always a comfortable experience for the clients, especially since this type of research can often expose 'taken-for-granted' assumptions or can challenge a 'comfortable status quo'. Nevertheless, phenomenological research can deliver valuable insights that can help shape the overall corporate strategy (Lester, 1999).

4.4.2 DATA COLLECTION

As mentioned above, there are several methods that can be used for collecting data in phenomenological research, but the main one is through interviews. Here, participants are usually selected by different criteria than those used to meet statistical requirements. The key is to find participants who have been through the experience that is the focus of the study, and most importantly they need to be willing to talk about their experience. The participants need to be diverse enough from each other, as this will enhance the possibility for gathering rich and unique stories of the particular experience (Laverty, 2003: 18).

According to David W. Smith (2008), the focus of the interview should investigate the following: How people experience things? How do they perceive these experiences? What meanings things have in these experiences? What is their significance? This is an unstructured interview in which both the researcher and the participant need to work together in order to arrive at 'the heart' of the matter. The researcher first asks the participant to describe their everyday experiences related to the phenomenon in question, and then carefully listens for meaningful cues in participants' responses, which can often be quite subtle. In this type of interview it is also important to look for what has not been said, or what has been said 'between the lines' (Laverty, 2003: 19).

Similarly to the ethnographic interview, the researcher needs to observe the participants' expressions, record the questions that the participant might ask back, and examine any occasional sidetracks that might occur. A typical phenomenological interview should appear like an informal conversation in which the participant is doing most of the talking, and the researcher most of the listening (Leedy and Ormrod, 2010: 141). The researcher should continue engaging in interviews with participants until the point when saturation is reached. Saturation is reached when the researcher feels that there are no new moments or clearer understanding of the experience that can be found through further discussions with the participants (Laverty, 2003: 18). There are three types of interviews that you could use for this type of study: focus groups, oral history, and in-depth interview.

FOCUS GROUPS

In a focus group, the researchers want to observe several things: how people interact in a group when they are confronted with the same questions; how they moderate their views; how they react to different perspectives; and how manage their disagreements. Good focus group interviews are essentially group discussions where everyone participates and comments at the same time. The researcher in this case acts as a moderator who chairs the discussion, ensuring that everyone has a say. Normally, focus groups cover about three or four related issues. Anything more and there is a risk of losing the depth of the information. In line with this, Moore (2000: 124) highlights an example of a successful focus group that has covered only three issues: What health information did people need? What did they receive? What additional information would they have liked?

The size of the group is also important. Ideally, the group should have between five and eight participants. It might be difficult to get a sufficient range of views with less than five participants. With more than eight participants the group will be difficult to handle, or some people might feel that they have not had a sufficient opportunity to participate. Focus groups normally last between one-and-a-half hours to three hours, or longer in some cases (Moore, 2000: 124).

ORAL HISTORY

At times you may need to do a research about a particular event that has occurred in the past, and you would like to interview eyewitnesses, people who have experienced or participated in this event, or people who have organized the event. Your participants do not need to be very high-profile people to have something interesting to say. In any case, you will need to be very well prepared before the interview, so read as much as you can about the subject of your interview and try to understand the main issues and debates surrounding this particular event. This will also help you define your main research question, and any additional sub-questions that you would like to discuss with the interviewees. Send a list of the questions to your participants in advance and give them some time to prepare. Begin the interview by asking your participants to clarify relevant facts, such as their names, job titles, periods of employment, or whatever details are relevant to the topic of your interview. Do not expect them to know specific details such as particular government legislations or specific dates of historical events that might be relevant to you. They may know them, or have a recollection of them, but they do not necessarily need to know such details for the purpose of your interview. Give your participants absolute respect; do not argue or contradict them. Let them do most of the talking, and only interfere if you need clarification or to keep them on the subject. Make sure you record the interview – with the participants' permission, of course (Stokes, 2011: 124–5).

IN-DEPTH INTERVIEW

In-depth interviews are based on a set of predetermined questions. However, the sequences in which the issues are raised do not need to be formally set. Once the participants are informed about the topic of the interview and the issues that are to be discussed, the interview should start with casual dialogue and it needs to progress from there. In this way, the participants will be gradually engaged in a conversation rather than feeling that they are being interrogated. This will make the participants feel more relaxed and the responses will be more candid. As the interview carries on, the participants should be given time to think and to reflect on the questions. They should also be encouraged to elaborate on and explain in as much detail as possible their motivations, attitudes, beliefs, experience, behaviour, or feelings in regard to the issues in question. What you also need to be aware of is that in-depth interviews can be time consuming. This includes both the time it takes for the interview to be completed, and the time for data to be analysed – especially since the collected data is unstructured and unquantifiable (Yin, 1994: 84–5; Moore, 2000: 122).

In-depth interviews are complex tasks that should be undertaken by skilled researchers. According to Moore, there are several barriers that may interfere with the collection of reliable information. First, participants may try to portray themselves as more rational than they normally are. This may impede their ability to disclose their true emotions, views, and beliefs. Most people are often unaware of their own attitudes or beliefs, as they are a part of their subconsciousness. It takes considerable skill on the part of the researcher to get people to articulate things that are not part of their daily thoughts, and most people may be uncomfortable to admit or disclose revelations about themselves that are contrary to their projected self-image. Also, people may simply try to be polite and provide answers that they feel the researcher expects to hear. For you to overcome these barriers, you will need to be as unobtrusive as possible. Even the way you dress for the interview should be acceptable and unsurprising to the people you interview. Your participants should not feel that they are somehow different from you (Moore, 2000: 123).

EXAMPLE

In-depth Interview with Dana Arnett, CEO of VSA Partners

This example is an edited and abridged transcript based on an in-depth interview that I have conducted with Dana Arnett, the founding Principal and CEO of VSA Partners. VSA Partners is one of the most influential design and branding consultancies in the US and abroad. As a CEO, Dana Arnett heads a team of more than 180 associates in the creation of design programmes, digital and interactive initiatives, and brand marketing solutions for clients such as Harley-Davidson, Nike, IBM, Coca-Cola, Caterpillar, Proctor & Gamble, General Electric, and many more.

The main topic of this interview was the role of research and strategy in design and branding, especially when it comes to working for high-profile clients. The interview took place on 22 May, 2012 during the International Research Conference: Design for Business, which was presented at the Melbourne International Design Week (Australia). An extended version of this interview was published in *Design for Business, Volume 1* (Muratovski, 2012b). While this interview was not strictly done as a part of a larger research project, it follows the same principles and it sheds light on the research practices of one of the most prestigious design consultancies in the world. What you can also see here is how the interview questions were formulated and how the conversation was moderated.

Interview topic: The role of research and strategy in design and branding

Gjoko Muratovski: Dana, you place great importance on strategy in your company, and good strategy is always based on research. Can you tell us, how do you use research in your practice and how do you develop design and brand strategies?

Dana Arnett: Well, first of all, the front half of our process focuses on the strategic proposition of 'what a brand is' – that is, how a brand's purpose and meaning is contextualized and defined. This approach requires a blend of insights that are typically uncovered through research, facts and knowledgeable inquiry. With that data we can then solve the design problem. From there, the marketer can ultimately position their brand in more meaningful ways to their customer.

Depending on the scope and scale of project, research can tap into many viable sources – understanding consumer behaviours, habits, preferences, market conditions, channels and other influences. Armed with the knowledge derived through these insights, we can then shape a design direction that expresses and completes the other half of the equation: 'what a brand does'.

As social and digital information sources have progressed, we also have the advantage of incorporating data into the modelling of these solutions. By understanding behaviour, we can make the best recommendations for influencing choice along the path to purchase and adoption. It is particularly interesting these days because there are so many non-linear paths to making purchases.

The rise of mobile and social medias and technologies has provided immense variety in the ways of reaching people and driving demand. With better knowledge of how and where people are interacting with content, we can now influence and measure purchasing behaviour along these paths.

There is so much more than just click data being discovered through social and mobile media. We're finding out where people are, what they like and dislike, and how they're forming opinions, choices and preferences around brands. This helps us to detect new possibilities and new purchasing patterns. With this depth of information and insight we can personalize data and use design to shape and express unique brand experiences.

Gjoko Muratovski: What can you tell us about your day-to-day operations?

Dana Arnett: Perhaps the most important aspect of my job is figuring out how to get the thinkers and the creators to seamlessly come together. In our organization we have a strategy practice with a diverse roster of thinkers, a design practice with close to a hundred creatives, a technology practice that includes developers, information architects, writers and technologists, and a consumer marketing practice that has a rich mixture of marketing experts. My job is to provide the best environment where these diverse individuals can come together as a collective. We always stress collaboration so that holistic and inspiring solutions can blossom and thrive.

We also foster a process where strategists can think creatively and creatives can think strategically. In our work setting we don't have strategists sitting on one side of the office, throwing their research and thinking over the transom and hoping the designers will interpret their ideas. We intentionally blur the lines by insisting on total team interaction and collaboration. It's all about executing in a truly integrated way. Additionally, we encourage our clients to interact with us in the same way. We love it when our clients engage and work with our team to solve the problem. The results are generally phenomenal. I often refer to this process as 'the making of meaning'.

Gjoko Muratovski: In your opinion, beyond creating meaning, can a designer also create value?

Dana Arnett: Paul Rand once shared this thought on the designer's ultimate role and responsibility: 'Providing meaning to a mass of unrelated needs, ideas, words and pictures – it is the designer's job to select and fit this material together and make it interesting.' This ideology helped companies like IBM understand the real value of engaging a designer by having them think, create and contribute on the larger strategic level. Rand's elevated view also cleared the way for designers and organizations to realize design's catalytic force to inspire change, accelerate competitive metabolism, create irresistible marketplace attraction and fulfil a greater state of enterprise potential.

Like many of his twentieth-century design contemporaries, Rand was at the beginning of what would become an unprecedented run of design's higher purpose. Whether he knew it or not, he was 'justifying' design's worth. That's a much bigger deal than simply delivering results or pushing more products out the door. But at the very heart of his success and all the fruitful outcomes was an equally significant force: creativity. For two of his most cherished clients, Thomas Watson Jr. of IBM and Steve Jobs of Apple, creating meaning and reaping returns from business investment was never about 'selling more stuff'.

Gjoko Muratovski: Speaking of great companies with great brands, can you talk about the process that goes into brand development for companies such as Harley-Davidson and Nike?

Dana Arnett: I'll start by saying that both of those companies have been fortunate to have visionary leaders running them. Their CEOs have a genuine passion and belief in the brand and they support these intentions with a strong investment commitment. Cultural buy-in is equally important. Nike and Harley-Davidson have cultivated and groomed highly motivated workforces that are instilled with a deep sense of the brand, its value and its purpose in the world.

On a purely functional level, both companies also know what the customer wants and uniquely expects. And on an emotional level, brands like Nike and Harley-Davidson are charged to deliver customer and lifestyle experiences that are truly unmatched. By managing both sides of this equation, these companies have been able to ground their agency partners in the right way, with the best intentions. Together, we've been able to build potent and sustainable brand equity over time.

From an agency perspective, we always start by asking the simple question: How can we create a customer experience that is uniquely and exclusively Harley-Davidson? This may seem rudimentary, but it's so grounding if you're genuinely embracing a customer-driven approach to brand marketing.

From there, your team can be inspired to express the brand in so many powerful ways – ways that eclipse conventional and predictable thinking. We never lose sight of this, nor do we underestimate the level of emotional and personal impact we can generate. You have to capture the head and the heart of the customer.

Nike has a similar perspective on branding but their product offering and marketing universe is much more vast. In a recent interview, Nike's CEO Mark Parker explained to Fortune that connecting with customers used to be: 'Here's some product and here's some advertising. We hope you like it.' He continued: 'Connecting today is a dialogue.' So with the case of work we do for Nike, our challenge is never focused on simply communicating; it's more about finding the consumer and connecting with them in new and powerful ways. With that 'outside-in' mindset, we can shape vivid and unique connections that feel both familiar and very fresh.

Gjoko Muratovski: How do you determine where the emotional and the financial impact return is the greatest? How do you define that?

Dana Arnett: There are many formulas to quantify and qualify results. Each is very distinct to each of our client's own unique situations. At a broad level, we typically use a number of research and measurement techniques to determine impact and return. It starts with conducting research that uncovers key customer behaviours and inflection points. With that data and those insights, we can better understand ways to create experiences, motivate actions and drive and measure results. It's important to note that the goal isn't simply to measure but to inspire actions that move your buyer towards a purchase or a deeper level of brand attraction. Understanding the actions and behaviours along the way is key.

Today we're lucky to have better avenues and opportunities to utilize data and digital content. By mining and synthesizing research and insights we can then determine how to influence key moments along the path to purchase. Taking action on these insights also represents the greatest opportunity to build business results and brand value. By deepening our knowledge of customer behaviour and motivation we can design the right tools and methods that generate opportunities and create value. The return should outweigh the investment, ultimately leading to an entirely new way of defining marketing's role and worth in today's world.

Gjoko Muratovski: Do you think designers can paint a more vivid picture by making research findings and recommendations more emotionally compelling to their clients?

Dana Arnett: Designers have a talent and an opportunity to tap into a unique set of human needs. And the best designers understand how to shape content well beyond a set of rational directives. At its core, design is about shaping understanding by combining words, pictures and messages. When these elements work at the highest level, the final creative solution can stimulate passion, desire, curiosity, and interest. And by utilizing insights and research up front, a designer is armed with better input that can directly influence preference and create measurable value.

There's also a great deal of emotional and human insight you can gather by being close to the customer. Over the years, I've spent many hours with Harley-Davidson owners, at rallies and on personal rides. I observed how they shopped at Harley dealerships. I looked at what they wore, ate, and how they interacted. We also listened to what Harley-Davidson enthusiasts were telling us. So beyond all the data and the information that marketers can glean through research and insights, a designer can uncover a great deal of emotional intelligence by simply 'being there'. I would attest that these real-time experiences have been crucial to helping us better understand and define the brand's intangible value. This is the hard work that goes on in the background, and it feeds the design process.

Gjoko Muratovski: How do you present your research to the clients?

Dana Arnett: We typically present the facts and the insights in combination with our design recommendation. We present the research, package it and model the content into a set of recommendations that are supported by a creative and strategic position. And while no two projects are alike, our clients value our thinking best when there's a clear case for how it will effectively work in the marketplace. This makes us different in comparison to many of the pure-play research firms that focus solely on providing findings.

Gjoko Muratovski: When you work on large-scale corporate projects, research is absolutely necessary prior to designing. But brands of this nature also require a certain level of authenticity. How do you design to create authenticity?

Dana Arnett: I take an archaeological perspective; not in the true sense of archaeology, but I dig. I dig deep. In concert with the research work we uncover, we also have a wall in our office where we create giant mood sketches. We throw everything up there – from pictures, to words, to current and historical content, to a competitor's design and brand assets. This montage becomes a living representation of what the brand can look like, feel like, and sound like. By digging into this content, we can model and paint the ultimate visual and verbal picture of the brand.

The real challenge is to tap into that content and confront those influences, so that the full creative potential is realized. We try to find elements that are unique in terms of words, pictures, colour, and so on. We also do a lot of competitive analysis. We put our work up against the competition, exhausting every aspect of uniqueness.

We also pay close attention to how design can evolve a brand's identity and voice over time. By embracing design as a creative and strategic force, companies can build and enhance the life of their brands. More and more of our clients are placing a high premium on design's ability to create distinct and competitive advantage. As a result, we're seeing a renaissance in design.

Gjoko Muratovski: Dana, you've raised some very interesting points. You have identified research as a cornerstone of business strategy, and design as a key element that communicates and transforms this strategy into unique consumer experiences. It was interesting to hear how you have managed to develop a nexus between research and design as a part of the corporate culture at VSA. Introducing design research in your practice has proved to be highly effective, as can be seen in the success of your clients such as Harley-Davidson, Nike, Proctor & Gamble and IBM. Your experience shows that such research is one of the most efficient ways for a company to understand not only the needs of its customers but their emotional gravitation as well. Then again, the importance of generating authentic creative solutions at VSA has not been underestimated either.

Thank you for your time today, Dana.

(Muratovski, 2012b: 16–23)

4.4.3 DATA ANALYSIS

The main task of phenomenological data analysis is the identification of common themes in people's descriptions of their experiences. Once the interviews are transcribed, you will need to follow these four steps:

Step 1: Data segmentation

Step 2: Data categorization

Step 3: Comparison of data

Step 4: Description of the findings

First you need to identify the statements that relate to the topic. You can do this by separating the relevant from the irrelevant information in the interview. Then you will need to break this information into segments such as phrases or sentences. Each of the segments should reflect a single, specific thought. Once this is done, you will need to group the segments into categories that reflect the various aspects (the meanings) of the phenomenon as the participants have experienced it. The next step is for you to identify and compare the various ways in which different people experience the phenomenon. Finally, you will need to develop an overall description of the phenomenon as seen through the eyes of the people who have experienced it. The focus should be on the common themes in the experience, despite the diversity of the participants and the settings (Leedy and Ormrod, 2010: 141).

4.4.4 PREPARING A REPORT

There is no specific structure for preparing a phenomenological study report. But, as is the case for any research report, you can use the structure outlined here (see Figure 4.3):

Approximate Content Distribution Ratio

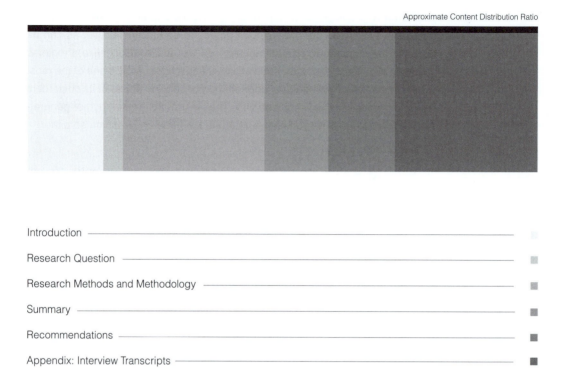

Introduction ——

Research Question ———————————————————————————————————

Research Methods and Methodology ——————————————————————

Summary ——

Recommendations ———————————————————————————————————

Appendix: Interview Transcripts ———————————————————————

Figure 4.3 Structure of a report on phenomenological research

1. Introduction

2. Research Question

3. Research Methods and Methodology

4. Summary

5. Recommendations

6. Appendix: Interview Transcripts

First, you need to provide an introduction to the phenomenon that you have been investigating, followed by your research question. Then, you need to introduce your methodology, including your methods of data collection, followed by an explanation of your data analysis process. In the summary you will need to present your conclusions about the phenomenon that has been studied, and this can take the form of a composite of your participants' experiences. Then, you will need to relate your findings to an existing body of theory and research and discuss the practical implications of your study (Leedy and Ormrod, 2010: 142). The success of the report can be measured by how vividly and accurately the experience has been described. If this is done well, the readers should be able to see the text as a statement of the experience itself (Laverty, 2003: 23). If deemed necessary, you can also include transcripts of your interviews as an appendix to your report.

4.5 HISTORICAL RESEARCH

History is an ever-flowing stream of events and continuing changes of everyday life. Historical research deals with the meaning of these events and changes, and tries to make sense of them by considering currents and counter-currents of present and past events with the hope of discerning patterns that can tie them all together. Conducting historical research, however, is not the same as studying history. The study of history is mainly concerned with the gathering and organizing of significant facts about a significant event, or occurrences of some kind that may involve a certain person or a group of people, various institutions, or the origin of certain ideas and concepts. This type of study is usually conducted for the purpose of conveying a 'historical narrative' that describes the event or the occurrence in question. Historical research, on the other hand, continues where studying history ends. While historical research is also concerned with the accumulation of facts and their organization, its main focus is their interpretation (Leedy and Ormrod, 2010: 164). As a designer, there are two ways in which you can use historical research: for conducting research related to design history; or for trends forecasting. One focuses on the past, and the other on the future.

DESIGN HISTORY

Design history, according to Daniel J. Huppatz and Grace Lees-Maffei, is 'the study of designed artefacts, practices and behaviours, and the discourses surrounding these, in order to understand the past, contextualize the present, and map possible trajectories for the future' (2013: 311). In a similar way, Clive Dilnot (1984a: 12) describes design history as a field of study that examines the history of professional design activity, or more precisely, the results of that activity. This includes designed objects and images, but also the people and the ideas behind this activity, such as designers, design movements, design schools, and design philosophies. To Victor Margolin (1992: 115), design history is not only a study of the history of design, but also a study of design itself, bringing a variety of influences together. According to him, the historical component is only a part of this study.

Understanding the social, cultural, and historical context of design is very important for any professional designer, and as Dilnot (1984b: 20) argues, without such grounding, design can only be 'incidental' and it is bound to fail. This also corresponds with the new trend in design practice that tells us that an object or an image might be beautiful, and may even fulfil a need, but unless this is a result of a conscious problem-solving process, it is not design – it is art or craft (Muratovski, 2006: 91). Ultimately, design history (or design studies) can provide us with a fundamental understanding of the design field and the design profession by answering essential questions such as: Who are we? What is it that we do? Where do we come from? And most importantly: Where are we going from here?

TREND FORECASTING

Following the same principle, we can generate the same level of understanding for other areas that might be of interest to us and even establish a process to explore ways in which the future could develop. This can be particularly useful if we want to forecast new trends or alternative futures in a particular area of interest, including design (see Engeler Newbury, 2012). But first, I need to clarify one thing: trend is not the same as fashion. Fashion can be the style of dress, behaviour, way of living, or other expressions that are popular at the present. Trend is a projection of the society and the future. Fashion can be made, trends cannot. Trends can only be followed, much like a weather forecast, hence the term 'trend forecasting' (Muratovski, 2006: 76).

Trend forecasting is done in the same way as historical research, but with one main difference. Rather than examining past information, the data is being gathered as it emerges. Trend forecasting experts identify and document trends across the globe as they surface. This is done by monitoring and examining new developments and changes in fashion, arts and culture, colour, consumer behaviour, architecture, textiles, and everything in between, including the latest developments in politics, business, and technology. Once this information is gathered, the data is then carefully analysed to ensure accuracy, validity, and influence. Then, future themes are identified and this analysis is presented in the form of key themes called 'macro trends'. According to WGSN, a global leading trend forecasting agency, these trends may influence businesses up to two years in advance, and can forecast a comprehensive profile of the future consumer (WGSN, 2013). Then again, if you are interested in looking at long-term strategic planning, you can broaden your research into past and current trends and start looking for various patterns that might occur in the future as well. These patterns are called 'mega trends'. Mega trend analysis can give you a future projection of up to 50 years, and this can be used for predicting massive changes in the way we live our lives. Major mega trends represent the industrial revolution, the rise of the consumer society, and more recently the emergence of the digital era that is characterized by rapid advances in the global information and telecommunications technologies that have changed the way people learn and interact with each other (Muratovski, 2006: 77). Mega trend forecasting is not as precise as macro trend forecasting in terms of the details that it can provide to the businesses' day-to-day activities, but it can certainly help an organization to plan its vision for the future. Since the size of the company is no guarantee that the company will survive a major shift in trends if the company is not prepared in advance, the shift in mega trends can equally affect both small businesses and major corporations alike.

A recent example of this includes the shift from film-based to digital photography. According to Christian Sandström (2009), many legendary and highly innovative companies for their time – such as Polaroid, Bronica, Contax, Agfa, Konica Minolta, and Ilford – have gone out of business since the emergence of digital imaging. Some of the other well-established companies in this industry – such as Kodak, Hasselblad, Pentax, Mamiya, Leica, and Fujifilm – have suffered huge losses but have managed to survive. Others, like Canon, Nikon, and Olympus, were prepared for the shift and have continued their business as usual. What makes it striking, as Sandström points out, is the extent to which companies with no past experience in photography have prospered in this field. Consumer electronics firms like Casio, Sony, HP, and Samsung have entered the industry after the shift to digital imaging and are quickly filling the gaps in the market. And if we take into account the advances in mobile phone cameras, we can safely say that this trend will continue to shift until saturation in digital technologies is achieved (Sandström, 2009).

If trend forecasting means thinking about the future, it also implies a systematic or strategic approach to predicting the future, planning for disruption, and managing change. There are many ways for facilitating future thinking, including historical research that can lead to data and trend analysis, as well as pattern recognition, alongside intuition and imagination. Foresight is an iterative, structured process that considers a range of possibilities and perspectives that can lead to multiple desirable and sustainable paths of action. Therefore, trend forecasting is not about predicting the future, but it is about asking 'what if' questions. Asking the right questions can eventually help society and organizations to understand the potential impacts and consequences of today's decisions and actions, and shape better pathways forward (Engeler Newbury, 2012: 30).

4.5.1 CONDUCTING HISTORICAL RESEARCH

While often on the surface it may appear that things happen randomly, this is rarely the case. If you study the sequence of events and occurrences and the broader context that surrounds them, then you will begin to see patterns that tie them together and make them meaningful. Therefore, by conducting historical research your task is not merely to describe 'what' has happened and 'when', but to present a factually supported rationale that explains 'why' these things might have happened (Leedy and Ormrod, 2010: 164).

Good historical research asks questions that deal with relevant and perennial issues that can be of benefit to the overall body of knowledge within your discipline and beyond, or can provide you with information that can be relevant to your practice. After you have formulated your question, you will need to identify a gap in the existing historical scholarship. This means that you will need to become quite familiar with the literature that has examined this topic before and identify any possibilities for new research. This does not necessarily mean that you need to discover a 'missing link' in the literature; it is equally valid if you reconsider how existing historical data are interpreted and provide new, or an alternative way of interpreting, historical evidence (Hines, 2009: 148–9).

What you also need to take into account is that you should not be judging or evaluating earlier people, events, or concepts using today's values and standards. Rather, you should try to understand the circumstances when these things occurred (Hines, 2009: 146–7). In order for you to do that, you need to look at the things that you are investigating not only chronologically, but also within the context of 'historical time' – other similar things that were happening around the same time, and in consideration of 'historical space' – similar things that were happening at other locations, but not necessarily at the exact same time (Leedy and Ormrod, 2010: 172–5).

There are several reasons for this. The historical data related to certain events and occurrences that happened a long time ago often has a tendency to create an illusion that these things appear closer together in time than they really were. Also, as is often the case, events and occurrences do not normally appear in a vacuum and there might be other indirectly associated events that might have triggered the occurrence of the events that you are studying. A particular design trend, for example, might appear not simply because it is fashionable, but because this trend appears as a reaction to certain external influences, such as lack or abundance of resources in a particular location; local or global economic crisis; war; social, political or environmental concerns in a particular era; and so on (see Hines, 2009: 147). Such was the case with the design of the iconic British car, the Mini – a product of the Morris design team at the British Motor Corporation (BMC). The design and the production of small and efficient cars for the British market have not been triggered by fashion, but by the fuel shortages caused by the 1956 Suez Canal crisis. The Mini was officially launched in 1959 and in the light of the circumstances the car has become a design icon of its era (Coulter, 1989). This is a good example of how a problem in one area can influence the design in another.

4.5.2 DATA COLLECTION

Historical research is a type of research that aims to reconstruct or interpret historical events or occurrences through the gathering of relevant historical materials. These materials can come from both primary and secondary sources.

PRIMARY SOURCES

Primary sources are data created during the time of your own investigation. This often includes statements or oral interviews from people who actually witnessed or experienced an event. In addition to this, you can consider including a variety of documents or artifacts as supporting primary sources, including newspaper articles, letters, personal journals or diaries, photographs, films, personal items, or other culturally significant objects. Primary sources can also include public records or documents published by government or non-government bodies (Hines, 2009: 152–4).

Researching public or a private archival collection of documents and artifacts can be a very rewarding research experience, especially if you are examining an archive that has not been previously studied. A good archive can give you an exciting insight into something that no one has looked at from a scholarly perspective before. This type of research can allow you to generate first-hand data from primary sources, and this can result in an original contribution to the knowledge of the field that you are studying (Stokes, 2011: 114). Documentary evidence also plays an important and explicit role in any data collection. When used in conjunction with other sources of information, such as archival records, interviews, or observations, you will be able to create a consistent picture of a given situation or a certain period of time and project a fairly certain assumption of what has actually occurred (Yin, 1994: 81–2). Research of this kind can be highly important and can become the object of extensive retrieval and analysis, but not always – in some cases they may hold only a minor relevance. Therefore, before using archival or documentary records in your research, you will first need to establish whether this kind of research is suitable for your project, and if so, you will need to understand the context and the audience for which these records were produced in the first place (1994: 83–4). While oral history interviews can create new primary sources, you need to be aware that participants' recollections of certain events may not always be accurate. That is why you need to conduct interviews with several people, cross-reference their statements, and then establish whether your participants recall these events in the same or a similar way. If they do, then you can have reasonable confidence that the interviews have provided you with factual information, but you should also be careful not to resort to overgeneralizations of personal experiences (Leedy and Ormrod, 2010: 165).

SECONDARY SOURCES

Secondary sources, on the other hand, are any interpretations or histories about the past developed by other researchers. These include books, journal articles, and documentaries. Secondary sources are useful at the beginning of your research because they can present you with an existing knowledge on the topic or the period, they can provide you with starting points for your own research, and they can help you identify your primary sources (Hines, 2009: 156).

Once you have located the historical data that is relevant to your research question, you should also determine the validity of the data – in terms of whether the data that you have found is authentic or not (Leedy and Ormrod, 2010: 169–71). In doing so, you need to look for two things:

- Is the material that you have found genuine, or is it a fabrication?
- If this material is genuine, does it represent a biased, one-sided view, or an objective view of the situation?

Gathering historical data can be a daunting task because of the sheer volume of information that you can gather on a topic. Therefore, it is important for you to set up a system of how you will gather and use the information. A good way to deal with this is by setting up various categories, such as by topic, type of document, date, author, location, and so on. However, what you will see is that many of your findings will need to appear in several categories at the same time and that you may need to have multiple copies of the same material that will be placed in different categories. One way of dealing with this is if you apply a system of classification and list your materials in terms of chronological order, geographical position, historical figures, and specific subtopics that relate to your overall research topic (Leedy and Ormrod, 2010: 168–9). This is a very pedantic system of working, and it might take you a significant amount of time to set up this system. However, this way of working will significantly ease your data analysis process later on.

4.5.3 DATA ANALYSIS

Analysis and interpretation are key elements of any historical research. Without them you will be simply compiling facts or you will be telling stories. As a part of your analysis you need to take into consideration these three steps:

Step 1: Explain the context of the information

Step 2: Establish the validity of the facts

Step 3: Identify the causation and the motives behind the event

At the very least, historical research analysis calls for consideration of information within its multiple contexts, weighing of facts, and careful consideration of any reasons and motives behind the event or the occurrence in question (Hines, 2009: 147).

4.5.4 PREPARING A REPORT

Historical research reports can vary in style and format. A good historical research report can be very engaging, and unlike most other types of research reports, many well-written histori-cal studies often appear on best-seller lists for the general public as well (Leedy and Ormrod, 2010: 175). Here is a suggestion on how you can structure your report (see Figure 4.4):

1. Introduction

2. Examples

3. Discussion

4. Reflection

5. Conclusion

You should start by stating your argument early in your report. The reason behind this is that you are not only presenting the data, but you are also interpreting it. Be upfront with

Approximate Content Distribution Ratio

Introduction ————————————————————————————————————

Examples ————————————————————————————————————

Discussion ————————————————————————————————————

Reflection ————————————————————————————————————

Conclusion ————————————————————————————————————

Figure 4.4 Structure of a report on historical research

your findings and do not keep your readers guessing. Then, you should provide several case studies that can support the assertions that you have made in the introduction. This will help you to make a more credible case for your overall research and will add a level of credibility to your position. It is not unusual if you present an interpretation that is different from those of other researchers. It might be very likely that you have discovered some unknown elements that now cast a different light on a certain event or occurrence. Whatever might be the case, you need to describe any relevant competing interpretations and provide evidence that supports them, as well as evidence that questions them. By the same token, you should identify and point out any concerns or weaknesses related to your own findings. It is better for you to identify any potential problems and to be upfront with that, rather than to let others do that for you. In this way, you will portray yourself as a credible and objective researcher. As long as you have been systematic in your work, identifying some gaps or problems in your own research is not necessarily a negative thing. Many good research reports conclude by highlighting any issues of this kind as opportunities for further research. In this way you are enabling other researchers to conduct research on the same topic by building on your work (Leedy and Ormrod, 2010: 177).

4.6 GROUNDED THEORY

Grounded theory is a form of research that is least likely to begin from a particular theoretical framework. Instead, grounded theory first begins by gathering data which the researcher uses to develop a new theory on a particular issue. The term 'grounded' refers to the idea that the theory that emerges from this research is grounded in data that has been collected from a variety of sources (Leedy and Ormrod, 2010: 142).

Grounded theory is an advanced form of research that calls for strong understanding of various research techniques and cross-disciplinary knowledge of many areas that are directly or indirectly associated with the topic of interest. As such, this research approach is best suited to conducting transdisciplinary research. Researchers who conduct grounded theory research tend to look at areas that have not been studied in great depth before, or do not have clear and definite theories associated with them. In fact, grounded theory relies on the absence of an existing theory and its purpose is to set up a new theory (Jones et al., 2005). Due to its complex and broad nature, this research approach is not recommended for novice researchers.

Developing new theories as a form of 'blue-sky' research is not a common practice in industry. This is because it takes a significant amount of time and funding for a new theory to be developed and implemented in practice. Unless an organization is prepared to invest considerable resources in research and development of this nature, grounded theory research is better conducted in university environments first, at various research centres, or at a PhD level, and then applied in industry or government later. Also, out of all research approaches, grounded theory is perhaps the most suitable for studying the field of design – considering that this is an ever-changing field that resists any clear definition (see Muratovski, 2006: 26–9).

4.6.1 CONDUCTING GROUNDED THEORY RESEARCH

Grounded theory is a research approach aimed at developing new theory through the use of multiple forms of data collection and interpretations (Leedy and Ormrod, 2010: 108). In most cases, this type of research focuses on a process of some kind, and the final goal is the development of a theory about this process. A study of this type can examine rarely explored transdisciplinary areas (e.g. how methods of religious and political propaganda can be used for developing persuasive brand strategies) (see Muratovski, 2010b).

4.6.2 DATA COLLECTION

There are no prescribed data collection methods when it comes to grounded theory – the use of all available methods is applicable. Because of this, the research process is quite flexible and it is likely to change over the course of the study. What makes this research approach different from the others is that the data analysis process begins simultaneously with the data collection process. Researchers working in grounded theory start classifying the data as it comes. As the process of data collection continues, the new data should be used for further saturation of the categories (learning as much as possible about each particular problem), and for finding any disconfirming evidence that may suggest revisions in the categories or in the interrelationships between them. As the work progresses, the positions shift and the data analysis begins to drive the data collection process. This constant loop of data collection and analysis needs to continue until a clear theory begins to form. This means that the new theory is based on numerous concepts and their interrelationships (Leedy and Ormrod, 2010: 142–3).

4.6.3 DATA ANALYSIS

There are numerous ways in which you can approach the data analysis process in grounded theory, and experts often disagree on what is the best way to do that. One widely used approach includes these five steps:

Step 1: Conduct open coding

Step 2: Conduct axial coding

Step 3: Revise the data

Step 4: Synthesize the findings

Step 5: Develop a theory

According to this approach, first you should begin by dividing the data into segments. Then, you should start looking for commonalities that reflect different categories or themes. When you have finished this categorization, you need to begin looking for specific 'properties' in each of the categories, such as certain attributes or subcategories. This is called 'open coding'. Open coding is a process of reducing the data to a small set of themes that describe the phenomenon under investigation. Axial coding, on the other hand, is about establishing interconnections between categories and subcategories. The focus here is on determining the following for each category:

- What are the conditions that have given rise to this process?
- What is the context in which this process is embedded?
- What are the strategies that people use to manage this process or to carry it out?
- What are the consequences of these strategies?

At this stage you will need to go back and forth among data collection, open coding, and axial coding, continuously refining the categories and their interconnections until a level of saturation is reached. Then, if you are confident that you have gathered sufficient data, the categories and their interconnections will need to be combined to form a storyline that describes the mechanics of this process. This then leads to the development of a theory that explains the process. The theory can take the form of a statement, visual model, or a series of hypotheses, and should depict the evolving nature of the process and describe how certain conditions lead to certain actions or interactions (Leedy and Ormrod, 2010: 143).

While these steps are structured in a rigorous and systematic way and can be useful for narrowing down a relatively large body of data into a concise, structural framework, according to Leedy and Ormrod (2010: 143), some researchers find this way of dealing with grounded theory 'too structured', in that it can limit the researcher's flexibility and may predispose a premature identification of categories. As this is a highly complex form of study, I would recommend further reading on the topic and a consultation with a senior researcher or with a supervisor familiar with grounded theory prior to engaging with this kind of research.

4.6.4 PREPARING A REPORT

The style of reporting a grounded theory is generally formal, objective, and impersonal. Your report can be based on the structure outlined here (see Figure 4.5):

1. Introduction

2. Research Question

3. Literature Review

4. Methodology and Data Analysis

5. Presentation or Theory

6. Implications

7. Conclusion

In the introduction you should set the context of your research. Then you should begin by describing your research question. Following this, you should explain how you have delineated your question more precisely during the course of the study. When you move to the section on the literature review, make sure that you are using the literature not as a means for providing concepts or theories for your study, but as a way of building a rationale and context. Then you will need to describe the approach that you have taken at the beginning of the study, and you should also explain how your approach evolved over the course of time. Here you also need to outline any specific methods or supporting methodologies that you have been using. You can also explain the categories and their properties, and how your data collection was driven by your data analysis. In the end, you should present your theory. Here you can use some excerpts from the data to illustrate and support your statements. Then you should explain how your

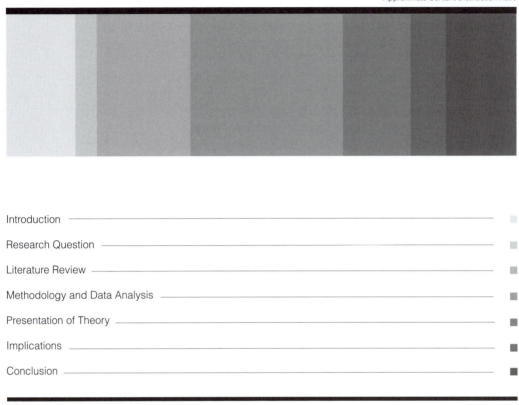

Introduction

Research Question

Literature Review

Methodology and Data Analysis

Presentation of Theory

Implications

Conclusion

Figure 4.5 Structure of a report on grounded theory

theory is similar to or dissimilar from other theoretical perspectives, how your theory relates to existing knowledge in the field, and what the potential implications of the theory are for practice or further research. You can conclude by providing a summary of your research and by reiterating the key points of your findings (Leedy and Ormrod, 2010: 143–4).

4.7 HALLMARKS OF GOOD QUALITATIVE RESEARCH

Most researchers agree that there are nine general hallmarks that characterize good qualitative research:

- Purpose
- Disclosure

- Rigour

- Open-mindedness

- Completeness

- Coherence

- Persuasiveness

- Usefulness

- Consensus

In a good qualitative study, the research question clearly drives the purpose of the research through the methodology for collecting and analysing data. The research methods are rigorous, precise, and thorough. Also, at the beginning of the study, the researcher has disclosed any assumptions, beliefs, values, and biases that he or she might hold. Furthermore, the researcher has managed to maintain objectivity throughout the research process.

In addition to this, the study shows that the researcher has been willing to modify hypotheses and interpretations when newly acquired data have conflicted with previously collected data. The work itself shows that the object of the study has been depicted in all of its complexity. This means that the researcher has spent sufficient time studying all nuances of the problem in question and is able to provide a total, multifaceted picture of the research in return. Furthermore, the study presents consistent findings and demonstrates that any contradictions within the data have been examined and reconciled. Also, the argument has been presented in a logical and convincing manner and it has been supported by empirical evidence. The conclusion has promoted one of these three things:

- A better understanding of the phenomenon in question.

- A sustained prediction of a future event or a series of events.

- A list of specific interventions that can enhance the quality of life.

Finally, the study has been peer reviewed or examined by the relevant stakeholders and the interpretations and the explanations have been accepted as valid and useful (Leedy and Ormrod, 2010: 157).

4.8 CONCLUSION

Qualitative research is an in-depth research method that you can use when you need to generate more understanding of a particular topic. This research is primarily based on open-ended questions and interpretations of data. As such, this research includes a collection of various forms of data from a wide range of sources, which are then examined from many angles. Qualitative research, as any form of research, requires considerable planning and preparation, and this includes a solid understanding of previous research conducted on the same or similar topic.

You can use qualitative research if you want to understand the nature of certain situations, settings, processes, relationships, systems, or people; test the validity of certain assumptions, claims, theories, or generalizations within real-world contexts; or as a means through which you can judge the effectiveness of particular policies, practice, or innovation. Because of its ability to deal with complex issues, qualitative research can be quite beneficial for designers – especially when it comes to building an understanding of contemporary problems.

4.9 SUMMARY

In this chapter I have explained the benefits of using qualitative research in design and I have introduced some of the most commonly used qualitative research approaches in the field. This includes case studies, ethnography, phenomenology, grounded theory, and historical research.

Case study research is an approach that can provide you with the tools to study a complex or a little known phenomenon by using a variety of data. This approach can allow you to conduct an in-depth investigation into a particular person, programme, or event for a defined period of time and within a set context. Data collection for case studies may come from various sources: direct observations, participant observations, interviews, documents, newspaper articles, official records, physical artifacts, and various audio-visual materials. There are five steps that you can follow when you analyse the data. You should organize the details about the case, categorize the data, identify patterns, and synthesize and generalize the information. There is no set formula on how you should prepare your case study research report; you can either tell a story or provide a chronological report, or you can address systematically each proposition – it all depends on what you have to say, to whom you are reporting, and what do they expect to see.

Ethnography is the study of social interactions, behaviours, and perceptions that occur within various groups and communities. The main aim of the ethnographer is to prepare an interpretation of the culture that is being studied. As such, ethnographic research can play a valuable role in the design field. By studying the social and the cultural contexts in which we are working, we can create better everyday experiences for the people for whom we design. This type of study involves an in-depth, systematic study about groups of people by observing, or participating in, the lives of the people who are being studied. In ethnography, talking to people is crucial. However, while it is essential to know the language of the community that you will be investigating, depending on the context, it is not always advisable to use this language. Also, you need to be aware that there is always the risk that if you spend long time conducting fieldwork, you can become too emotionally involved and lose the ability to assess the situation accurately. Due to the dynamics of the work, data collection and data analysis in an ethnographic study often occur simultaneously. That is why timely and detailed write-up of field notes is essential. In addition to taking field notes, you should also consider taking photographs as well as video and audio recordings as a way to complement your notes.

Phenomenology is a research approach that attempts to understand participants' experiences in relation to various phenomena. In other words, this research studies how people experience things and events. This approach can be used as a one-off study, or depending on the overall problem in question, it can also be used in conjunction with other research approaches. The main method in phenomenological research is the in-depth interview. A typical phenomenological interview should appear like an informal conversation. However, you have to note that if you have a personal experience with the phenomenon in question, you must maintain an unbiased position.

The purpose of the historical research is essentially an interpretation of the past by examining various ideas, beliefs, and values that shaped earlier times. By conducting historical research your task is not merely to describe 'what' has happened and 'when', but to present a factually supported rationale that explains 'why' these things might have happened. This type of research is based on evidence coming from primary and secondary sources, and its analysis. If you are studying design history, this will be your key research approach. But you can use historical research for other purposes as well. By learning about the past, we can also learn about the future. Good historical research asks questions that deal with relevant and perennial issues that can be of benefit to the overall body of knowledge within your discipline and beyond, or can provide you with information that can be relevant to your practice. Through historical research you will be able to learn about causalities and patterns of current behaviour that you can use to predict future trends and possible occurrences in your own field, or in other areas that you may be investigating. Reports of historical research can vary in style and format.

Grounded theory is a research approach that uses a range of research techniques and calls for a broad understanding of many areas that are directly or indirectly associated with the topic of interest. The main purpose of grounded theory is the development of a new theory for an area that does not have a theoretical foundation, or lacks a clear theoretical focus. There are no prescribed data collection and analysis methods when it comes to grounded theory – the use of all available methods is applicable. The research process can be quite flexible and it can continuously evolve during the course of the study, but it must remain rigorous. What makes this type of research different from the others is that the data analysis process begins simultaneously with the data collection process. The style of reporting grounded theory is generally formal, objective, and impersonal.

QUANTITATIVE RESEARCH

KEYWORDS Quantitative Research   User-Centred Design (UCD)
              Surveys   Prototyping
              Experiments   Scientific Method

If you are interested in working in the corporate sector, or intend to prepare design proposals for prospective clients in the corporate sector, you will need to develop a proficiency in quantitative research. Many business executives are more accustomed to seeing quantitative research coming from various market or business reports rather than qualitative research – which is often wrongfully perceived as speculative.

According to Peter Zec, President of the Red Dot Design Awards, the whole purpose of quantifying design's value in the corporate sector is to achieve a better financial understanding of the risks and rewards associated with the proposed design. As Zec argues further, quantifying design facilitates developing concepts and objectives that can help a company define its strategic design management. Quantitative research often serves as a basis on which financial objectives and future planning are calculated, but by the same token, this research can also be used for comparing competitor companies and industry branches (Zec, 2011: 39). This, however, is not an easy process. Measuring design in statistical terms can prove to be costly and problematic – especially since design outcomes cannot be easily extracted from the broader commercial context (Whicher et al., 2011: 47). Regardless of this, there are some basic types of quantitative research, such as surveys and experiments, that would be relatively easy for you to adopt in your design practice. But let us begin with the essentials first.

5.1 WHAT IS QUANTITATIVE RESEARCH?

Quantitative research is an empirical research that uses numeric and quantifiable data to arrive at conclusions. In other words, this is the type of research that uses data which can be measured and independently verified. The conclusions in quantitative research are based on experimentation, or on objective and systematic observations and statistics. That is why this type of research is often described as being 'independent' from the researcher in terms that it is based on 'objective measurement of reality' rather than on personal interpretations by the researcher (Williams, 2007: 66). Unlike qualitative research, which is an in-depth research used for construction of new theories, quantitative research is primarily used for simplifying and generalizing things, describing a certain phenomenon, or identifying 'cause-and-effect' relationships (Belli, 2009: 60).

While qualitative research is used for developing a new theory, quantitative research is mainly used for two things: testing or verifying an existing theory, or gathering statistical data (Creswell, 2003: 125–6). In this capacity, quantitative research is concerned primarily with measuring attitudes, behaviours, and perceptions based on a systematic observation, or by collection of numerical data. Gathered data is then used to prove or disprove ideas or assumptions. The analysis and the conclusions are based on deductive reasoning – a logical process where repeated observations of a certain phenomenon will lead to a conclusion based on high probability or predictability of occurrence (Lewis-Beck et al., 2004: 896).

There are many kinds of quantitative investigations that can be done. For example, you can use quantitative research to conduct surveys for various design or market research purposes, or you can conduct user-testing experiments for new products or applications (both visual or tangible). Some examples of quantitative research questions might include the following:

- What are the mobile phone usage habits of teenagers?
- What are the attitudes of the elderly towards retirement housing?
- What is the correlation between the brand's 'likes' on a Facebook page and the actual sales of the brand's products?
- What are the effects of a new website interface on typical users?
- What do people think of the new product features?

In comparison to the qualitative research questions, quantitative questions are focused on more specific things – things that can be measured or quantified in some way. For example, we can measure how often teenagers use their mobile phones, for what purposes, and the peak of their usage times. We can measure the general attitudes of senior citizens towards retirement housing by conducting a survey, and this survey can tell us what percentage of the elderly are opposing or accepting retirement housing as an option for them. We can measure the relationship between how many 'likes' a brand gets on Facebook and how this relates to the actual sales of their products. We can easily compare whether a new website interface proves a positive or negative experience for the typical users by conducting user-testing experiments. And in the same way, we can measure the effects of new product features over the old ones.

We use these types of investigations so we can create a 'snapshot' of the issue that we are studying. Depending on what we want to know, we can use quantitative research at all stages of our research: at the very beginning (when we want to identify particular problems); during the design development stage (when we want to test the current status of our design and its reception by the target market); and in the final stage (when we want to measure the acceptance rate of certain designs, or their effect).

There are many ways of conducting quantitative research. Here, however, I will discuss two main ways of conducting quantitative research: by using surveys and experiments. In both cases, what you need to be aware of is that there are two key things that you need to take into consideration: the setting – where and how you are conducting your research; and the sampling – how are you selecting your participants. Your choice on the setting and the sampling can have a significant effect on the results of your research.

5.1.1 SETTINGS

Quantitative research can be conducted externally (in a natural setting during fieldwork) or internally (in a controlled environment within a research facility). In terms of validity, there are advantages and disadvantages to both. Validity in an internal setting can be easily stablished in a laboratory because the researcher can set up an experiment in which all of the factors that may cause an effect can be controlled. The problem with this type of research is that the testing conditions are ideal and therefore not likely to resemble a real-world environment. As a result, this type of research cannot be easily generalized and cannot be easily applied in practice.

Laboratory-based research is often considered to be the 'gold standard' for many scientific researchers; however, when it comes to applied practice, external research is seen as more valuable to the profession. Then again, because external research is conducted in a real-world environment, the researcher cannot control all the variables that may influence the results. 'Variable' is a term that stands for 'something that can vary', and it is a technical term for something that you can measure.

What this means is that the results can often be compromised due to the unpredictability of the environment itself. This is often a problem because validity in external settings can only be achieved when the study results can be generalized and applied with certainty to other groups and settings beyond those in the current study. Therefore, the external study needs to be repeated several times, and sometimes in various settings, until the researchers are confident that the results are validated and are general in nature (Cottrell and McKenzie, 2011: 172–3). In either case, once the testing is completed, researchers assess and analyse the results, and then draw a general conclusion about their participants in a statistical manner (Lewis-Beck et al., 2004: 896).

5.1.2 SAMPLING

Another important factor that needs to be taken into consideration here is the selection of the participants. This process is called 'sampling'. When you are conducting quantitative research, you need to select your participants from a particular population – a group of people or a community that is of interest to you. Since it is impossible to test everyone, you can test people that are randomly selected from this group. These randomly selected participants should be identified as average representatives of this population. You can never be certain that you have the ideal representative sample, and you probably never will, but if your sample of participants is large enough, the validity of your study will be higher (Moore, 2000: 104–5). In your research proposal, and subsequently the research report, you will need to provide the information that is listed here (see Figure 5.1):

1. Introduction

2. Population Description

3. Size

4. Individual Characteristics

5. Stratification

6. Access

7. Procedures

8. Sample Size

9. Instrumentation

10. Summary

11. Appendix: Cover Letter

First, you should set the context by introducing your research briefly. Then you need to identify and describe the population that you will study. Following this, you will need to provide an indication of the size of the population – if size can be determined. Also, you will need to discuss how you will identify individuals in this population and what their individual characteristics are. You can use qualitative research for this, or you can use your literature review if such information is already available. Then, you will need to identify whether your study will use stratification of the population before selecting the sample. 'Stratification' means that specific characteristics of the individuals (e.g. gender, age, income level, education) are represented in the sample, and whether the selected sample reflects the true proportion of such individuals in the entire population. You will also need to provide an indication of the number of people in your sample. Then, you will need to discuss how you will gain access to this population. For example, if you are investigating an ethnic minority group, you may want to visit their local community centre. Once you have provided an answer to these questions, you will need to describe what kind of procedure you will use for sampling. You can answer the following questions in the process:

- Will you advertise your research project?

- Will you approach people directly?

- How will you determine who is a suitable participant?

- What kind of survey instrument will you use to collect data?

Once this is done, you should provide a summary of all of these things. Finally, in your appendix you should also include the cover letter that you used to invite the participants (Creswell, 2003: 156–8).

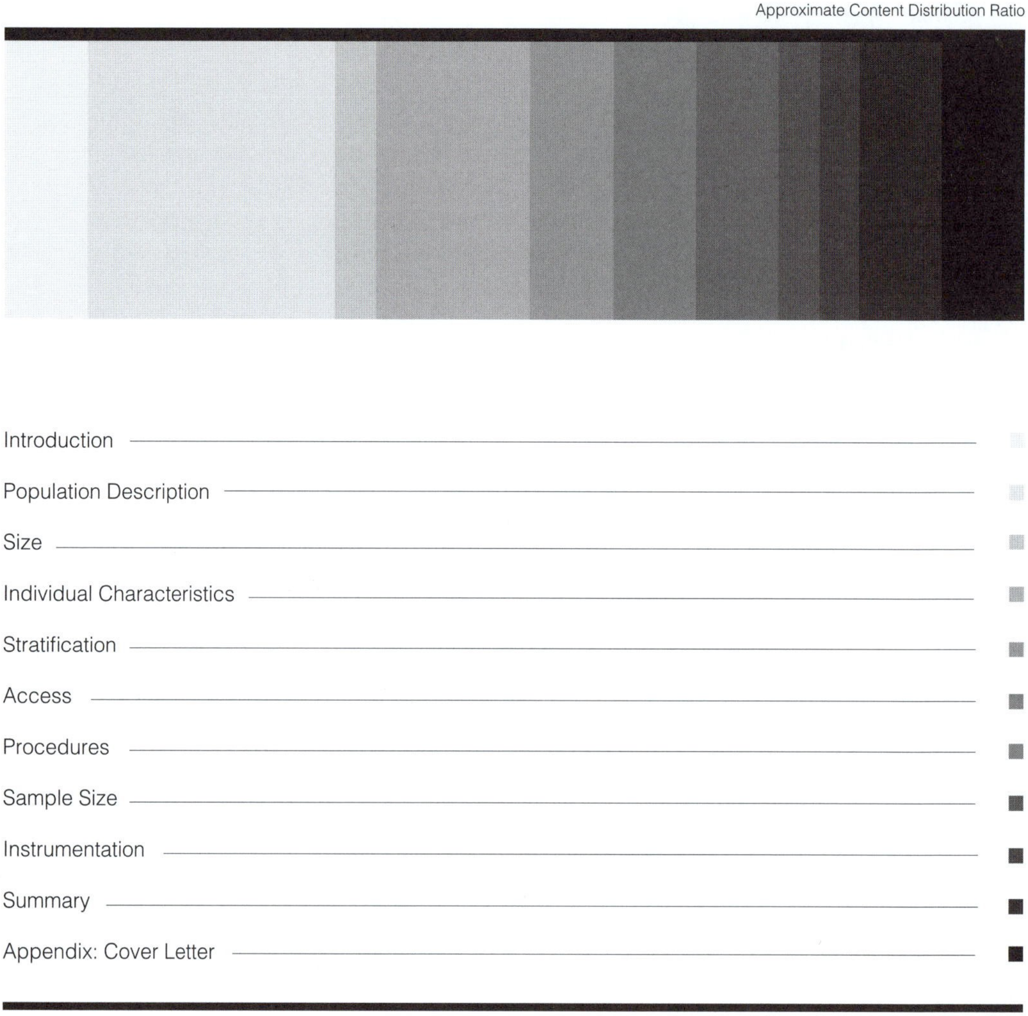

Approximate Content Distribution Ratio

Introduction

Population Description

Size

Individual Characteristics

Stratification

Access

Procedures

Sample Size

Instrumentation

Summary

Appendix: Cover Letter

Figure 5.1 Structure of a sampling report

5.2 SURVEYS

Surveys are the best-known form of statistical research and they are perhaps the most widely used form of quantitative research. The purpose of the survey is to document people's characteristics, opinions, attitudes, or previous experiences (Leedy and Ormrod, 2010: 182–7). This kind of research involves acquiring information about a particular group of people by asking them questions and then arranging these answers in a structured and systemic order.

From a simple petition form circulated by a group of neighbours or a poll that aims to discover people's attitudes towards certain political candidates, to a nation-wide census conducted by the government, surveys are commonplace features in our everyday lives. Surveys are deceptively simple in their design, and despite their seeming simplicity, they do require a considerable level of knowledge in developing them correctly. However, as it is virtually impossible for a researcher to conduct a study on an entire population of interest, the survey can involve a carefully selected sample of that population instead.

5.2.1 CONDUCTING A SURVEY

There are few things that need to be noted when it comes to conducting survey research. At a glance, surveys appear to be quite simple in their design, but planning survey questions is not an easy task. This type of research is no less demanding or easier to conduct than some other types of research. Despite your best intentions to develop clear and concise questions, you may produce questions that are ambiguous, misleading, or can lead to answers that are difficult to interpret. At times, some questions may even prove to be useless for the purpose of your research. For example, you should not try to get too much information in any single question because you may get confusing answers in return. Therefore, try to restrict each question to one single idea. A good survey can be quite demanding in terms of planning and execution, and framing the right questions can take a considerable time. The basic procedure in survey research is this: the researcher prepares a set of questions, finds willing participants who represent a sample of the population of interest, asks them questions, summarizes their answers, calculates percentages in terms of types of responses per question or per individual characteristics (e.g. age, gender, location, etc.), and then draws a conclusion about that population on the basis of the received answers (Leedy and Ormrod, 2010: 187; Stokes, 2011: 141–2).

The core of the survey research comes from the questions. While the reliability and validity of the survey depends on how it was planned and executed, its most essential component is the way the questions are formed (Alreck and Settle, 1985: 97). When working on a research survey, you will need to take into consideration the same things that were discussed for qualitative interviews. When it comes to preparing questions and setting the survey, the procedure that you will need to follow is the same as if you were preparing to conduct an interview. The main difference between the two is that in survey research you will need to frame the questions in a way that you can quantify the answers. Also, you need to take into account that in survey research you need to code people's responses as numbers and then conduct a statistical analysis on those numbers. That is why you need to identify an appropriate coding scheme ahead of time. Then again, this does not mean that you will need to quantify everything. A few open-ended questions might give you a new perspective or may provide you with some valuable additional insights. This combination of quantitative and qualitative research methods is called 'mixed methods' research.

What you need to be aware of is that this type of research captures only a 'moment in time' – like a snapshot. What this means is that the results of the survey are valid only for that particular time and cannot be accepted as a constant for all times. People's attitudes tend to change with time, and in the future the same population might respond differently to the same questions. Furthermore, you need to be aware that you are relying on so-called 'self-report' data. This means that people are telling you what they believe to be true, or what they believe that you want to hear.

You also need to bear in mind that people's opinions are often constructed on the spot, which means that they have probably not given enough thought to the issue that you are asking them. In other cases people may misinterpret the question or even misrepresent the fact – especially if they want to present themselves better. You also need to be aware that very few people are prepared to consciously admit that they have been engaged in a behaviour that can be construed as negative by the broader public (Leedy and Ormrod, 2010: 187–8; Stokes, 2011: 142).

Here are few more tips. If you want to ask some controversial or sensitive questions, leave them for the latter part of the survey. This will give you some time to engage the participant in the survey and establish a better rapport before you move on to more difficult topics. Also, be aware that some responses may be vague or difficult to interpret. A follow-up question such as 'Can you tell me more about that?' may often provide that additional information you need. Finally, you should conduct a small pilot study with a few volunteers, so that you can test the survey before you distribute it. This will give you the opportunity to fine-tune your questions, and this may save you a great deal of time in the long run (Leedy and Ormrod, 2010: 191–2).

5.2.2 DATA COLLECTION

Contrary to qualitative research where the interviews are quite open-ended, in survey research interviews are fairly structured. In a structured interview, the researcher asks a standard set of questions alongside a multiple choice of answers that the respondent can choose from. In a semi-structured interview, in addition to the standard set of questions, the researcher usually asks one or more individually tailored questions to get additional clarification. In addition to this, there are several things that you should consider when planning a survey: brevity, clarity, focus, options, bias, consistency, and design (see Figure 5.2).

BREVITY

For many people, a request to complete a questionnaire can often be seen as a nuisance and a waste of time. That is why you need to keep the questionnaire as short as possible. You can do this by asking only for the information that is essential to your project. You can determine what is essential by asking yourself two questions:

- Why do I need to know this?
- How will this help me to resolve my research problem?

Do not use more than two or three open-ended questions in your questionnaire. This will be a strain to your participants, and to you as well. If you feel that there is a need for more discussion, then you should have chosen a qualitative method instead. Also, it might be helpful if you indicate at the beginning of your questionnaire how long it will take to complete it. This is only an estimate, of course, and the results can vary, but this might help the prospective participants to decide whether to take the survey now or later. Most often people will be concerned that this will take too much of their time, so if they see that the questionnaire is a short one, they will be more inclined to respond. You can estimate the completion time when you conduct the pilot questionnaire.

Brevity

Clarity

Focus

Options

Bias

Consistency

Design

Figure 5.2 Things to consider when planning a survey

CLARITY

You will need to make sure that the questionnaire is easy to read and use, and that everyone understands the questions in the same way. That is why you need to use simple and unambiguous language. Therefore, avoid complex terms, obscure words, and jargon. Also, avoid words that have no clear meaning, such as 'several' and 'usual' – such words can mean different things to different people. Provide clear instructions at all stages. Your participants should be able to understand exactly how you want them to respond to each of your questions. Do not assume that they already know how to respond to a questionnaire. And try to keep your questions as short as possible. Long questions might confuse the participants, or as is sometimes the case, people might forget the first part of the question by the time they get a grasp of the last part.

FOCUS

The questions should have a clear focus on a single, specific issue or a topic. While this appears to be obvious, in practice it is not so easily achieved. For example, you may be interested in identifying and measuring the purchasing preferences of your participants. An obvious thing to ask might be: What brand do you like the most?

This, however, would be the wrong question to ask. People often tend to like brands that they cannot normally afford, and they settle on buying brands that they can afford instead. Therefore, the right question would be: What brand do you normally purchase when you are buying [certain product]? Or, as an alternative, you could frame the question like this: Which of these brands are you most likely to buy?

In both cases there is a clear focus on what you want to know. An example of this problem might include the question: When do you usually go to work? A non-focused question such as this can provide you with a multiple answers. For example, a person might provide you with any of the following answers:

- I start work at 9 am.
- In the morning.
- I leave my home at 8 am.
- I take the 8:30 am train to work.

Therefore, a better question might be: What time do you typically leave home for work? A follow-up question to this might be: Do you leave home for work always at the same time, or do you leave for work at different times on different days?

In this case, you will also need to include the option for the participants to explain their working patterns if they do not conform to a typical working week – 9 am to 5 pm, Monday to Friday. Another problem with the focus can be identified in the so-called 'double-barrelled' questions. A double-barrelled question is when two issues that are not necessarily related are combined in one question. An example of this might be: Do you often go to the movies and buy popcorn?

A person may indeed often go to the movies, but may not necessarily often buy popcorn there. So what should the participant respond here? A better way to ask this question is: Do you buy popcorn when you go to the cinema? If yes, how often: every time, sometimes, very rarely?

OPTIONS

Do not assume or imply anything. Before you start asking specific details about some kind of activity, always provide options for the participants to specify whether they are engaged in this activity at all, and if so, with what frequency. For example, before you ask someone what kind of things they normally post on their Facebook wall, you first need to establish whether this person uses Facebook at all, and if so, how frequently. If you do not ask these two questions first, you may get a misleading answer: first, the person may not use Facebook at all, but may respond to your question anyway because you have not provided any option for the person to opt out; and second, active and passive Facebook users tend to exhibit very different online behaviours. Mixing them together without even being aware of that may lead you to a misleading result at the end.

BIAS

When the questionnaire can exhibit a prejudice of favour for or against something, and tends to lead the participant to answer in a particular way, we say that the questionnaire is biased. There are two types of questions that can make a questionnaire biased: leading questions and loaded questions. A leading question is a question that leads the participant to a particular answer. An example of this might be: Would you agree that option A is better than option B?

This question asks the participants to 'agree' with the researcher, and some people might do that in order to leave a good impression. The correct way to frame such a question is: Which of the following options do you prefer?

On some occasions, loaded questions are purposefully developed in such a way, and this is an example of unethical behaviour. For example, let us say that a particular sponsor might commission a survey in the hope of proving a point of some kind, or to obtain results that are in their best interests. In order to ensure that the results of the survey will lead to favourable data, some sponsors may try to insert leading questions, or may insist on certain wording to be included in the survey. This is considered to be a fraudulent practice, and researchers who follow through with such requests will be risking their reputation. Loaded questions are similar to leading questions. While leading questions tend to direct the participant towards a specific type of response, or may suggest an answer, loaded questions do so in a less obvious way. Loaded questions tend to include the 'reason' for doing something in the question. An example of this could be: Would you support more speeding cameras to save human lives?

Saving human lives is a very desirable thing and those who choose to answer this question in a negative way would appear not to value human life. If we ask the question in the following way, we may get a completely different answer: Would you support more speeding cameras as a way of increasing the state revenue budget? A correct way would be to remove the emotions out of the equation and to ask an objective question: Does traffic safety need more speeding cameras? While the chances are that no survey is completely free of error and bias, if such types of questions are consciously introduced and they are identified as such, the data may be rendered completely invalid.

Double-barrelled questions can also lead towards bias in some cases. For example: Do you wear seatbelts when driving so you can feel safer? This question already implies that seatbelts lead to increased sense of safety, but ignores the issue that some people might wear seatbelts only to avoid being fined. So, if this question is asked in this particular way, the results can be interpreted that people who say 'yes' wear seatbelts because they want to feel safe, not because they are required to do so.

CONSISTENCY

On many occasions, when faced with a controversial question, people's instinct will guide them to provide a socially acceptable answer, rather than their true opinion. That is why for some studies that involve complex psychological traits such as personality characteristics, motivations, or attitudes, researchers tend to include several questions framed to assess the same issue from different angles. These 'follow-ups' should be introduced at some distance from each other; for example, several other questions should appear between each of these questions. This strategy allows for you to test the consistency of the answers. The distance between the questions increases the likelihood that the participants will answer the second or the third question without recalling how they responded to the first question. This strategy is only advisable when you are conducting lengthy and complex questionnaires that deal with sensitive topics.

DESIGN

Pay attention to the design of the questionnaire – especially on issues of legibility, layout, and colour. An attractive and professional looking questionnaire may solicit you a higher response rate (Alreck and Settle, 1985: 97–128; Leedy and Ormrod, 2010: 194–7).

Also, you need to be aware that there are several ways in which you can conduct a research survey. However, regardless of how you conduct the survey, the principles are always the same. Nevertheless, what you need to be aware of is that each form of survey has its own advantages and disadvantages. There are several data collection methods that you could consider – face-to-face interviews, telephone interviews, written questionnaires, online questionnaires – and these are discussed below.

FACE-TO-FACE INTERVIEWS

The advantage of face-to-face interviews is that the researcher can establish a better rapport with the participants, which means better cooperation. Face-to-face interviews have the highest response rate (in terms of the percentage of people agreeing to participate). The disadvantage is that this type of research draws heavily on resources such as time and money, especially if the researcher has to travel to meet with the participants.

TELEPHONE INTERVIEWS

As an alternative, telephone interviews are less time consuming and less expensive (since travel is not needed). Also, with the use of Skype, the cost of conducting a telephone interview is significantly reduced, so there is no need for making expensive long-distance calls anymore. The response rate of such an interview is probably not as high as a face-to-face interview, but still significantly high compared to a mailed questionnaire. A minor drawback is that the researcher cannot establish the same kind of rapport as with face-to-face interviews. Also, the sample tends to be biased in terms that people without a telephone or access to the Internet cannot participate. In some cases, depending on the target population, this may not be a problem, but if the researcher deems this to be a problem, than another form of communication, or a distribution of a written questionnaire, needs to be devised. An additional advantage to both face-to-face and telephone interviews is that the researcher can ask for clarification of an ambiguous answer whenever appropriate.

WRITTEN QUESTIONNAIRES

Written questionnaires, on the other hand, can be distributed to a large number of people, including those who live far away. This means that the researcher does not need to travel, but there is some cost that needs to be factored in for mailing questionnaires if this is so. In this case, the researcher also needs to provide a stamped, addressed envelope so that participants can return their responses.

The distance between the researcher and the participant can be a disadvantage and an advantage at the same time. While lack of personal touch may result in a lower level of rapport, willing participants may respond more truthfully than in a personal interview if their anonymity is guaranteed. This is particularly the case when it comes to addressing sensitive or controversial topics. One drawback with this type of research is that most people do not bother returning the questionnaires, and so people who do return them may not necessarily be typical representatives of the planned sample. Another drawback is that the gathered data needs to be processed manually. If there is a large number of responses this may take some time (Leedy and Ormrod, 2010: 188–9).

ONLINE QUESTIONNAIRES

Online questionnaires are the same as the written questionnaires with the main difference being the distribution. Online questionnaires can reach even more people than written questionnaires, there are no associated expenses with mailing, and generally the response rate is somewhat larger because people can submit their responses more easily. An added benefit to this type of questionnaire is that the results are easier to process; or in some cases, the software automatically generates the results.

When it comes to recruiting participants, you can often target specific groups of people through various social media platforms such as Facebook or LinkedIn, or through group emails that may be supplied by various stakeholder institutions or organizations. In some cases you may need to provide some incentives in order to find participants, such as gift cards, or a prize draw.

When it comes to the actual gathering of data, you can either develop your own survey instrument if you have the skills, or you can use an already existing one. One popular online instrument that you can use for conducting research surveys is SurveyMonkey (www.surveymonkey.com). Companies such as Facebook, Philips, and Samsung use this instrument to conduct their market research or gather customer feedback.

If you plan to do an online questionnaire, the first thing that you need to be aware of is whether the population that you are interested in surveying has access to the Internet, and whether those that do have access are typical representatives of this population. If this is the case, then you can proceed with planning an online questionnaire.

EXAMPLE

Online Survey by 99designs.com

This example shows an abridged case study of an online survey. However, in this case the designers are not the ones conducting the study; they are the subject of the study. While so far I have discussed how you can conduct surveys, this example is intended to place you on the other side of the table, and to show you how it looks when designers are being surveyed. While I could have chosen any random example to illustrate how surveys work, I have decided to share this particular example because I believe that you might be curious to see how a sample of graphic designers have responded to the questions in this survey.

Survey topic: Client–designer relationship

Introduction

The survey was conducted in 2012 by the website 99designs.com, which is an online marketplace for crowd-sourced graphic design; 99designs is a type of business where the goods being sold are essentially the designers themselves, and positive client experiences are the primary source of new business. The business model of 99designs is based around their ability to provide customers with original graphic design work quickly and inexpensively. In order for them to do so, they rely on a network of over 180,000 designers based in 192 countries. A part of their business also includes helping designers to develop their professional skills and build strong and lasting client relationships.

Research Question

For an online business such as 99designs, increasing the number of their vendors – in this case, graphic designers – is as important as increasing their customer base. Keeping designers happy is essential to achieving this. One of the major concerns that they have identified in their business is that designers and clients often struggle to understand one other. In light of this, their research question was fairly straightforward: How to woo a designer?

Methods of Data Collection, Distribution and Data Analysis

In order to understand why is this the case, and to find ways to improve the designer–client relationships, 99designs used SurveyMonkey.com to gather quantifiable data from over 250 graphic designers in the US. Based on a formula provided to them by SurveyMonkey, they needed at least 200 respondents in order to have statistically correct results. They needed to develop an educational content that designers can use to bridge the communication gap with their clients, and this was the position from which they analysed the data.

Summary of Results

Designers' ability to communicate effectively with their clients is seen as critical to the business success of 99designs. Their survey confirmed that there is discontent between clients' needs and designers' wants. For example, as major sources of conflict, designers identified lack of clear direction from their clients, unclear understanding of the project, and unrealistic expectations (see Figure 5.3 Q1). In terms of what kind of client they would like to work with, almost 60 per cent preferred a client that is responsive – a

Question 1: What is your biggest challenge when working with clients? (Select up to two)

Getting paid on time

Getting pad what I am owed

Client's lack of direction

Client doesn't understand

Client doesn't provide

Client has unrealistic expectations

0%   50%   100%

Answered: 234 / Skipped: 23

Question 2: What are the most important characteristics a client can have? (Select up to two)

Always pays on time

Unlimited budget

Gives creative freedom

Knows exactly what they want

Very responsive

0%   50%   100%

Answered: 233 / Skipped: 24

Question 3: How do you most often source new clients? (Select up to two)

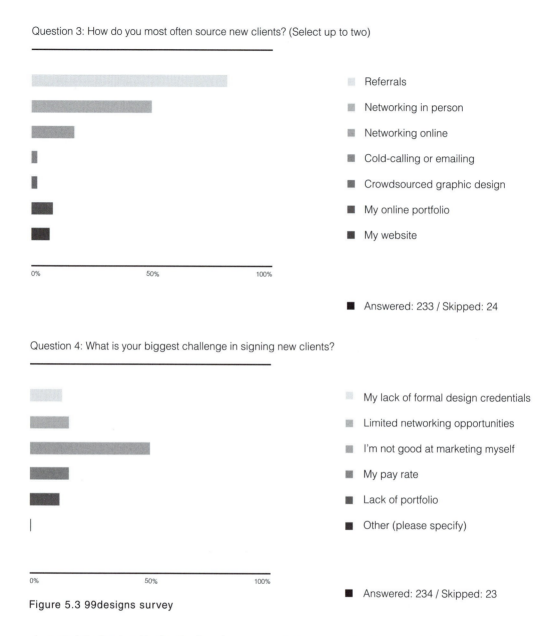

Referrals

Networking in person

Networking online

Cold-calling or emailing

Crowdsourced graphic design

My online portfolio

My website

0%   50%   100%

Answered: 233 / Skipped: 24

Question 4: What is your biggest challenge in signing new clients?

My lack of formal design credentials

Limited networking opportunities

I'm not good at marketing myself

My pay rate

Lack of portfolio

Other (please specify)

0%   50%   100%

Answered: 234 / Skipped: 23

Figure 5.3 99designs survey

characteristic that is critical to the iterative process that comes with refining a design. Clients that know what they want were the second most popular option, alongside clients that are willing to give them creative freedom (see Figure 5.3, Q2). When asked how they source new business, the survey showed that graphic designers largely source new business in relatively traditional ways, mostly relying on referrals based on personal relationships, or in-person networking (see Figure 5.3, Q3). Yet, when asked what their biggest challenge is in procuring new clients, nearly 50 per cent responded that they struggle to market themselves successfully. Half of the participants felt that their lack of personal marketing skills is preventing them from winning new business, outweighing other professional challenges such as lack of experience, access to networking opportunities, pay rate, and even lack of formal design qualifications or a design portfolio. By far the biggest challenge in getting new business, as the graphic design community in the US believes, is their inability to sell themselves (see Figure 5.3, Q4).

Recommendations

For 99designs, attracting and retaining designers is crucial. This also means helping designers build better client relationships and develop their portfolios. This survey helped them to understand how graphic designers felt about their own profession, and where their main issues lie. What they concluded is that the key to a successful project is straightforward communication with clients. When clients have a clear vision of what they want, the designs are better, they are produced more quickly, and this in turn becomes more cost-effective for both parties. Consequently, 99designs used this information to develop educational content for their blog where they provide expert advice to their network of designers and clients.

(SurveyMonkey, 2012)

5.2.3 DATA ANALYSIS

The analysis of the data is closely related to how the survey has been constructed. There are two main things that you need to consider first: how you will frame the questions, and how you will gather the answers.

PREPARING QUESTIONS

Sometimes, asking direct questions is the best way of finding out what people do in a certain situation, or think about a particular issue. However, constructing a questionnaire can prove to be a lot harder than it looks. When conducting a questionnaire, what we are trying to do is compare a number of people along a list of variables. As mentioned previously, the term 'variable' stands for 'something that can vary' and is a technical term for something that you can measure. In most cases, variables are characteristics that differ between people, such as age or gender, or place of birth, or level of income, or how many hours a person watches TV per day; and this is something that we can identify and quantify. As with any form of research that involves asking people questions, there is always a possibility that the responses might not be necessarily true. Participants may misinterpret the questions or misreport their answers for various reasons. For example, the participants may want to conceal something, or they may want to present themselves in a better way. You will need to take these things into account when preparing a questionnaire and when analysing the answers (Stokes, 2011: 141–2). Here is a straightforward six-step procedure that you can follow when working on a questionnaire:

Step 1: Define the purpose of the questionnaire

Step 2: Prepare the questions

Step 3: Specify the sequences of the questions

Step 4: Outline the distribution process

Step 5: Decide how will you administer the responses

Step 6: Pre-test and review the questionnaire if necessary

Once you have established what it is that you want to know – or in other words, what is your key research question – and once you have specified how you will administer or distribute the questionnaire (e.g. face-to-face, telephone, mail, or online), you will need to start thinking about asking questions and gathering answers. There are number of ways in which you can do this. The format of the questions does not necessarily need to be fixed, and it can vary throughout the questionnaire.

The way the questions are framed should depend on what it is that you want to know about a certain topic or an issue. Examples of different types of questions include dichotomy, multiple choices, checklist, categorization, frequency of occurrence, ranking, quantity, scale, and open-ended questions (see Figure 5.4).

1. Dichotomy

Dichotomy implies a division between two things that are seen as being opposite to each other, or entirely different. These types of questions are normally required for binary answers by which the participant is asked to choose one option out of two available alternatives. An example of this can be seen in Table 5.1.

Table 5.1 Dichotomist questions

What is your gender?

O Male

O Female

Do you own a car?

O Yes

O No

Dichotomy ————————————————————————————————————

Multiple Choices ——————————————————————————————

Checklist ——————————————————————————————————————

Categorization ————————————————————————————————

Frequency of Occurrence ————————————————————————

Ranking ——

Quantity ——————————————————————————————————————

Scale ——

Open-Ended Questions ——————————————————————————

Figure 5.4 Types of questionnaires

2. **Multiple Choices**

A multiple-choice option allows for the participant to choose only one option out of several possible alternatives. In some cases, this is a preferred option to an open-ended question – especially since it is easier for a researcher to quantify the responses. This may not always be an option, but in many cases, the researcher can predict what the possible responses to a particular question might be. Then the possible alternatives are listed, and the participant is invited to select one. An example of this can be seen in Table 5.2.

Table 5.2 Multiple-choice question

Which one out of the following brands of sports shoes are you most likely to buy?

○ Nike

○ Adidas

○ Reebok

○ Converse

○ Puma

○ Other (Please specify) _____

---

3. Checklist

The checklist option, on the other hand, allows the participant to select several options to a single question. In this case, the participant is asked to read the question or the statement and to select the options that he or she believes apply the best. The participant is also provided with the option to make either a single or a multiple selection, or to advise the researcher that he or she does not own any of the listed items. An example of this can be seen in Table 5.3.

Table 5.3 Checklist question

Do you own any of the following items?

○ Desktop computer

○ Laptop computer

○ Tablet (e.g. iPad)

○ Smart phone (e.g. iPhone or an Android)

○ I don't own any of the above items

---

4. Categorization

Some questions can be constructed in such a way that the answer can fit only one category. An example of this can be seen in Table 5.4.

Table 5.4 Categorization question

Please select what type of car are you interested in buying:

○ Hatch

○ Sedan

○ Coupe

○ Convertible

○ Wagon

○ SUV

○ Van

○ Light truck

5. Frequency of Occurrence

If the purpose of your research is to establish certain behavioural patterns, you can ask questions that can provide you with behavioural-style answers. A good way to do this is by asking questions that can help you determine the frequency of occurrence of some personal activity. Examples of this can be seen in Table 5.5.

The second example is a follow-up question. This means that the participant has already stated that he or she has a Facebook account in a previous question. Therefore, the purpose of this follow-up question is for you to identify how frequently the participant uses this social network. If the participant has stated that he or she does not use Facebook at all, then the participant should have been provided with the option to skip this question.

Table 5.5 Frequency of occurrence

How often do you exercise?

○ Every day

○ 5 to 6 times a week

○ 2 to 4 times a week

○ Once or twice a week

○ Less than once a week

○ Less than twice a month

○ I don't exercise at all

How often do you use Facebook?

○ I rarely use Facebook

○ I use Facebook at least once a week

○ I spend less than 1 hour per day on Facebook

○ I spend between 1 and 2 hours a day

○ I spend between 2 and 4 hours a day

○ I spend 5 hours or more on Facebook each day

---

6. Ranking

On some occasions you may want to identify the participants' preferences for something. The best way for you to do this is to ask the participants to place their responses in a ranking order. For example, let us say that you are conducting a survey of secondary school students based in a metropolitan area and you want to learn about their Internet usage habits. The question could be framed as shown in Table 5.6.

Table 5.6 Ranking question

Where do you use Internet the most?

Rank the following places in order of importance by writing 1, 2, 3…, with 1 being the most important. Write 0 for the places where you don't use Internet at all.

__ At home

__ In a classroom

__ At a school's library

__ At a public library

__ In public transport on a mobile device

__ At a friend's house

__ Other (Please specify) _____

---

7. Quantity

In other cases, you may need to know the amount of something. The answer to a quantity-related question is simply a number. An example of this can be seen in Table 5.7.

Table 5.7 Quantity question

How many full-time employees do you currently employ?

Write in number _____

---

8. Scale

In some cases, certain questions that are aimed at measuring someone's attitude towards something cannot be answered simply on the basis of 'yes' or 'no'. Such questions need to be ranked on a scale of some kind. Some of the most commonly used scales are: Likert scale, numerical scale, itemized scale, graphic scale, semantic differentiation scale, constant-sum scale, and behavioural scale.

Even though there are some differences between them, all scales are essentially similar to each other. They do, however, vary in terms of visual appearance. Therefore, you may want to take this into consideration when you are deciding which kind of scale to use in your survey. You do not have to use one and the same format of scale throughout your questionnaire. For example, for the purposes of your report presentation you can diversify your use of scales by generating various infographics. Infographics are a highly effective form of data visualization and they are very useful in written reports, interactive media, or when conducting research presentations. Here are some explanations about the above-mentioned scales:

- **Likert Scale**: The Likert scale, named after the researcher Rensis Likert, is one of the most popular scales. This scale consists of a series of statements or items that the participants can evaluate on a 5-point scale ranging from 'strongly agree' to 'strongly disagree'. There are several variations on how you could design a Likert scale. Table 5.8 is one example of how a Likert scale could look.

Table 5.8 Likert scale

Bellow you will find a list of statements about the product that you just tested.

Please indicate your agreement or disagreement for each statement by selecting the appropriate number.

	Strongly Agree	Agree	Neutral	Disagree	Strongly Disagree
It's easy to use	1	2	3	4	5
It looks good	1	2	3	4	5
I like the quality	1	2	3	4	5
The price is reasonable	1	2	3	4	5
I would buy it	1	2	3	4	5

- **Numerical Scale**: The numerical scale is based on a series of bipolar words or phrases in relation to the issue in question. As with the Likert scale, participants also select numbers to identify their responses. See Table 5.9 for an example.

Table 5.9 Numerical scale

Please tell us how satisfied are you with the product that you have just tested.

    Extremely satisfied | 1   2   3   4   5   6   7 | Extremely dissatisfied

---

- **Itemized Scale**: The itemized scale is quite similar to the one above. The main difference is that the participants have a predetermined set of responses to choose from. See Table 5.10 for an example.

Table 5.10 Itemized scale

What is your opinion about the product that you have just tested?

1. Very bad

2. Bad

3. Neither bad nor good

4. Good

5. Very good

How would you describe your overall experience using this product?

1. Terrible

2. Not good

3. It was all right

4. Good

5. Very good

6. Excellent

- **Graphic Scale**: The graphic scale, on the other hand, allows the participants to rate an issue by making a point on a line, rather then choosing a number. See Table 5.11 for an example.

Table 5.11 Graphic scale

Indicate your opinion about the product by marking an X on the lines bellow.

Ease of use	Very bad ├───────────────────────┤	Very good
Visual appearance	Very bad ├───────────────────────┤	Very good
Quality	Very bad ├───────────────────────┤	Very good
Pricing	Very bad ├───────────────────────┤	Very good

- **Semantic Differentiation Scale**: The semantic differentiation scale is, again, very similar to the one above. The main difference is that rather than marking an X on a straight line, the participants are asked to rate their responses on a seven-point scale. See Table 5.12 for an example.

Table 5.12 Semantic differentiation scale

Indicate your opinion about the product by marking an X on the lines bellow.

It's easy to use	├──┼──┼──┼──┼──┼──┤	It's difficult to use
Looks great	├──┼──┼──┼──┼──┼──┤	Looks terrible
Very good quality	├──┼──┼──┼──┼──┼──┤	Poor quality
Affordable	├──┼──┼──┼──┼──┼──┤	Expensive

- **Constant-Sum Scale**: The constant-sum scale asks the participants to divide a constant by way of indicating the relative importance of each attribute in question. See Table 5.13 for an example.

Table 5.13 Constant-sum scale

In regards to the product that you have just tested, divide 100 points among the following characteristics, depending on how important they are too you if you were to purchase this product.

Please make sure that the allocated points add to 100.

Ease of use	_____ points
Visual appearance	_____ points
Quality	_____ points
Cost of maintenance	_____ points
Electricity usage	_____ points
Recyclability	_____ points
Packaging	_____ points
Price	_____ points
	100 points

- **Behavioural Scale**: The behavioural scale is normally used for identifying the likelihood of the participants to engage in some action, or to perform some function in the future. See Table 5.14 for an example.

Table 5.14 Behavioural scale

How likely are you to buy the product that you have just tested?.

○ I will definitely buy it

○ I probably will buy it

○ I might buy it

○ I probably will not buy it

○ I will definitely not buy it

9. Open-Ended Questions

Sometimes we need to ask questions whose answers cannot be easily quantified. These questions are called 'open-ended'. Even though they elicit qualitative responses, on occasions we do need them in order to accrue an additional layer of information from the participants. Examples of this can be seen in Table 5.15.

Table 5.15 Open-ended questions

If this brand was a person, how would you describe this person?

Describe your feelings when you look at this logo?

The second example indicates that a visual prompt (a logo in this case) is also included in the questionnaire. In this particular case, the logo should be placed next to or above the question. In some other cases, supporting visual material can be included as an appendix at the end of the questionnaire. Also, when including open-ended questions, you need to make sure that the participants will have sufficient space to write down their responses.

ANALYSING ANSWERS

Once you have received the answers, you can group them statistically in relation to the questions. You can do this in several ways. For example, you can group people by gender, age, location, or any other characteristic that you have found important to identify. Then you can see how the responses relate to each of these groups, as well as how they present themselves overall. In this way you can see what the preferences are for each of these groups and whether there are some patterns in their responses. Various combinations of participant characteristics can give you various data, and this can be very useful if you want to identify some particular behavioural or social patterns. If you have included some open-ended questions, summarize the responses and see if you can establish some categories based on what those responses indicate.

5.2.4 PREPARING A REPORT

When it comes to preparing a report on a survey research, you can use the following structure as a guide (see Figure 5.5):

1. Introduction
2. Research Question
3. Methods of Data Collection
4. Process of Distribution
5. Data Analysis
6. Summary of Results
7. Recommendations
8. Appendix 1: The Questionnaire
9. Appendix 2: The Responses

As with all research reports, first you need to provide an introduction to the issue that you have been investigating, followed by your key research question. Then, you will need to explain what kind of questionnaire you have developed and why, how did you distributed it, and how you have analysed the answers. Here you also need to state what the response rate was and whether there have been any limitations that you had to take into account, such as time and resources. Following this, you will need to summarize the results of the survey and point out any interesting patterns or unexpected responses that you have identified. The best way for you to present the results from your survey is to visualize them through infographics. Then, in the recommendation section, draw

Approximate Content Distribution Ratio

Introduction

Research Question

Methods of Data Collection

Process of Distribution

Data Analysis

Summary of Results

Recommendations

Appendix 1: The Questionnaire

Appendix 2: The Responses

Figure 5.5 Preparing a survey report

connections between the responses and the research question and present recommendations in terms of what might be the suitable course of action. Also, you will need to state here whether further research is needed, and if so, what kind of research. In most cases, in addition to the report, you will need to include the questionnaire and the responses in the form of appendixes. This is not only good for record keeping, but it also allows your supervisors or any external researchers to examine and evaluate your research, thus allowing for greater validity of your work.

5.3 USER-CENTRED DESIGN (UCD) RESEARCH

Technology often creates the illusion that it is here to make our lives simpler. However, we continue to be surrounded by things that make our lives more complicated because they are difficult or confusing to use. We often lose time and patience trying to understand how something works, and in doing so we tend to adjust ourselves to meet the functions of some particular product. When such situations occur, this means that we have been exposed to bad design. A well-designed product is a product that is designed to meet your needs and not the other way around.

User-centred design (UCD) is a design process that is driven by the information that is generated by the design users. Design-driven companies tend to use UCD research in order to discover intuitive ways for people to interact with their products, and they are constantly on the lookout to resolve any usability issues with their own products. Therefore, in UCD research the research participants are the subjects of the study. This type of research process enables companies to consistently design engaging and user-friendly products, interfaces, or environments. Companies that use UCD research know that products that are easy to use will lead to increased client satisfaction, and satisfied clients tend to become loyal consumers. However, this is a never-ending task, and the research process requires a constant review and update (IBM, 2007; UXPA, 2010).

When used as a strategic business resource, UCD can offer a number of critical advantages: it can enable businesses to develop user-friendly products; it can improve the customer satisfaction levels; it can decrease expenditures on technical support and training; it can assist with the promotional aspects of the product; and it can increase the company's market share. Yet, despite these advantages, many companies still do not conduct UCD research. Instead, they assume that they have an intuitive understanding of the needs of the common user and that UCD is somehow inherently present in their products. This misconception of how products should be developed often allows for new technology or market trends to drive the development of the products, rather than the actual needs of the users (IBM, 2007).

The use of UCD as a strategic business resource can be beneficial to both the end-users and the company. According to IBM, every dollar invested in UCD returns from $10 to $100 in profits. Such high return on investment is possible because, as IBM explains, 'usable products are desirable products'. This is especially important to be taken into account when products have to compete in highly competitive market environments where usable products tend to stand out more. Then again, increased sales are not the only benefit of UCD. When used to its full extent, UCD can save money and time to producers, clients, and end-users.

According to IBM, companies that do not use UCD research in their product development stage tend to spend up to 80 per cent of their service costs on unforeseen user requirements down the track. With this in mind, it can be argued that it is far more economical for producers to invest in UCD research, than not to. UCD research can identify any potential user-related problems in the early stages of the design and can factor them in on time. The alternative is that these problems will have to be addressed later on under pressure from the market, and this can be a very costly exercise. Therefore, one of the best ways for a company to protect its development investment is to keep its clients and end-users involved through the entire design development cycle (IBM, 2007).

For clients, on the other hand, better usability can often translate into higher efficiency and better productivity – and this is especially true for corporate clients whose business processes are based on products that require ease of use and intuitive systems of navigation by their employees. While these benefits can be financial, they can also be psychological. Ease of use reduces the operational stress for the end-users and can lead to higher levels of user satisfaction. Yet, regardless

UCD Team

UCD Team Leader ⎯⎯⎯⎯⎯⎯⎯⎯⎯⎯⎯⎯⎯⎯⎯⎯⎯⎯⎯⎯⎯⎯⎯⎯⎯⎯⎯⎯⎯⎯⎯ ●

User Experience (UX) Design Leader ⎯⎯⎯⎯⎯⎯⎯⎯⎯⎯⎯⎯⎯⎯⎯⎯⎯⎯⎯⎯ ●

Visual / Industrial Designer ⎯⎯⎯⎯⎯⎯⎯⎯⎯⎯⎯⎯⎯⎯⎯⎯⎯⎯⎯⎯⎯⎯⎯⎯⎯ ●

Human-Computer Interaction (HCI) Designer ⎯⎯⎯⎯⎯⎯⎯⎯⎯⎯⎯⎯⎯ ●

User Assistance (UA) Architect ⎯⎯⎯⎯⎯⎯⎯⎯⎯⎯⎯⎯⎯⎯⎯⎯⎯⎯⎯⎯⎯⎯ ●

Technology Architect ⎯⎯⎯⎯⎯⎯⎯⎯⎯⎯⎯⎯⎯⎯⎯⎯⎯⎯⎯⎯⎯⎯⎯⎯⎯⎯⎯⎯ ●

Marketing Specialist ⎯⎯⎯⎯⎯⎯⎯⎯⎯⎯⎯⎯⎯⎯⎯⎯⎯⎯⎯⎯⎯⎯⎯⎯⎯⎯⎯⎯⎯ ●

Service / Support Specialist ⎯⎯⎯⎯⎯⎯⎯⎯⎯⎯⎯⎯⎯⎯⎯⎯⎯⎯⎯⎯⎯⎯⎯⎯ ●

Internationalization and Terminology Specialist ⎯⎯⎯⎯⎯⎯⎯⎯⎯⎯ ●

User Research Specialist ⎯⎯⎯⎯⎯⎯⎯⎯⎯⎯⎯⎯⎯⎯⎯⎯⎯⎯⎯⎯⎯⎯⎯⎯⎯⎯ ●

Figure 5.6 UCD Team at IBM

UCD Team Leader

───────

Responsibilities: The UCD Team Leader has an overall responsibility for UCD deliverables and their integration into the product development plan.

Skills required: Project management skills, knowledge of UCD processes, and knowledge of product development processes.

Figure 5.7 UCD Team Leader

User Experience (UX) Design Leader

Responsibilities: The UX Design Leader has the responsibility
for the total user experience design of the project.

Skills required: Vision, leadership, technical expertise,
as well as project and people management skills.

Figure 5.8 User Experience (UX) Design Leader

Visual / Industrial Designer

Responsibilities: The designers have the responsibility for the overall product appearance, visual layout, as well as the consistent visual signature of the advertising, packaging, and product design.

Skills required: Ability to work in a team, design knowledge, creativity, as well as model making and prototype building skills.

Figure 5.9 Visual/Industrial Designer

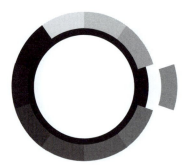

Human–Computer Interaction (HCI) Designer

Responsibilities: The HCI designer has the responsibility to specify the software task flow, to manage the overall interface and interaction design, and to divide the tasks to be carried out by the user and by the computer.

Skills required: HCI knowledge, conceptual modelling, and ability to synthesize information.

Figure 5.10 Human–Computer Interaction (HCI) Designer

User Assistance (UA) Architect

Responsibilities: The UA architect has the responsibility
to specify the most appropriate user assistance
mechanisms available.

Skills required: Knowledge of information architecture
and ability to work in a team.

Figure 5.11 User Assistance (UA) Architect

Technology Architect

Responsibilities: The technology architect has the responsibility
to specify the underlying technology required for the project.

Skills required: Technical skills in the relevant domain,
knowledge of the development process, programming or
engineering knowledge, and ability to work in a team.

Figure 5.12 Technology Architect

Marketing Specialist

Responsibilities: The marketing specialist has a responsibility to specify the target market and the user audiences; to identify the key competitors, the market objectives, the key promotional messages and the communication channels; needs to provide advice on the packaging; and will need to specify the terms and conditions of sale.

Skills required: Marketing knowledge, market intelligence, knowledge of market trends, ability to synthesize information, and ability to work in a team.

Figure 5.13 Marketing Specialist

Service / Support Specialist

Responsibility: The service and support specialists have to specify what kind of support and service should be delivered with the product offer.

Skills required: Knowledge of service and support technologies and knowledge of product options.

Figure 5.14 Service/Support Specialist

Internationalization and Terminology Specialist

Responsibilities: The specialist in Internationalization and Terminology needs to make sure that the product offer addresses the needs of international audiences and has a responsibility to specify the most suitable terminology that is to be used for the offer.

Skills required: Internationalization and localization specialization, as well as knowledge of relevant terminology and languages.

Figure 5.15 Internationalization and Terminology Specialist

User Research Specialist

Responsibilities: The user research specialist has the
responsibility for the design, and to facilitate, analyse,
and interpret the UCD studies as well as articulate the recommendations based on the applied research.

Skills required: Knowledge of UCD research methods,
technical abilities, and knowledge of Human Factors and
Usability Architecture.

Figure 5.16 User Research Specialist

of these benefits, many producers still do not invest in UCD capabilities and act reactively by relying on their knowledge alone, or on current and often short-lived market trends when developing their products – in other words, by imitating their competitors. These companies are easy to spot because they tend to show the following signs: dissatisfied customers; unproductive users; expenses related to heavy training and support costs; and they exhibit decrease in market share, or lack of market growth (IBM, 2007).

5.3.1 CONDUCTING UCD RESEARCH

Above all, UCD research is a human-focused experimental research. By definition, an experiment is a study where a systemic effort is made to identify and impose control over all variables except one (Punch, 2005: 68–9). Research by experiments is often conducted in pure sciences (fields such as mathematics, physics, or chemistry), but can also be found in social sciences (fields such as psychology, economics, or politics). Experiments in pure science are primarily carried out in a laboratory where the researcher can easily control the environment. Experiments in social sciences, on the other hand, are primarily carried out in the real world where the environment is unpredictable and subject to changes brought about by various external factors (Moore, 2000: xii). Experimental research in design, such as UCD research, can be conducted both in a laboratory setting and in the real world. This mostly depends on the purpose of the study: whether design prototypes are being tested, or whether final designs are being evaluated. In either case, the research participants can be randomly assigned, or identified in naturally occurring groups (see Leedy and Ormrod, 2010: 108). Now I will introduce you to four key principles in UCD: team formation, problem identification, prototyping, and product review.

TEAM FORMATION

UCD research starts with the formation of a multidisciplinary project team. This team will work with the prospective end-users throughout the design process and beyond. Ideally, the members of the UCD research teams will come from a range of disciplines. As IBM points out, getting the right set of people with the right set of skills is essential. From one organization to another, the structure of the UCD research teams will certainly vary, depending on the projects or the available resources. As a company that uses UCD research on a regular basis for developing products, websites, software packages, apps, and other interfaces, IBM has its own specific UCD structure (see Figure 5.6).

PROBLEM IDENTIFICATION

Once the team is set, there are seven basic steps that you will need to address when identifying the problem that needs to be solved:

Step 1: Identify the business aims and objectives

Step 2: Conduct user analysis

Step 3: Conduct competitors' analysis

Step 4: Start with the design process

Step 5: Review the design process

Step 6: Provide an overview of the user experience

Step 7: Continue with the observations

The first thing that you will need to do is to set the right business goals by determining the nature of the target market, who the end-users are, and identifying the primary competitors. Therefore, the first task begins with an internal question: Who will be using the product? Once the target audience is identified and sampling has been made, participants are recruited to work with the team.

For a successful UCD, a commitment to understanding and involving the end-users in the design process is necessary. Therefore, you will need to be able to understand and determine the core user needs and desires that must be fulfilled in order for the product to be successful. A good way of achieving this is to ask the participants to rate their levels of interest in a new product or product enhancement. For this task, the UCD researchers at IBM use the following questions:

- What do you want the product to do for you?
- In what sort of environment will you be using the product?
- What are your priorities when using this product?

or:

- Which functions will you use most often?
- How are you doing these tasks today?
- What do you like and dislike about the way you've been getting your tasks done?

The last two questions identify issues related to the product's competition. These questions do not necessarily refer to products by other companies. The purpose of these questions is to identify whether there are any other means that the participants might have been using to complete these tasks. For example, people often tend to improvise and adjust things to serve them for other purposes (IBM, 2007).

Superior design calls for an ongoing awareness of the competitors and the customers. Therefore, it is advisable that at the same time when you are testing how the participants perform their tasks with your product, you should test how they perform the same tasks with products by your competitors. At this stage you can ask your participants to list and prioritize their needs; identify current products that they use at the moment; and list any other products they would prefer to use instead. Then, you should ask them to perform their normal tasks with your product and with other, competitive products. You should also ask your participants to list the strengths and the weaknesses of the competition in order of importance. This is a very useful exercise and it will help you to set the initial benchmarks for your new product design and development. After completing this task, you should be able to identify how your product performs when compared with other, competitive products.

Once you have gathered the information from the user analysis and the competitors' analysis you will need to start by proposing design solutions and soliciting new user feedback. Typically, at this stage you should introduce low-fidelity prototypes and conduct evaluation sessions. Feedback needs to be gathered throughout all stages of the design development, and at regular intervals. Based on the input that you are receiving, you should start updating the design solution and conduct further evaluations. This should continue up to the stage when you will have a fully working prototype. Then you will need to do another series of tests on the feedback obtained regarding your competitors, and see whether your product is achieving its goals. If the test is conducted by a third party and the results are in your favour, then this is something that you can also use for promotional purposes.

You also need to be aware that the user experience neither starts nor ends with the product alone. The design team must have an overview, and provide input, on all of the interactions that the users have with the product, regardless of whether these interactions are direct or indirect. This includes how the product is advertised, ordered, paid for, packaged, maintained, installed, administrated, documented, upgraded, and supported. The UCD researchers will need to continue to monitor the product through its lifecycle, while gathering market intelligence, monitoring any market changes and competitor activities, and continue to listen to user feedback. This knowledge will then be used for the development of the next generation of products (IBM, 2007).

PROTOTYPING

Once the users task requirements are identified and the competitive methods are understood, the design process can begin. This includes the development of a prototype. As the research progresses, prototypes will assume different complexity and should be rolled out accordingly, at different stages of the research process. First you can start with basic, low-fidelity prototypes. These basic prototypes can be as simple as pieces of paper put together to form the shape of the product. If the design is a screen-based interface, the prototypes can feature visuals resembling the interface. As the testing progresses and the feedback is processed, more advanced prototypes can be introduced for further testing. Advanced prototypes should be developed to resemble the finished product as closely as possible. In most cases, prototypes may not have all the functionality that the final product will have, but they will have enough functionality for the researchers to test some parts of the design.

The observation studies come to the forefront during the prototype testing stages. As the participants try out the prototypes, the researchers record their task performance, reactions, and comments. This information will help the design team to decide which design elements to keep and which to change. On the basis of this input, design refinements need to be implemented in the subsequent prototypes and tested again. This cycle of modification and retesting should continue until the end result meets the required functionality and usability criteria.

At this point, a 'beta' version of the product might be introduced and distributed to a restricted set of users for their evaluation. Unlike the prototypes, the beta version should be a fully functional product. The information gathered from the beta release can help UCD researchers to identify any unforeseen problems with the design and to 'fine-tune' the product before its formal market release. This, however, does not mean that the user input ends here.

PRODUCT REVIEW

The UCD research team should continue to monitor the product and should invite the users to participate in 'benchmark assessments' in which the product is rated against the users requirements and against other competitive products. At the same time, the company's customer services should also record any problems that are reported by the users. This information should help the design team to improve the next iteration of the product (IBM, 2007).

5.3.2 DATA COLLECTION

Data collection in UCD research is often done in combination with questionnaires and observation studies because together they complement each other. For example, in most cases, you will be asking a set of structured and semi-structured questions prior to the observations, during the observations, and once the observations have concluded, so you can establish what the attitudes and the opinions of the participants are.

What you also need to be aware of is that observation studies in quantitative research are somewhat different from those in qualitative research. Qualitative observation studies are exploratory and tend to record things in great detail by using field notes and documenting events, phenomena, or behaviours. Quantitative observation studies, on the other hand, tend to be descriptive in nature and have a clearly outlined focus. Their purpose is to measure certain aspects of human behaviour, and to quantify that in some way. For example, in some cases particular types of behaviour can be monitored for the purpose of determining the frequency by which these types of behaviour occur, and in other cases, the behaviour can be rated for accuracy, intensity, maturity, or for whatever dimension is deemed important. In order for researchers to record this information, they prepare charts in which they define and categorize various types of behaviour that they would like to study in a precise and concrete manner. This helps researchers to record behavioural characteristics in a systematic way as they occur. In the case of design-related observation studies, design researchers often develop a design prototype, or a series of prototypes, that are then tested by groups of participants while observations take place.

Observation studies, like most forms of research, involve considerable advance planning, attention to detail, and time. Unlike some other forms of research, observation studies often require the help of one or more research assistants. If this is the right research approach for you, conducting a pilot study first is highly recommended. A pilot study will help you test whether you have managed to define and categorize all types of behaviour that you plan to monitor, and whether you have anticipated every action, segment, or time sequence correctly (Leedy and Ormrod, 2010: 182–3).

The nature of the data collection process in UCD research often calls for highly advanced research capabilities. For example, in addition to well-established research teams, large corporations use a range of state-of-the-art UCD labs that are based around the world. In the case of IBM, this includes the Usability Test Lab, Electronic Group Lab, and Prototype Design Lab.

- **Usability Test Lab**: The Usability Test Lab is the longest established UCD lab at IBM. This lab is used for carrying out hands-on tests on products, ranging from small focused tests to large-scale product tests. The lab consists of two rooms: a participant room and an observation room. The participant room is set up in such a way as to simulate as close as possible the environment in which the product would be most likely used. This room has cameras that capture the participants' facial expressions, their hand movements, and their use of manuals. The cameras are kept hidden or out of sight, because the participants might not behave naturally if there was a camera right in front of them. This room is separated from the observation room by one-way glass and a sound-resistant wall. In this way, researchers can observe the participants without causing much interference in the test procedures. The researchers in the observation room use a microphone to communicate with the participants, ask them questions, or direct them to begin with their tasks.

- **Electronic Group Lab**: For experimenting with groups of people, IBM uses a so-called Electronic Group Lab equipped with local area network (LAN) based groupware that can collect a variety of data from various groups of users. The data that they collect includes information such as task requirements, task flow, current products, as well as feedback on early mock-up designs. In these labs, IBM can gather information from 20 users simultaneously, while still ensuring that all users' views are heard, and the input is viewed anonymously by all of the participants at the same time. This lab also has technologies for studying users remotely. Once the test is complete, the information is automatically collected and securely stored in a database for further use.

- **Prototype Design Lab**: In their Prototype Design Lab, IBM uses rapid prototyping technology to produce alternative designs based on user feedback during the participatory design sessions. They begin with low-fidelity paper-made prototypes and ask participants to make amendments to the design by using pencils and coloured sticky notes. This feedback is processed and reflected into more advanced types of prototypes. While design researchers at IBM do have the capacity to immediately produce realistic looking prototypes, through practice they have identified that participants are more willing to propose changes when the prototypes are of basic quality. Based on their observations, it appears that the participants seem to be more reluctant to challenge realistic looking prototypes. As with the other labs, user feedback is also recorded and securely stored in a database for further use.

At IBM, UCD research tests are conducted on a regular basis and various teams conduct user feedback sessions once a week or fortnightly. In addition to this, IBM uses portable labs for conducting fieldwork studies. Such labs can be bought ready-made from various vendors, or they can be custom made. IBM uses portable labs when visiting customers in their place of work, or presenting at conferences (IBM, 2007).

While the research approach by IBM that I have presented here is the best-case scenario, this does not mean that smaller companies cannot conduct UCD research with smaller teams and with basic facilities. Even IBM started its UCD research programme as a very small operation, with only a couple of rooms available for conducting their research (see IBM, 2007). As the importance of UCD for the company begins to grow, so will the UCD research budget and the related facilities.

5.3.3 DATA ANALYSIS

The key to data analysis in an observation study of this kind is the objectiveness by which the data collections are being made and assessed. Once you have prepared the chart with the behaviours that you are interested in monitoring, you can start dividing the observation period into segments or time intervals and record what kind of behaviour occurs during each segment or time interval. Segments could be based on particular sets of actions that the participants will perform. The time intervals can be based on whatever time span might be suitable for the observed behaviour. In addition, you should create a rating scale by which you can score the participants' behaviour; for example, from bored to very excited, or from happy to sad. It might be beneficial if you have two or three assistants or research partners, independently from each other, who can help you with the rating of the same behaviour. Then, when you compare the reports you will be able to see whether the results correspond with each other, or not. You will need to continue with the study until you receive consistent ratings for any single occurrence of the behaviour (Leedy and Ormrod, 2010: 183).

5.3.4 PREPARING A REPORT

Preparing a report for a UCD research is not much different from preparing a report for a survey research. Therefore, a similar guide applies (see Figure 5.17):

1. Introduction
2. Research Question
3. Prototype Description
4. Methods of Data Collection
5. Data Analysis
6. Summary of Results
7. Recommendations
8. Appendix 1: The Questionnaire and the Responses
9. Appendix 2: Records from the Observation Study

As with all research reports, first you need to provide an introduction to the issue that you have been investigating, followed by your key research question. Then, you will need to explain what kind of prototype you have developed and why. This should be followed by an explanation of how you have collected the data and how you analysed it. In addition to this, you will need to summarize the results and point out any interesting patterns or unexpected responses that you have identified. The best way for you to present the results from your survey is to present charts that document the behaviour and the responses. Visualize the results by using infographics whenever possible. In the recommendation section, draw connections between the responses and the research question, and present a recommendation on how the design can be improved further. In

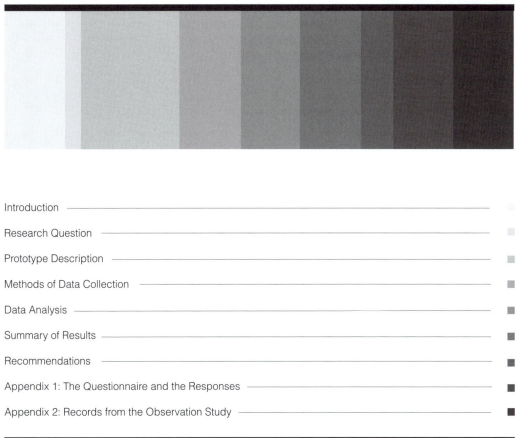

Approximate Content Distribution Ratio

Introduction

Research Question

Prototype Description

Methods of Data Collection

Data Analysis

Summary of Results

Recommendations

Appendix 1: The Questionnaire and the Responses

Appendix 2: Records from the Observation Study

Figure 5.17 Structure of a UCD report

most cases, in addition to the report, you will need to include the questionnaire, the responses, and the records from the observation study in the form of appendixes. As with the survey research, this is not only good for record keeping, but it also enables your supervisors or any external research-ers to examine and evaluate your research, thus allowing for greater validity of your work.

5.4 HALLMARKS OF GOOD QUANTITATIVE RESEARCH

A good rule of thumb for beginners in quantitative research is to follow the so-called 'scientific method' – an empirical scientific inquiry based on five to seven steps (Gimbel, 2011: xi). The steps in this process are (see Figure 5.18):

- Observations
- Question
- Hypothesis
- Prediction
- Test (Experiment or Additional Observation)
- Negative Result (Introduce New Hypothesis)
- Positive Result (Verification)

First, you need to make observations about something that is unknown, new, or unexplained. This is where you identify a problem that you will investigate further. On the

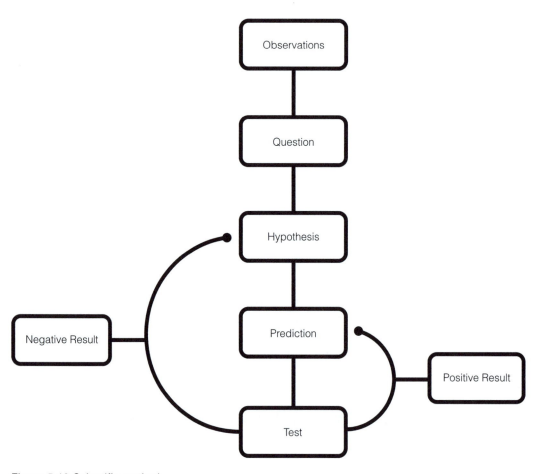

Figure 5.18 Scientific method

basis of your observations, you will need to form a question that can focus your investigation further. Then you should read about the current theory surrounding this problem and form a hypothesis that provides an explanation for the observations. On the basis of the hypothesis, you can make initial predictions on the possible outcomes and formulate a plan to test these predictions by conducting experiments or further observations. As you collect and process your data, you will see whether your predictions are correct or not. If your initial predictions are correct, go back to step four (Prediction), make additional predictions, and test them again. If they are also correct, that means that you have verified your findings. Then make your final conclusions and present your findings in your report. If your predictions were not correct, that means that your hypothesis has been proven false, in which case you will need to go back to step three (Hypothesis) and form a new hypothesis based on your new knowledge. Then follow the process again. What you also need to be wary of is to what extent the variables have been identified, whether they were relevant to the problem, and whether they have been controlled or not. You will need to take everything into account and report all variables that may have affected your investigation.

5.5 CONCLUSION

Unlike qualitative research, which is used for building new theories, quantitative research is often used for generating statistics, describing a certain phenomenon, or identifying cause-and-effect relationships. This type of research is often described as 'independent' and 'objective', because it relies on an empirical process that uses numeric and quantifiable data to arrive at conclusions. This is in contrast to qualitative research, where the conclusions are often made on subjective interpretations (Williams, 2007: 66; Belli, 2009: 60).

There are two ways in which you can approach quantitative research: externally – in a natural setting during fieldwork; or internally – in a controlled environment within a research facility. In either case you will need to select your participants randomly from a particular group of people (or a community) that is of interest to you. A good rule of thumb for beginners in quantitative research is to follow the so-called 'scientific method' in the research process – an empirical principle of scientific inquiry based on five to seven steps.

While this type of research is frequently used in marketing, now it is also gaining a wider acceptance in the field of design as well. This is especially beneficial when you are presenting your design proposal in a corporate environment, because most corporate clients will be accustomed to seeing quantitative research from various market or business reports, and this is the type of research they more readily accept. Communicating quantitative research in the form of metrics that matter to corporate clients can often be the key to helping businesses understand design as a strategic investment (Sato and Mrazek, 2013).

5.6 SUMMARY

In this chapter I have provided an outline of what quantitative research is, discussed its relevance to designers, and explained how it is conducted. In addition to this, I have presented you with two of the most common quantitative research approaches in design: surveys and experimental research, or in this particular case, UCD research.

Survey research is one of the most commonly used types of quantitative research. This kind of research involves acquiring statistical information about a particular group of people by asking them questions and then arranging these answers in a systemic order. The purpose of the survey is to document people's characteristics, opinions, attitudes, or previous experiences. Contrary to qualitative research where the interviews are quite open-ended, in survey research interviews are fairly structured. You can conduct a research survey based on a face-to-face interview, a telephone interview, a written questionnaire, or via an online questionnaire (Leedy and Ormrod, 2010: 182).

Experimental research tries to establish the cause-and-effect relationship among a group of variables. Experimental research in design can be conducted both in a laboratory setting and in the real world, depending on what kind of designs are being tested and how these designs are intended to be used. A true experimental study follows a systemic procedure that imposes various level of control over the variables and then measures the effects as they occur (Punch, 2005: 68–9).

This type of research is fundamental to UCD – a design approach that grounds the planning, design, and development process in information about the people who will use a particular product, environment, or service. Data collection in experimental research is often done in combination with questionnaires and observation studies. Quantitative observation studies are descriptive in nature and have a clearly outlined focus. Their purpose is to measure certain aspects of human behaviour, and to quantify them in some way. The key to data analysis in an observation study is the objectiveness by which the data collections are being made and assessed.

The introduction of UCD as a strategic business resource can be beneficial to both the end-users and the company. UCD can enable businesses to develop user-friendly products, it can improve the customer satisfaction levels, it can decrease expenditures on technical support and training, it can assist with the promotional aspects of the product, and it can increase the company's market share. Companies that do not use UCD research in their product development stage tend to spend up to 80 per cent of their service costs on unforeseen user requirements down the track.

VISUAL RESEARCH

KEYWORDS   Visual Research   Visual Connoisseurship
           Hermeneutics   Compositional Interpretation
           Visual Culture   Content Analysis
           Material Culture   Semiotics

We live in a society that is dominated by images and objects. Whether we remember or forget the things we see around us, we need to accept that even for a moment they stimulate our imagination by way of either memory or expectation (Berger, 1972: 129). The ability to critically examine the effects images and objects have on people's lives is particularly important for all designers regardless of their disciplinary focus. Therefore, the type of visual research that I will introduce here is concerned with the study and interpretation of images and objects. This means that this research is 'hermeneutic' in nature. Hermeneutics is a philosophical inquiry that focuses on the interpretation of linguistic and non-linguistic expressions that can be found in symbolic communication, symbolic interaction, and culture in general (Ramberg and Gjesdal, 2013).

6.1 WHAT IS VISUAL RESEARCH?

There are many ways of looking at visual research, but for the purpose of this book visual research will be defined as a study of images, forms, and objects in both visual and material culture. For the same purpose, culture can be described as 'the arts and other manifestations of human intellectual achievement regarded collectively' (Oxford Dictionaries, 2013c). A form can be described as 'The visible shape or configuration of something' (Oxford Dictionaries, 2014a); an object can be described as 'A material thing that can be seen and touched' (Oxford Dictionaries, 2014b); while an image can be described as: 'A representation of the external form of a person or thing in art', or 'A visible impression obtained by a camera [. . .] or other device, or displayed on a computer or video screen' (Oxford Dictionaries, 2013d).

As such, this kind of research can cover everything from typography, illustration, and advertising, to product design and architecture. The reason why visual and material cultures are grouped together under the banner of visual research is because we perceive both of these cultures in visual terms, regardless of whether we deal with two-dimensional images or three-dimensional forms.

The focus of this chapter will be on the study of existing images, forms, and objects that have been found or identified by the researcher. One traditional way of visual analysis (or a critique) has been termed as 'the good eye' principle. This type of analysis is neither methodological nor theoretically explicit practice. Therefore, this practice can best be described as 'visual connoisseurship' (Rose, 2012: 52). Visual connoisseurship focuses on various aspects of the social modality of the production of images, forms, and objects in the following terms:

- Who commissioned the work?

- Why was the work commissioned?

- Who was the creator behind the work?

- How is this work being used?

- Who is using this work?

Visual connoisseurship also examines compositional and technological modalities of the making of an image, a form, or an object, but with the purpose of identifying the influences of other creators in a particular work. Experts who use this method have acquired extensive knowledge of works of art and design, and can confidently attribute these works to artists or designers, or to particular schools and styles. These people can establish the sources of the works they are studying, and likely the influences behind them – and as a result they can judge and critique the quality of these works. Developing a 'good eye' requires a lot of experience, as well as broad and specialist historical and contextual knowledge in the area of study (Rose, 2012: 52–7). This approach has been long established in the field of art history and theory, and from there it has been adopted to design history and theory. Nevertheless, this way of looking at things will not be introduced further here, because it requires a substantial knowledge of the field as a prerequisite, and as such it is more appropriate for providing a critique rather than conducting research.

In this chapter, however, I will introduce you to other ways of looking at images, forms, and objects that are more practice-based and that do not require extensive previous knowledge in the field. This includes three research methods: compositional interpretation, content analysis, and semiotics. You can use these methods to conduct systematic and empirical visual research under the framework of visual and material culture studies.

6.2 VISUAL AND MATERIAL CULTURE STUDIES

Visual and material cultures are not only a *part* of our everyday life; they *are* our everyday life. Visual culture focuses on the importance of images in people's lives. As such, it takes into account issues such as image making, the formal components of the image, and the cultural reception of that image (Mirzoeff, 1999). Material culture, on the other hand, takes into account the social relationships people have with objects and looks at what kind of symbolic meanings these objects project (Woodward, 2007: 3). The term 'form' in this case stands for many things and can include any inanimate thing or object, ranging from a pencil or a spoon to a building or a mobile phone.

For many years, Western culture has privileged the spoken and written word as the highest form of intellectual practice and has seen visual representations as 'second-rate illustrations of ideas' (Mirzoeff, 1999: 5). However, I have to clarify that observing visual culture is not the same as understanding it – and this is where studies of visual culture come in. The emergence of visual culture studies has challenged the assumption that text is a higher form of intellectual practice, and Western philosophy and science have recognized the value of visual representations alongside the textual representations of the world. Given that certain visual experiences may not be fully explicable in purely linguistic terms, visual literacy is also necessary. From this point it can be argued that visual culture is not an independent field of study, but an interdisciplinary subject that exists within a broader social, historical, and cultural context (Mirzoeff, 1999: 5–6; 2009).

The field of material culture studies brings together a range of disciplines into the study of uses and meanings of forms, and provides a perspective into the human–object relations (Woodward, 2007: 3). As Ian Woodward (2007: 4) argues, by studying culture through material objects we can better understand social structures and social differences, as well as human action, emotion, and meaning. Objects can signify sub-cultural affinity, occupation, personal interests, or social status. In addition to this, objects are incorporated into, and represent, wider discourses related to social norms and values. Furthermore, objects can carry personal and emotional meanings, can mediate interpersonal interactions, and can even define one's social identity. As such, objects can help particular social groups or classes form a sense of integration, belonging, and identity; they can assist in the formation of self-identity; and they can even help people achieve self-esteem (2007: 4). In addition to this, material culture is particularly useful for studying consumer society and consumer behaviour, especially since people need to establish and negotiate their own meaning of the consumer objects before they incorporate them within their own personal culture (2007: 4).

6.2.1 DATA COLLECTION

As a researcher of visual and material culture you can examine the effects of images, forms, and objects that are already out there in the world – this is the data that you are collecting. The sampling process of your research can vary from highly rigorous to very subjective. However, regardless of this, I would advise you to define an ideological platform around which you will frame your selection. The ideological approach that you can consider may be placed within a range of contexts – historical, geographical, commercial, political, cultural, or social. This in turn will give you a strong research focus and will allow you to analyse images, forms, and objects better. The processes of data collection and data analysis are often closely intertwined in visual research, and therefore I will address aspects of data collection alongside data analysis.

6.2.2 DATA ANALYSIS

In addition to being able to identify and select a sample of images, forms, and objects around some kind of ideological platform, you will need to be able to critically examine your selection. There are five points that you can take into consideration while doing this, which are discussed in detail below:

- What does my selection depict?

- Who is the audience?

- How do people look at this?

- How are these things embedded in a wider cultural context?

- What is the interrelation between the image, the form, or the object and the accompanying text (if any)?

WHAT DOES MY SELECTION DEPICT?

Images, forms, and objects often depict social differences. Social scientists have argued that social categories are not natural, but constructed – and these constructions can take visual or material forms (see Rose, 2012: 11–12; Woodward, 2007: 3–16). What you need to be aware of is that there are a number of ideological platforms through which these things could be studied. For example, feminist and postcolonial scholars have studied how gender and race have been represented and visually communicated in the context of Western culture, both in a historical sense and in a contemporary one.

One particular example of this would include the studies by Jean Kilbourne, a prominent advertising critic, whose critical studies helped develop and popularize the study of gender representation in advertising. Her books such as *So Sexy So Soon* (Levin and Kilbourne, 2009), and her award-winning films *Killing Us Softly* (1979) and *Still Killing Us Softly* (1987), have been highly influential in establishing the connection between advertising and several public health issues, including violence against women, eating disorders, and addiction. In her film *Slim Hopes: Advertising and the Obsession with Thinness* (1995), Kilbourne uses over 150 magazine and TV advertisements to offer an in-depth analysis of how female bodies are depicted in promotional imagery. She also reports on the negative effects of such imagery on women's health. By addressing the relationship between these images and the obsession of girls and women with dieting and thinness, Kilbourne offers a new way to think about life-threatening eating disorders such as anorexia and bulimia, and provides a well-documented critical perspective on the social impact of advertising. In her film *Killing Us Softly 4: Advertising's Image of Women* (2010), Kilbourne reviews whether and how the image of women in advertising has changed over the last 20 years. In doing so, she uses over 160 advertisements and commercials to critique advertising's image of women. Through creative and productive dialogue, she invites viewers to look at familiar images in a new way – one that moves and empowers them to take action (see Kilbourne, 2013).

Another example worth noting would be the studies of Tanner Higgin (2009). Higgin studied the 'disappearance of race' – Black race in particular – in massively multiplayer online role-playing games (MMORPG) such as Ever Quest, Ever Quest II, and World of Warcraft. In his study, Higgin argues that the disappearance of blackness is evident in contemporary fantasy role-playing games. MMORPG privileges whiteness and contextualizes it as the only selection by not allowing options for alterations in coloration or racial deviations. Higgin believes that because Blacks are generally hypermasculinized and ghettoized in the world of gaming fiction, players and game designers do not see blackness as appropriate for the discourse of heroic fantasy. As a result, Eurocentrism proliferates while other disruptive racial profiles are removed and eliminated through fantastical proxies (Higgin, 2009).

This way of analysing culture allows us to reflect on how images, forms, and objects portray social categories such as gender, race, class, sexuality, or disability. According to Gillian Rose (2012: 12), understanding the social context in which these things exist can help us to critically examine:

- What kind of social work do these things perform?
- What are the underlying principles of inclusion and exclusion that are evident here?
- What is the distribution?
- What kind of codes, signs and signifiers are used for communicating meaning?

WHO IS THE AUDIENCE?

Images, forms, and objects are usually produced with a specific audience in mind, or with a broader idea of what kind of effect they should draw from the viewers. What you need to be aware of is that each audience brings its own interpretations of what certain things stand for, and that not all audiences will be able or willing to respond in a way in which they might be expected to respond. A way of understanding audiences can be done through a culturographic analysis. This is a research process that uses research methods such as interviews and ethnographic observations for the purposes of studying people and their reactions, or visual and material objects – more specifically their content, physical qualities, and presentational form; and techno-anthropologies (communication technologies that display images, forms, and objects) (see Rose, 2012: 261–96).

HOW DO PEOPLE LOOK AT THIS?

Critics of visual and material culture are concerned not only with how images, forms, and objects look and who looks at them or uses them, but also *how* they are looked at and used. For example, Rose (2012: 13) argues that visuals work by producing effects every time they are looked at or used. John Berger (1972: 8–9), however, argues that we never look at just one thing; instead, we are always looking at the relation between 'things' and ourselves. The way we see, as he points out, is affected by what we know or what we believe in (1972: 9).

There is an underlying connection between visuals and viewers, and objects and users. Taking images, forms, and objects seriously involves thinking about how the viewers and the users are positioned in relation to the image, the form, or the object – and whether this might be a historical, cultural, commercial, or philosophical placement.

HOW ARE THESE THINGS EMBEDDED IN A WIDER CULTURAL CONTEXT?

The seeing of an image or the use of an object always takes place within a particular cultural context that mediates its impact – whether this is a gallery, private home, public space, museum, or shop. Each place has its own economy, discipline, and rules – and all of this creates a culture that influences the behaviour of the individual, which then leads to how an image is being seen and experienced, and how an object is being used (see Rose, 2012: 15). As mentioned before, culture in this context can be understood as 'the ideas, customs, and social behaviour of a particular people or society' (Oxford Dictionaries, 2013c).

WHAT IS THE INTERRELATION BETWEEN THE IMAGE, THE FORM, OR THE OBJECT AND THE ACCOMPANYING TEXT (IF ANY)?

Images, forms, and objects are often used in conjunction with other kinds of representations, such as written or spoken text. It is very unusual, in fact, to encounter 'something' without a text of some kind. Even paintings and sculptures in a gallery will very likely have written labels on the walls that provide some kind of information about them, or a price. I will not go into detail by providing obvious examples such as images used in newspapers and magazines, signage on buildings, or products in shops, but the point is that virtually all images, forms, and objects may be accompanied by some kind of text at some point. This interrelation between images, forms, objects, and text can often provide an additional context in which culture can be studied further (Rose, 2012: 16).

Furthermore, there are a number of methods that you can take into consideration when analysing data on visual and material culture. However, if you are at an early stage of your research career it is best to begin by using three methods: compositional interpretation, content analysis, and semiotics.

COMPOSITIONAL INTERPRETATION

From the first year of their studies, design students are trained to develop an ability to describe and discuss their work and the works of others. Therefore, designers should be able to critically examine and describe images, forms, and objects by using correct terminology and vocabulary, and compositional interpretation is a method that can be used for this purpose (Rose, 2012: 51). However, unlike its name suggests, compositional interpretation is a descriptive research method with limited interpretative abilities.

The main benefit from using this method is its inherent vocabulary that allows you to describe in correct terminology what it is that you are seeing. While this method focuses strongly on the visual appearance and pays most attention to compositionality, it also pays attention to the production aspects – but only when the knowledge of the technique of production helps in describing some characteristics of the image or the objects. Compositional interpretation does, however, have its limitations. This method focuses on the visual aspects of the work in question, but it ignores socially specific ways of seeing and experiencing things, as well as the visual and material representations of the social. In visual research, images and objects cannot be seen as isolated occurrences and they also need to be looked at and interpreted in terms of how they are produced, for whom, and why (Rose, 2012: 55). That is why other methods such as content analysis and semiotics are necessary for further exploration. Nevertheless, despite its limitations, compositional interpretation offers a particular way of looking at content and form (2012: 55–6).

Compositional interpretation is a method that examines images, forms, and objects by breaking them down into a number of components related to things such as content, colour, type of form, spatial organization, light, movement, expressive content, and so on. Nevertheless, in practice most of these components are related to each other and the notion of composition refers to all of these components seen together (Rose, 2012: 58–79).

There are a number of questions that you can ask in the process of compositional interpretation. First, you should begin with some really basic questions and then progress to those that require specific details. These questions are for the purpose of providing pure description of the image, and answers should not contain value judgements, analysis, or interpretation. You can use the following set of questions to describe some of the key elements of the image or the object, but please note that not all questions will be applicable in all cases:

- What do you see? Does this work represent a form of art, architecture, design, advertisement, a motion picture, or something else? Are there any iconographic elements that you can identify (e.g. is this image a form, or an object based on, or inspired by, a historical event or a period, particular style, or something else)?

- Can you provide the location and date of when the work was made, and by whom?

- What is the medium in which the work is presented? Is it painted, photographed, filmed, made out of stone, metal, and so on?

- What kind of techniques and tools were used in the production of the work? Are there any particular or characteristic tools and techniques used in the production of the work?

- What is the size, scale, or length of the work? Depending on what it is that you are analysing, you can assess the relationship of the work to a person – in terms of scale; you can provide the actual dimensions if you are studying a product or a building; or if the image is a film, you can provide information on its length. In some cases, you can assess these issues in terms of context as well.

- What kinds of objects or forms are represented in the image, or vice versa? Can you identify any elements, structural systems, or general shapes within the composition?

- What kind of direction does the composition follow? Is the axis of the direction vertical, horizontal, centred, or diagonal? If it is diagonal, does the axis go from left to right, or from right to left?

- What kinds of lines dominate? Is the line soft, hard, thick, thin, variable, irregular, planar, jagged, intermittent, indistinct, curved, and so on?

- What is the relationship between the shapes in the work? Are they grouped in terms of large and small, are they overlapping, are they positioned gradually next to each other, and so on?

- Can you describe the texture of the surface, or provide any other comments about the execution of the work if the issue of texture is not applicable?

- Can you describe the dominant colour, or the colour palette of the work? There are three terms that you can use to describe the colour palette: hue – this is a reference to the basic, dominating colours in the image (e.g. red, blue, and green); saturation – this is a reference to the purity of a colour in relation to the colour spectrum (e.g. the saturation is high if the colour is vivid, and low if it is nearly neutral); and value – this is a reference to the lightness or darkness of a colour (e.g. if a colour is in its near-white form, than its value is high; if it is its near-black form, than its value is low).

- Can you describe the composition of the design? Is it stable, repetitious, rhythmic, unified, symmetrical, harmonious, geometric, varied, chaotic, horizontal or vertically oriented, and so on?

- Can you describe the spatial organization? How is the work positioned within the space or the environment where it is found? If the work is an image, then you can answer this question in terms of perspective: How are elements of the image presented in relation to each other – in terms of height, width, depth, and position when viewed from a particular point? How is the effect of distance is achieved? While answering these questions, you can also describe from what kind of point of view the image is being presented – is it 'bird's-eye' (a top-down perspective, also referred to as an 'aerial view'); is it a an eye-level angle (when the image is presented as seen through the eyes of the image maker); is it a 'worm's-eye' perspective (the opposite to a bird's eye view); and so on? The second question refers to two-dimensional images that try to give an impression of depth (Barrett, 1994; Rose, 2012: 51–80).

These are only some of the questions that you can consider when providing a compositional interpretation. As your knowledge and experience progress, you will be able to describe images, forms, and objects in even greater detail by using some additional descriptive elements to do so. In time, by developing a proficiency in this method you will be also able to develop visual connoisseurship skills.

CONTENT ANALYSIS

Content analysis is a quite different method from compositional interpretation. This is a quantitative method that involves counting and summing phenomena in images or texts. As with other quantitative research methods, this method can also be used to support your qualitative research. One of the main advantages of content analysis is that it can enable you to conduct primary research and come up with new and original data that you can use as evidence in your argument (Stokes, 2011: 56). This method is based on a set of rules and procedures that must be rigorously followed for the analysis of images, including images of objects and forms – but not of the objects and the forms themselves (Rose, 2012: 81).

Content analysis is best used for visual culture studies related to mass media, such as TV, newspapers, magazines, and the like. As a designer, you may need to study the frequency with which certain types of images appear in the media. For example, let us say that you are conducting a study on advertisements in fashion magazines and you would like to know how multicultural high fashion is, or what kind of products have placements on a particular TV show. You can get a definitive answer to this by comparing the number of product placements in that TV show, or by counting models with different ethnicities that have appeared in selected magazines within a given period. In the case of the TV show, you can choose to watch all seasons of the show and categorize all product placements. Or, in the case of fashion magazines, you can select a representative number of issues from, for example, *Vogue*, *Elle*, and *Cosmopolitan* from the selected period, and you can count the number of models in each of these categories – 'Black', 'White', 'Asian', and 'other'. In addition to this, you can have other categories representing selected product brands in the first example, or fashion labels in the second. Using the same principle, you can also identify how much each brand is presented, or how multicultural each of the fashion labels is. Once this study is completed you will have factual evidence on which you can make an informed statement about the object of your study (see Rose, 2013: 82; Stokes, 2011: 56–7).

In any case, please bear in mind that the above examples are only a generalization. If you are conducting such a study you will probably need to develop a more detailed system of analysis. For example, you could conduct content analysis based on counting the frequency of certain images, or visual elements in a clearly defined sample of images. This approach also includes an analysis of these frequencies. In order for this research process to be reliable and replicable, each aspect of the process needs to follow certain requirements (Rose, 2012: 87). The breakdown of the process has been outlined by Jane Stokes in her book *How to Do Media & Cultural Studies* (2011: 61–4), and this process can be easily adapted to content analysis in visual research. Here is a 12-step process that you can follow to achieve this:

Step 1: Establish your research question or hypothesis

Step 2: Read widely on the topic

Step 3: Define your object of analysis

Step 4: Define your categories

Step 5: Create a coding sheet to record your findings

Step 6: Test your coding categories

Step 7: Collect your data

Step 8: Summarize your findings

Step 9: Interpret the findings

Step 10: Relate this back to your research question

Step 11: Present your findings

Step 12: Discuss the findings

As with any other research process, first you will need to establish your research question or hypothesis. This is important, because you will need to have a clear idea of what you would like to find out before you start looking. Then look at previous work focused on the medium in which you are interested. Has there been any previous research done on the topic of your interest? Has any of this research been done by using content analysis? If not, examine some other similar work based on content analysis so you can see how and why this method has been applied. Then you can refine your research question and hypothesis to incorporate your secondary findings (Stokes, 2011: 61).

Now you will need to isolate the material that you have chosen to study and think about how your selection will help you answer your research question or test your hypothesis. State what kind of images you will study and why. You also need to think about how many images you are going to examine. As with any quantitative research, your sample should be large enough to be representative, but also manageable (Stokes, 2011: 61). For research students, it is best if you first consult your supervisor on the amount of images you are planning to study before you proceed.

The next thing you will need to do is decide what categories of content you are going to count in your analysis. This is called 'coding'. The coding categories must be associated with a number of characteristics. Rose (2013: 91) outlines three criteria that you need to consider when defining coding categories:

- **Exhaustive**: Every aspect of the images that you are studying must be covered by one category.
- **Exclusive**: The categories should not overlap.
- **Enlightening**: The categories should be analytically interesting and coherent.

Taking these criteria into consideration can prove to be difficult, but it is necessary. What you also need to be aware of here is that different people might interpret the same code in different ways. That is why your coding must be clearly defined and unambiguous. To make this process valid, your content analysis needs to be replicable. Other researchers independently from you should also be able to code similar images by using the same categories in the same way. A good way of testing your codes is by conducting a smaller-scale pilot study alongside other fellow researchers who will be following the same principles of work independently. The process needs to be refined until an agreement is reached on the final codes. However, this does not mean that the codes are final; you can continue refining your categories as you progress with your research if deemed necessary (Rose: 2013: 96). Based on this process, you may need to further refine your research question or hypothesis. Also, you should keep a careful record of all the changes that you make, as you will need to discuss this process in your research report (or thesis). It is very important to show in your report how your ideas have developed (Stokes, 2011: 62–3).

Once the categories have been defined and tested, and you are confident that your coding parameters will provide you with the information you need in order to answer your research question or to prove or disprove your hypothesis, then you can start processing the images. Make sure that you note down any exceptions or particularly difficult decisions. Then you will need to start summing up your findings. Make a note of how many occurrences of each category there are. This raw data can then be converted to percentages. This will allow you to make easier comparisons across your sample. Once this is done, you will be able to observe whether the patterns of the relationships in each of the categories can answer your research question or confirm your hypothesis (Stokes, 2011: 63–4).

Do not worry if your research question is not answered or your original hypothesis is not confirmed. Think about why this might have happened and allow the data to lead you to a new question or hypothesis if necessary. This is all part of the learning process. Reflect on what you could have done otherwise and how you would do things differently. Repeat the study if necessary. In any case, present your findings in a clear and organized manner, using appropriate charts, tables, and infographics. Finish your study by discussing the strengths and weaknesses of your research, and discuss how you might have conducted your study otherwise. Explain what you have learned from this study (Stokes, 2011: 63–4). What you also need to take into consideration here is that numbers do not transfer easily into significance. If something occurs very often, this is not necessarily a sign that this thing is more important than something that occurs rarely. Sometimes something that is kept out of the picture can also be significant to your research (Rose, 2012: 102). That is why content analysis can be a powerful method for making explicit facts about content that may not be immediately obvious (Stokes, 2011: 66).

SEMIOTICS

Semiotics, also referred to as 'semiology', is a study of signs and their interpretation. This method is neither descriptive (in the way compositional interpretation is) nor quantifiable (as content analysis). Instead, this is an interpretative method that allows you to analyse images or objects and understand how they work in relation to broader systems of meaning (Rose, 2012: 105). Semiotics as a method can provide you with an elaborate analytical vocabulary for describing how signs make sense. Due to the nature of their work, this method is particularly useful to creatives working in graphic design, advertising, branding, fashion, and photography, but it can be very beneficial to other designers as well (e.g. product or spatial designers). By addressing how various elements of your work interact with cultural knowledge to create social meaning, semiotics can provide an intellectual context to your work (see Stokes, 2011: 72).

This is a particularly popular method for studying both visual and material culture. The method involves describing how images and objects create meaning by observing them from a particular ideological platform. This is an interpretative method that requires relatively few resources, and unlike content analysis, it does not need to be applied to a large number of images or images of objects. Nevertheless, this method does require a high level of knowledge about the topic of your study. For example, you will need to have a good knowledge on what various visual or material codes represent in order to be able to fully understand the conventions that you are analysing (Stokes, 2011: 72–3). In any case, there are seven steps that you can follow when conducting a semiotic analysis:

Step 1: Define the topic that you will analyse

Step 2: Decide what kind of data you will gather

Step 3: Describe the data you have gathered

Step 4: Interpret the data

Step 5: Highlight any relevant cultural codes

Step 6: Discuss your findings

Step 7: Write a conclusion

Before you begin gathering data, you will need to decide what your topic of analysis is. This should be related to your research question or hypothesis. Then, you will need to decide what kind of images or objects you are going to look at and what kind of media will you be studying (e.g. TV, magazines, newspapers, showrooms, museums, etc.). The first stage of your analysis begins with the description of the content of the images or the objects. Here you will need to provide detailed information of what the images or the objects represent. The next stage involves a discussion of the meanings and implications of each separate sign, both individually and collectively. For example, if you are studying an advertisement, then you will need to explain what the relationships are between the linguistic signs (the text) and the visuals (the image or object) and how they work together. Here you also need to think about whether there are any cultural codes and conventions that one would expect from the audience of this particular media. In other words, for whom are these images or objects intended? Is there a specifically targeted audience for these codes, or are they meant to have a broad appeal? Is there any particular cultural knowledge that you need to have in order to understand the meaning behind them, or do they have a universal appeal? Discuss what these things actually represent, and what they mean to their audiences. Finally, discuss whether your analysis has answered your research question, as well as whether this has supported or refuted your hypothesis. Then, sum up your findings in the conclusion (Stokes, 2011: 74–5).

In order for you to conduct a semiotic analysis, first you will need to have a good understanding of what signs are. According to the *Oxford Dictionary*, a sign can be 'an object, quality, or event whose presence or occurrence indicates the probable presence or occurrence of something else' – for example, flowers are often given as a sign of affection. On the other hand, a sign can also be 'a gesture or action used to convey information or an instruction' – the type of function performed by traffic signs, for example (Oxford Dictionaries, 2013e).

Sign are often made up of two parts. The first part of the sign is the 'signified'. This stands for an object or a concept; for example, a young human that has not yet reached the age to walk and talk can be described as a baby. The second part of the sign is the 'signifier' – an element that is attached to a signified that in return sums up the meaning of the sign. The difference between the signifier and signified is very important in a context of semiotics, because these two may not always be connected in an obvious way. For example, in the English language, the word 'baby' may not refer to an actual baby and may also be used as a term of 'endearment between adults' – when one person calls the other 'baby' (Rose, 2012: 113). The distinctions, however, do not end here. You also need to take into consideration that there are three kinds of signs: icons, indexes, and symbols.

ICON

An iconic sign is a sign in which the signifier provides an instant recognizability to the signified. This type of sign is especially important for all types of design forms and visual images. For example, a photograph of a baby is an iconic sign of that baby (Rose, 2012: 119). In some cases, certain design objects can also acquire an iconic status. For example, the Eames lounge chair and ottoman developed by Charles and Ray Eames in 1956 can also be described as an icon of modern design (see Image 6.1). This is because the object is an instantly recognizable design artifact that is highly characteristic for its era. The chair's design has endured time and style and over half a century later it still remains a desirable object. The chair is even exhibited in places such as the Museum of Modern Art in New York, the Art Institute of Chicago, and the Vitra Design Museum in Germany, and it continues to be featured in various design publications.

Image 6.1 Eames lounge chair and ottoman

The Eames lounge chair and ottoman (1956), designed by Charles and Ray Eames, were originally produced by Herman Miller in the US. (Photography courtesy of Herman Miller, Inc.)

INDEX

An index is a sign that demonstrates a clear relationship between the signified and the signifier. In communication design, for example, indexes are often used for environmental graphics for the purpose of providing instructions or directions. Pictograms are the best examples of designed indexes. Whether they are used for ways of showing or ways of finding, they have an unmistakable universal appeal and command instant recognition (see Mollerup, 2005). One of the most commonly found pictograms is that of a woman and man used as a sign for a restroom (see Illustration 6.1). The pictogram of the baby, if used in the same context, indicates the location of a changing room for infants (Illustration 6.2).

SYMBOL

The word 'symbol' comes from the Greek *symbolon*, which means contract, token, insignia, and a means of identification. The symbol, regardless of whether it is in the form of a picture, a sign, a word, an object, or a gesture (or all of them, or parts of them together), requires an association

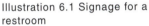

Illustration 6.1 Signage for a restroom

Illustration 6.2 Signage for a changing room for infants

with a certain and consciously held idea in order to fully express its meaning. As a rule, a symbol depends upon a group of people agreeing upon its meaning – thus this is a somewhat unfamiliar meaning of 'contract' (Goldammer, 1995: 591).

If we take this into consideration, a baby can also be interpreted as a symbol that stands for a new beginning or can represent notions of 'the future' (Rose, 2012: 119). Some other examples of widely accepted symbols include the following signs (see Illustrations 6.3, 6.4 and Image 6.2) – all of them standing for peace, and Che Guevara's stencilled image, which is often seen as a symbol of revolution and rebellion (see Illustration 6.5).

A word or an image, and even a gesture, becomes a symbol when it implies something more than its obvious and immediate meaning. The symbol has a wider and 'unconscious' appeal, which is never precisely defined or fully explained. Symbols work precisely because in the

Illustration 6.3 The peace symbol

This sign was created by the British artist Gerald Holtom in 1958. The sign was originally designed as a symbol for the Direct Action Committee Against Nuclear War (DAC) and was an emblem for the Campaign for Nuclear Disarmament (CND) in Britain, but in 1960 in the USA the sign was used as a symbol of the peace movement.

Illustration 6.4 Dove of peace

This illustration, drawn by Pablo Picasso as an emblem for the First International Peace Conference in Paris in 1949, became one of the world's most recognizable symbols of peace.

everyday context we do not perceive anything fully, or comprehend completely. We can see, hear, touch, smell, and taste; but how far we can see, how well we can hear, what our touch tells us, and what we taste, depends upon both the quality of our senses and our willingness and capacity to process all of this. It is our senses that limit our perception of the world. In this regard, it can be argued that we often rely on unconscious appeals when it comes to perceiving reality. Even when our senses react to real phenomena, such as sights and sounds, they are translated from the realm of reality into the realm of the mind. Within our mind they become psychic events whose ultimate nature is inexplicable (Jung, 1964: 4).

Since we cannot know the ultimate nature of matter itself, it can be argued that every experience contains an indefinite number of unknown factors, while every concrete object remains unknown in certain respects. In reality, events constantly occur, but they often remain hidden below the threshold of our consciousness. Since people select with reason and knowledge,

Image 6.2 The 'V' hand sign

This sign has a number of meanings that range from victory (most famously used by Winston Churchill during the Second World War), to insult, or happiness. Nevertheless, one of the most popular meanings of this sign is that of representing a symbol of peace by anti-war protestors and counterculture activists.

Illustration 6.5 Stencilled image of Che Guevara

This image was based on the iconic photograph taken by Alberto Korda in 1960, which was titled *Guerrillero Heroico* (Heroic Guerrilla Fighter). Because of Che Guevara's strong personal image as an idealist and revolutionary, his stylized image became a widely accepted symbol of revolution and rebellion in popular culture.

logical analysis is the prerogative of consciousness. The unconscious thought, on the other hand, seems to be guided mainly by instinctive trends and is represented by a different set of corresponding thought forms – archetypes (Jung, 1964: 67). When 'unconscious' events occur, they are subliminally absorbed. People become aware of them only in a moment of intuition; by a process of profound thought that leads to an unconscious conclusion; or as a sort of after-thought that such events must have happened – even though they have been originally ignored (1964: 5). Without us realizing it, our unconscious perception of subliminal messages influ-ences the way in which we react to both events and people (1964: 20). Consequently, when a mind explores a symbol, it is led to ideas that lie beyond the grasp of reason. Since there are innumerable things beyond the range of human understanding, we frequently resort to the use of symbols in order to communicate concepts we cannot exactly define or fully comprehend.

As Carl, Jung (1964: 4) argues, this is the reason why the employment of symbolic language and images is common to virtually all religions.

During the historical development and use of symbolization, a variety of categories and relationships have been developed. While some symbols, such as those of religion, have been and still are used to convey concepts concerned with people's relationship to the sacred, or holy, such as the Christian cross in Christianity (Illustration 6.6) and also to the social and material world, such as the *Dharmacakra* – the Wheel of Buddhist Law (Illustration 6.7), other non-religious types of symbols have achieved increasing significance as well. In the nineteenth and twentieth centuries, for example, symbols dealing with people's relationship to the material world and its conceptualization (such as scientific-technical symbols) have assumed ever-increasing importance in modern science and technology. These types of 'secularized' symbols are also rooted, to a degree, in the realm of religious symbolism. They function in a similar manner to religious symbols and their purpose is to associate particular meanings to particular signs. There are numbers of tropes and modes of signification that can operate within the concept of the religious symbol. This includes allegory, personifications, figures, analogies, metaphors, parables, pictures (as in pictorial representations of ideas), emblems, and individually conceived artificial symbols with added verbal meaning, as well as attributes used as a mark to distinguish certain individuals. They are all formal, historical, literary, and artificial categories of the symbolic. Whether it is religious or not, the symbol is intended primarily for the circle of the initiated and involves the acknowledgement of the experience that it expresses. Therefore, the meaning of the symbol is not to be kept hidden – on the contrary, it should have a revelatory character. The symbol indicates the need for communication, but at the same time it conceals the details and the innermost aspects of its contents (Goldammer, 1995: 591–2).

Essentially, semiotics is a method that is concerned with the analysis of meaning-making processes that are socially significant. As such, semiotics can provide you with an excellent

Illustration 6.6 The Christian cross

The cross is a Christian symbol that represents the crucifixion of Jesus Christ. This symbol is fully integrated within the whole process of worship. It appears on churches, in paintings, in books, on vestments, in jewellery, and at different stages in the church service as part of the ritual. With an intimate and all-embracing hand movement, the cross is even made by individuals – both priests and worshippers.

Illustration 6.7 The Wheel of Buddhist Law

The wheel represents the teachings of Buddha. The wheel has a number of meanings, including that it also stands for an endless cycle of birth and rebirth.

foundation for understanding the fundamentals of both visual and material culture. If you want to develop a better understanding of people's aspirations and motivations within our consumption-driven society, a particularly interesting area for conducting semiotic analysis is the field of advertising. That is why mainstream semiotics often looks at advertisements and the messages they convey. Often, these messages are core to the ideologies that structure contemporary society (Rose, 2012: 109). Given that advertising is a form of brand communication, similar semiotic analysis can also be extended to the field of branding. Below, I will provide you with some examples on how you can examine both fields from a semiotic perspective.

6.2.3 PREPARING A REPORT

There are no set formats on how you should prepare a report in visual research. As with most research reports, formats can vary depending on your audiences or style of work. Nevertheless, you can use the following list as a guide or starting point (see Figure 6.1):

1. Introduction
2. Research Question or Hypothesis
3. Visual Analysis
4. Social Awareness
5. Ideological Platform
6. Critical Reflection
7. Conclusion

After you have provided an introduction of what have you written and why, and presented the research question or the hypothesis that is the key driver behind your research, then you will need to show your selection and answer the question: What do you see? Images, forms, and objects often have underlying meanings that need to be identified, acknowledged, and deciphered. Regardless of what most people think, images, forms, and objects are not always self-explanatory or capable of being examined in a simple and generalist fashion. This means that in addition to showing what you are studying, you will also need to provide an accompanying description by using compositional interpretation and content analysis. Then, you also need to take into account that images, forms, and objects depend on and produce social inclusions and exclusions. Finally, you will need to take into consideration that there are many ways of 'seeing' and 'experiencing'. Because of divergence between ideologies (different ways of seeing the world), one and the same thing can be examined and interpreted in a number of ways (Rose, 2012: 16–17). At this point you can use semiotic analysis to explain the situation further. Therefore, think of your ideological platform as a system of ideas that aspire both to explain the world and to change it (Cranston, 1995: 768). All of this sets the context for your reflection; here you can discuss things such as:

- Why was this work created, and what does it mean?
- Was the intended effect on the audience achieved?
- On what criteria should the work be judged, and what is the evidence that relates to these criteria?

In conclusion, you can present your interpretation and judgement of the things that you have selected based on the criteria that you have set and the evidence that you have identified (Barrett, 1994).

DISCUSSION

Semiotics and advertising

If you are interested in studying how advertisements represent social or gender differences, you will need to define three key points before you begin. First, you will need to develop a clear definition for the type of ads that you will be looking at. Second, you will need to provide information on where you will be gathering the data. Third, you will need to explain how ads are constructed (Rose, 2012: 111). In order to address the last point you can ask yourself the following questions:

- What are these ads representing?
- What kind of values they are endorsing?
- How are they doing that?

Advertising works by shifting or transferring social meanings onto products. The signs in the ads usually signify aspirational or positive notions such as taste, luxury, health, happiness, friendship, and so on. The key point here is the transfer of the signifiers from these signs onto the products. This is crucial to how advertising works (Rose, 2012: 123).

The signs used in advertisements bring connotations to meanings that stem from our culture. Some of them can be easily recognized, while some are only unconsciously registered. For example, a picture of a female model in a perfume ad can be perceived as a 'sign' with connotations such as youth, slimness, beauty, health, and so on. This will mostly be perceived as such because the featured female will neither be overweight, elderly, nor below average height, and will have no physical blemishes. Since the sign has positive connotations that are then associated with the ad, the ad can work as a signifier of the mythic concept of 'feminine beauty'. This concept is identified within our society as a positive myth of the attributes of a sexually desirable woman. The ad works by showing one key visual sign: the 'feminine beauty' myth (the featured model), which has been placed next to the linguistic sign, the name of the perfume (often supported with a smaller image of the bottle itself). In this way, the signs endow the product with a mythic meaning and the perfume itself becomes a sign of feminine beauty. This is how semiotics works. People identify signs in the ad, register which social myths are evoked, and transfer the mythic meaning to the product being advertised.

The next step is to consider how the mythic meaning of the ad relates to our understanding of the real world, thus identifying the ideological function of the ad. While the perfume ad does not claim that someone will become beautiful by buying the perfume, people still might resort to buying the perfume in order to possess, or align themselves with, the myth. This is an example of how ads communicate their message by a structure of signs (Bignell, 1997: 30–55).

According to Jean Baudrillard (1998: 95–6), myths such as that of 'feminine beauty' draw on the notion of the narcissism of the individual within the consumer society. With such ads, the individual is invited to enjoy or indulge himself or herself. In this particular case, the notion of 'woman' is sold to women. This addresses not only one's relation to others, but also one's relationship to oneself. A woman is consuming herself and by that it can be said that she is 'personalizing' herself. Alternatively, a masculine model in a similar scenario is likely to be perceived as a representation of 'particularity' and 'choice'. Therefore, advertising aimed at men can often be seen to stress the 'rule of choice'. The modern man is usually portrayed as 'distinctive' and 'demanding'. He will not tolerate failure and he will neglect no detail. His aim is to achieve distinction. These qualities connect to such military and puritan virtues as 'persistence', 'decisiveness', and 'fearlessness'. The typical masculine model in advertising is a model of competitive or selective virtue that confers the status of social power. Fundamentally, in most advertisements men are invited to play soldiers, while women are invited to play dolls (1998: 97).

Nevertheless, it needs to be taken into consideration that there is a limiting factor to this analysis. Due to various cultural and social backgrounds, different people might decode signs in different ways from those intended by the advertiser. These myths are closely associated with contemporary Western culture, and therefore may be perceived differently in different cultures. For example, youth, slimness, or height do not necessary signify the ideal representation of female beauty within a historical Western context, nor within other cultures presently. Therefore, it must be understood that some conceptions might be specific to particular cultures, traditions, or particular historical periods. Further references on semiotic analysis of Western advertising, more particularly American advertising, can be found in *Decoding Advertisements: Ideology and Meaning of Advertising* (1978), a classic study by Judith Williamson. While this study reflects the 1970s' American advertising, which is quite different from today's advertising, the principles behind Williamson's semiotic analysis can be equally applied even today (Muratovski, 2010b: 84–5).

DISCUSSION

Semiotics and branding

Advertising is a form of brand communication. As much as brands use advertising to sell their products, they also use advertising to project their values and what they stand for. That is why the first and perhaps the most complex role that brands carry out in the eyes of their audiences is symbolic – they project a sense of identity. People often use brands as a signal or indicator of personality. Whether we like to admit this or not, we often assess others on first meeting by the car they drive, the clothes they wear, or the organization they associate themselves with; and it is at such times that the symbolic properties, rather than the physical properties, of the brands come forward. Therefore, the influence and the power that symbols and symbolism have within the context of identity formation should not be underestimated (Muratovski, 2010b: 134).

Any object, word, or action that stands for something more than its generic meaning can be considered as a symbol, but in corporate terms, the symbol most often takes the visual form of a sign or a logo. With time some logos even become symbols, but it has to be noted that every logo is not a symbol by default, and does not necessarily become one (Hatch and Shultz, 2008: 26). Carl Jung, the founder of analytical psychology, first explored this view in the book *Man and His Symbols* (1964). Jung's understanding of symbols began from the simple acknowledgement of the everyday use of spoken or written words. The auditory and graphic modes that constitute the language stand in for something (an absent referent), thus making language symbolic. Communities of speakers and writers continue to design new modes, which operate within the consensual system but are otherwise previously unknown. A good example is the twentieth-century rash of acronyms or words formed from strings of initials, like 'UN', 'UNICEF', 'UNESCO'. Meaningless in etymological terms (i.e. not developed with reference to any existing lexical cluster of common ancestors), these acronyms have acquired recognizable meaning, purely through common usage (1964: 3). However, as the Swiss linguist Ferdinand de Saussure (1983) theorizes, these acronyms are not symbols, but signs, and they do no more than denote the objects to which they are attached. Trademarks, names of patent medicines, badges, or insignias are likewise signs and not symbols. The sign as such is always less than the concept it represents, standing in for its absence. The difference between a sign and a symbol, as Jung (1964: 41) points out, is that the symbol always stands for something more. It adds to the obvious and immediate meaning represented by the sign, although it develops in much the same way: as a spontaneous process of cultural production, arising within a certain community through use, and by holding its denotations over a certain period of time. According to Jung (1964: 41), while signs can easily be created for a specific purpose, symbols cannot be created by deliberate and short-term intent. It takes a substantial period of time and an unambiguous programme of related action to reprocess a sign into a symbol, as a symbol cannot be associated with something that is not yet known to some wider groups of people.

Therefore, not by chance, design consultants involved in building visual identities put the sign (the logo) at the heart of the creative process and the corporate strategy. The prime purpose of the logo is to encapsulate the corporate identity by presenting the central idea of the organization with impact, brevity, and immediacy. If it is right, the logo can summon the very idea of the entire organization, but if it is wrong, then it can jeopardize the whole establishment. Corporate communication experts also agree that logos have the power to play upon emotions, memories, and sensitivities, as well as to evoke pleasure and smiles of recognition, or fear and horror from past contact. In corporate terms, when used for internal purposes, logos can be seen as concrete, visible objects meant to increase people's ability to identify with the organization. But when they are used for external audiences they are intended to increase the reflex recognition of the organization (van Riel and Fombrun, 2007: 103).

That being said, many corporations, unsurprisingly, look for a logo that inspires feelings of confidence, stability, comfort, and empathy – meanings that are uncontroversial, yet distinctive and embedded in the cultural past of their audience. At the same time, however, most major organizations want to present themselves as modern and timeless, as well as strong and memorable, while being offensive to no one (Olins, 1995: 11). It is often hard to produce an effective solution with that kind of mixed, even self-contradictory brief. Nevertheless, there are cases when certain organizations have chosen to strengthen their position within their constituencies by openly causing resentment to other groups or individuals (as in the case of the white supremacists and their adoption of the Nazi swastika), or simply by being provocative (as is the case with the UK's clothing label French Connection United Kingdom and their use of their alternative trademark, the FCUK acronym) (Muratovski, 2010b: 135).

EXAMPLE

The Persuasive Power of Advertising

This example is an abridged visual research report on advertising. Here I have reflected on the role that advertising plays in our society. For the sake of argument, the ideological position that I have taken here is anti-consumerist: I am examining advertising as a form of contemporary propaganda aimed at promoting consumerism as a way of life. However, please note that a full report of this nature should also include a deeper analytical discussion followed by a series of examples and case studies of a range of advertising campaigns that will be categorized in some way (e.g. historically or thematically) and interpreted in great detail.

Introduction

Through a series of appeals, symbols and statements, advertising is deliberately designed to influence the receiver of the message towards the point of view desired by the advertiser. The purpose of this is to prompt the receiver to act in some specific way as a result of receiving the message. It can be argued that the persuasive power of advertising lies in the fact that it is blended with other forms of popular culture, and therefore most people perceive it as a form of entertainment and information. This can be seen in the peculiar phenomenon of the proliferation of advertising slogans, labels and icons that people willingly wear or display, and even paying premium prices for the 'designer label'. Consumers accept their access to these brand-identifiers as a 'privilege', for which they often pay handsomely. Under these conditions it is no wonder that most people do not recognize advertising as the most ubiquitous form of propaganda in modern times (Jowett and O'Donnell, 2006: 146).

This statement is supportive of the work by one of the most prominent cultural theorists and advertising critics, Sut Jhally (2000), who argues that modern-day advertising constitutes the most powerful and sustained system of propaganda in human history. According to him, there has never been more thought, effort, creativity, time, and attention to detail invested in any propaganda campaign aimed at changing public consciousness as there has been with the advertising campaigns of the twentieth century.

Ideological framework: capitalist realism

The American sociologist Michael Schudson (1993: 6), who analysed advertising from a wider sociological and historical framework, describes advertising (with its omnipresent and repetitive system of symbols) as propaganda meant not only to sell products, but also to promote 'consumption as a way of life'. According to him, the world of advertising is an essential part of a deliberate effort to connect specific products in people's imaginations with certain demographic groupings, needs or occasions. For example, in some cases, a specific group that is most likely to consume the advertised product is abstractly represented and visualized in the ad – although there are other cases when it is more convenient not to include any people in the ads, in an effort not to exclude any category of person from identifying with the product. Schudson (1993: 209) also believes that abstraction is essential in contemporary mass-consumption advertising, as its purpose is to represent an alternative form of reality – one that he has called 'capitalist realism'. This is a concept where people in real life 'act out' and live social ideals as seen in advertising, thus presenting themselves in stereotypical pictures to the world. Driven by the need for mass-consumption, advertising has turned to a 'hyper-ritualization' where such behaviour is even more pronounced; but the key difference here is that life in advertising is 'edited' so that only the positive moments are presented to the public. In an attempt to explain this concept better, Schudson (1993: 209–33) associates 'capitalist realism' with 'socialist realism' – the official, state-sanctioned and state-governed art practised in the Soviet Union.

The First Soviet Writers' Congress, held in 1934, defined socialist realism as an art obliged to present a 'correct historically concrete representation of reality in its revolutionary development [and to do so in an educative form aimed at] the working masses in the spirit of socialism' (Fadayev, 1971: 299; cited in Schudson, 1993: 215). This meant that socialist realist art must be faithful to life, while following certain prescriptions:

- Art should picture reality in simplified and typified ways so that it communicates effectively to the masses.
- Art should picture life, but not as it is so much, as life as it should become, life worth emulating.
- Art should picture reality not in its individuality but only as it reveals larger social significance.
- Art should picture reality as progress toward the future and so represent social struggle positively. It should carry an air of optimism.
- Art should focus on contemporary life, creating pleasing images of new social phenomena, revealing and endorsing new features of society and thus aiding the masses in assimilating them. (Schudson, 1993: 215)

Considering the key concepts that encapsulated Soviet socialist realist art, Schudson concluded that the designs of the advertising in capitalist American society are nearly identical with those of communist Soviet society. Both forms subordinate everything to a message that romanticizes the present, or the potential of the present. The difference is that the visual aesthetic of socialist realism is designed to dignify the simplicity of human labour in the service of the state, and the aesthetic of capitalist realism glorifies the pleasures and freedoms of consumer choice in defence of the virtues of private life and materialism (Schudson, 1993: 233).

The use of cultural references in advertising

Advertising is a communication activity that absorbs and fuses a variety of symbolic practices and discourses. As a kind of shorthand, both the substance and the images in advertising are based on a wide range of cultural references. Advertising borrows its ideas, its language, and its visual representations from the fields of design, literature, media, history, and popular culture. After the right references are collected, they are masterfully recombined around the theme of consumption (Leiss et al., 1997: 193).

The manipulative power of advertising lies in the subtle mixes of reality and fantasy, which makes it harder to draw the line between what is a sensible behaviour and what is careless over-indulgence. Although many critics maintain the position that advertising exists primarily to create demand among people, some argue that people already know their needs and desires, and that advertising only makes them aware of certain items that can satisfy these needs and desires. What this argument implies is that advertising also 'helps' people to discover what their needs are. Nevertheless, these critics do not dispute the view that advertising has the potential to create new market demand by manipulating people's normal motivational impulses (see Leiss et al., 1997).

In line with this, Jib Fowles (1996: 167) adds that the work of the advertising industry is to uncover 'deeper veins of sentiment', while at the same time producing fresh symbols that can provoke new responses from the audience. According to him, symbols used in advertising must be comprehensible to the majority of people. However, I will make a comment that these symbols need to be comprehensible to the people at whom the advertising is aimed – the target audience – and not necessarily the wider public. Nevertheless, as advertising strives to enlist multitudes, it must be composed of familiar elements that 'articulate commonalities' within society. Yet at the same time, banality and over-familiarity must be avoided as such symbols elicit indifference and even rejection (Fowles, 1996).

Advertising formats

The primary role of advertising is to create a relationship between people (prospective consumers) and products (consumer goods). The way this is done is through four basic advertising formats: product-information format, product-image format, personalised format, and lifestyle format.

Product-Information format

The product-information format is the archetypical ad format. Here, the product is in the centre of attention in the ad. The focus of all elements in the ad is to explain the product and its utility. In such ads, the brand name is prominently displayed alongside a picture of the packaging or the product. The text in the ad is used to describe the product and its benefits, characteristics, performance, or construction. Usually additional information is not available, and little or no reference is made to the user or to the context of how and why this product is used – apart from instructions or special offers. Such advertising format was popular at the turn of the twentieth century, but it has been in decline ever since (Leiss et al., 1997: 240).

Product-image format

The product-image ad lends special qualities to the product by means of a symbolic relationship that has a more abstract and less pragmatic domain of significance. Unlike the product-information ad, the utility of the product is not in the focus of it – although the brand name and the packaging still play an important role in it. An ad like this works in such a manner that it positions the product in a symbolic context that imparts meaning to the product, above and beyond its constituent elements or benefits. Product-image ads tend to fuse two composite systems of signs together – the product and the setting – within a single message. These signs are not necessarily synthesized by casual or logical links. Instead, this is achieved through association, juxtaposition, or narration. The symbolic association brings the product into a meaningful relationship with the abstract values and ideas that the ad intends to send (Leiss et al., 1997: 245).

Personalized format

The framework of the personalised ad is defined by a direct relationship between the product and the human personality. In such ads, the person becomes the focus of the ad, but in a different manner than in the product-image ads. In personalized ads, people are explicitly and directly positioned in the world of the product. Social admirations, pride of ownership, anxiety about the lack of product use, and satisfaction in consumption have become important dimensions of the interpretation of the product. Here, the relationship between the consumer and the product becomes an important thematic focus. In this format, the product no longer stands as an independent autonomous object; instead, the product is displayed as an integral part of the codification of human existence and interaction (Leiss et al., 1997: 246–54).

Lifestyle format

By combining aspects of the product image and the personalized ads, lifestyle ads tend to create more balanced relationships among people, products, and settings. In most ads of this type, the setting usually serves as an interpretation of a positive stereotype. Stereotypes are fixed and oversimplified images or ideas of a particular type of people or things, and therefore people recognize them faster and more easily. These kinds of ads work by depicting desirable lifestyles and by linking them to products. In modern-day advertising, the reference to the consumption style is often very subtle – narratives are kept simple, yet they are presented in a sophisticated way; they blend visuals with text or they use dialogues to express different styles of consumption. Such ads do not focus on product satisfaction or utility; rather, they tend to offer the product or the associated consumer behaviour as appropriate to, or as typical of, a particular social group to which the consumer wants to belong (Leiss et al., 1997: 259–62).

Conclusion

Consumerism is the dominant ideology of today. Advertising, as a key propaganda component of this ideology, fulfils a crucial role in that it persuades people to consume. In order for advertising to achieve its ideological effect, advertisers tend to attach popular myths to products and services. In order for us to analyse ads in a cultural context, we will first need to separate these ads from the commercial environments in which they exist. The visual and the linguistic signs of the ad will need to be identified and analysed in terms of how they work together. What this means is that first we will need to identify the social myths from which the ads draw inspiration. Then we will need to establish whether these myths are being reinforced or challenged. Finally we will need to examine how the signs in the ads relate to each other (Muratovski, 2010b: 84–5).

6.3 HALLMARKS OF GOOD VISUAL RESEARCH

There are number of principles that you should follow if you want to deliver a critical interpretation of images, forms, and objects. John Barrett (1994, 2000) provides a set of principles that work in practice. Even though these principles are presented from the perspective of an art critic, they can also be applied in a design context (Barrett, 2000: 5–6):

- To interpret an image, a form, or an object is to respond to it.
- Images, forms, and objects need to be described and demand interpretation.
- Responsible interpretations present images, forms, and objects in their best rather than in their weakest light.
- Interpretations are persuasive arguments.
- There can be a range of competing and contradictory interpretations of the same image, form, or object.
- No single interpretation is exhaustive and final.
- Interpretations imply a world-view.
- Good interpretations say more about the work than they say about the critic.
- There can be different, competing, and contradictory interpretations of the same work.
- No interpretation can be absolutely correct.
- Good interpretations are meant to be reasonable, convincing, enlightening, and informative.
- Interpretations can be judged by coherence, correspondence, and inclusiveness.
- Interpretations are often guided by feelings.
- An interpretation of a work may not necessarily match what the creator wanted to convey.

Approximate Content Distribution Ratio

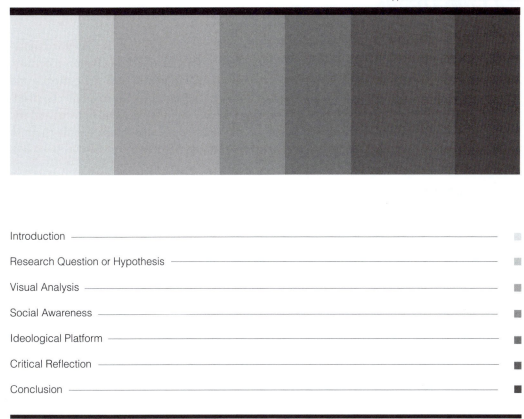

Introduction ———————————————————————————————— ▩

Research Question or Hypothesis ———————————————————— ▩

Visual Analysis ——————————————————————————————— ▩

Social Awareness —————————————————————————————— ▩

Ideological Platform ———————————————————————————— ■

Critical Reflection —————————————————————————————— ■

Conclusion ————————————————————————————————— ■

Figure 6.1 Structure of a report in visual research

- The work and not the creator must remain at the focus of the interpretation.
- All images, forms, and objects are in part about the world in which they have emerged.
- All images, forms, and objects are in part about other images, forms, and objects.
- Interpretations can be both an individual and personal, as well as a communal and shared endeavour.
- Good interpretations invite the readers to see for themselves and to continue on their own.

These principles are meant to account for both critical (from a contemporary point of view) and historical interpretation. The principles are drawn from theories that are diverse, but complimentary to each other. This list is comprehensive, but it is not final and the list can be expanded or shortened if necessary. Even though the list appears to be authoritative, the principles are tentative and open to revision (Barrett, 2000: 6).

6.4 CONCLUSION

Visual research is concerned with the study and interpretation of both visual images and material objects. This way of research can also be defined as a study of visual and material culture. This type of research is hermeneutic in nature and can enable you to look for patterns and meanings in sketches, drawings, illustrations, paintings, photographs, videos, objects, products, or architecture. The ability to critically examine meanings of images and objects, and the messages they convey, is particularly important for designers because it can enable them to better understand the effects of their work.

6.5 SUMMARY

In this chapter I have introduced visual research as a hermeneutical process of inquiry and I have presented you with a list of principles that you can follow when interpreting visual research. In addition to this, I have introduced you to visual and material culture studies – areas of study that examine images, forms, and objects that provide information, meaning, function, or pleasure. These are not independent fields, but cross-disciplinary subjects that exist within a broader social, historical, and cultural context. In addition to this, I have introduced three key research methods that you can use when conducting visual research: compositional interpretation, content analysis, and semiotics.

Compositional interpretation can offer you different ways of describing images, forms, and objects. This is a method that you can use at the first stage of your research to describe the visual impact that images, forms, and objects have. Compositional interpretation cannot be used for conducting an analysis because it does not encourage critical reflection (besides a discussion on the technological or the compositional production aspects), nor can this method engage with broader cultural meanings and contexts. That is why visual researchers need to combine compositional interpretation with other methods, such as those described below, in order to address the shortcomings that come with the use of only this method (Rose, 2012: 77–9).

Content analysis is a persuasive method that can generate reliable and replicable facts. This is a flexible and creative method for which a researcher requires only basic mathematical skills. The results can be presented in tables and charts that can be easily read, making this method broadly acceptable and comprehensible. The disadvantage is that content analysis can sometimes be an insensitive and blunt instrument (Stokes, 2011: 58). This method is only as sophisticated as the categories that the researcher defines in the course of the research. That is why the categories should be theoretically grounded and justifiable. If improperly developed and applied, this method will generate meaningless data (2011: 58–9). Nevertheless, content analysis offers a clear method for engaging systematically with large number of images (Rose, 2012: 101). However, you need to bear in mind that even though content analysis can provide you with factual evidence, the process itself is not entirely quantitative. At each stage of the process, ranging from formulating the research topic to developing coding categories and interpreting the results, you will need to make a range of subjective decisions. There are broader issues related to cultural meaning and significance of images that content analysis alone cannot address, and that is why you also need to support your visual research with a semiotic analysis.

Semiotics is one of the most influential methods for interpreting the materials of visual and material culture (see Rose, 2012: 105–6), and advertising especially (Stokes, 2011: 72). As a major part of the creative process of advertising, semiotics can provide us with a good vocabulary for talking about how advertisements add value to products by making them meaningful and socially relevant to the prospective buyers. Because of this, ads make excellent subjects for semiotic analysis (Stokes, 2011: 73). Furthermore, semiotics can be easily combined with other research methods, such as with content analysis. For example, you could use content analysis to determine how many images of a certain kind can be found in a particular medium, and then you can use semiotics to analyse a smaller selection of them in more detail. In addition to this, you can also include a participant observation or interviews with content creators or content providers, such as magazine editors, fashion photographers, creative directors, or publicists, in order to include their perspective as well. Or, once you conclude your analysis, you could conduct a small focus group to which you could present your findings in order to confirm or disprove your theory. In this way, you can add more breadth and depth to your research (2011: 75–6).

As a critic of both visual and material culture, you will be concerned with the examination of the effects of images and objects that are already out there in the world, and not by works that you are producing. This is the data that you are collecting. Your sampling process may range from highly rigorous to very subjective, and it is best if you frame your selection around some kind of ideological platform. There are no set formats on how you could prepare a report on visual research, and as with most research reports, formats can vary depending on your audiences or style of work.

APPLIED RESEARCH

KEYWORDS   Applied Research   Action Research
               Practice-Based Research Co-Design
               Practice-Led Research

Even though the conditions that have initially framed the field of design have changed significantly and designers now work in a post-industrial, rather than industrial society, designers are still perceived as people who 'make' rather than people who 'think'. Contemporary designers now work with complex political, environmental, and social issues where the focus is not simply on doing and acting, but also on thinking about action and its consequences. That is why designers have to first understand the complexities of their own practice before they can begin addressing issues related to other practices. In addition to this, designers should no longer see their practice as deterministic, monolithic, or fixed. Practices do change over time; sometimes this is led by new ideas about the practice, and sometimes by the introduction of new technologies within the practice (Crouch and Pearce, 2012: 35–7).

All designers, regardless of their area of specialization, engage in creative exploration in the process of designing. The main difference between design that is simply design and design that is a form of applied research can be found in the goals and the outcomes of each. Designers who are conducting research through their creative practice try to address a larger set of questions, alongside a design brief. Their work is experimental, interrogative, and inquisitive, and critical self-reflection is a necessary component of this kind of work (Burdick, 2003: 82). However, as design begins to emerge as a discipline in its own right, old ways of working will need to change; design needs to be 'demystified'. This means that designers must be able to provide a logical rationale behind their creative process (Swann, 2002: 51). In addition, this kind of research can also help you to engage better with the process of 'problem framing' and 'solution finding' (Crouch and Pearce, 2012: 143).

7.1 WHAT IS APPLIED RESEARCH?

Applied research is a type of research that enables practitioners to reflect on and evaluate their own work. This type of research approach can be found in a number of different disciplines, including design. In the case of design, this research approach has been primarily adopted from the field of art. This is no wonder, given that the contemporary design profession originally grew out of an applied arts tradition by bringing artistic skills and commercial practices together.

The works of many prominent twentieth-century designers have been based on an intuitive mode of operation often found in fine arts. Even though this was a quite typical way of working in the field of design, many designers found it difficult to articulate their creative process to the broader public. Given that design is an outer-directed occupation and designers are essentially service providers (unlike art, which is often inner-directed), the need to communicate the design process to the clients became increasingly important. As a result, in the second half of the twentieth century rational methods for making design decisions began to emerge. Between the 1960s and 1970s, a considerable amount of design thinking and writing was introduced and this had an enormous impact on the concept of the method and practice of design. With time, the field of design has been exposed to additional influences by a range of other disciplines such as architecture and engineering. For example, industrial designers coming from engineering backgrounds began to introduce a 'scientific method' in the design problem-solving process. Regardless of this, design in practice continues to be intertwined with a great deal of uncertainty, ambiguity, and intuition, as well as inspired guesswork, holistic thinking, and self-expressiveness (Swann, 2002: 50–51).

But there are some benefits to this approach too. One research study that compared the ways in which designers (in this case architects) and scientists work to address the same problem suggests that designers are predisposed to use 'solution-finding' strategies, while scientists tend to be 'problem-focused' in their approach. What this means is that designers seek a solution to a problem by synthesis: they suggest a variety of possible solutions until they find one that is good or satisfactory. Scientists, on the other hand, seek a solution on the basis of analysis: they look for underlying rules that would enable them to generate an optimum solution (Swann, 2002: 53).

If we accept that design is primarily a problem-solving activity, it can be argued that applied research, as a thought process, closely mirrors design. That is why some experts argue that design is synonymous with applied research, or at least it should be (see Swann, 2002; also Crouch and Pearce, 2012: 146). Nevertheless, research of any kind needs to be systematic and deliberate in its nature, but this is not always the case when it comes to design practice (Crouch and Pearce, 2012: 146). Design practice, as Swann (2002) points out, can be gener-ated without research (in a conventional sense) and design may be performed without the designer being involved in any kind of research. In many cases (and depending on the nature of the project), research in things such as material technology, production, or marketing has already been done, creative direction and art direction have been defined, and the designer is asked to synthesize this information into a solution (Swann, 2002: 53-4).

For designers who see themselves as technicians this way of working is quite sufficient. They see design as a 'trade' – a skilled job that requires manual skills and special training. For designers who see design as a 'career' – a profession that involves prolonged training and formal qualifications – design is a process that involves lifelong learning and ongoing self-development. These designers seek to establish an original way of thinking and they try to be innovative in their work. For them, applied research is an integral part of their work because this allows them to continually challenge themselves and the conventions of their profession.

Regardless of this, many designers would argue that they already do 'research' as a necessary part of their everyday practice. As Swann (2002: 56) correctly points out, design seldom takes place as a single flash of inspiration and the process usually involves several cycles of review, amendments, adaptation, and refinement before it is finalized. This process, however, is not equal to research. Therefore, it is important here to make a clear distinction between applied research and pure practice. Applied research aims to generate culturally novel apprehensions that are not just novel to the designer or to the client, but are novel to the field of design as well – the emphasis here is on the process. Pure practitioners, on the other hand, strive to improve and refine what they are doing and aspire to do their work faster, better, or more efficiently. The emphasis here is on the technical skills. While in the first instance applied research and practice might appear to be similar, the differences between the two are considerable (see Candy, 2006b).

There are two main areas of study when it comes to applied design research: practice-based research, where a creative artefact is the basis of the investigation; and practice-led research, where the research leads primarily to the new understandings about the design practice itself (see Candy, 2006a).

7.1.1 PRACTICE-BASED RESEARCH

According to Linda Candy, practice-based research is as an 'original investigation undertaken in order to gain new knowledge partly by means of practice and the outcomes of that practice' (2006a, para. 2). While the claims of originality and contribution to knowledge may be demonstrated through artifacts, as Candy argues, the significance and the context of these claims should be described in words, as only then can a comprehensive understanding of the investigation be gained. This is even more important in an academic environment, especially during practice-based doctoral submissions. In this case the creative outcome must be accompanied by a substantial textual contextualization. In addition to this, Candy (2006a) argues that this critical appraisal or analysis not only clarifies the basis of the claim of originality of the work and places the work within a broader body of knowledge, but it also allows the reviewers to establish whether the appropriate scholarly requirements were met.

7.1.2 PRACTICE-LED RESEARCH

Along the same lines, Candy goes on to describe practice-led research as a process that 'is concerned with the nature of practice and leads to new knowledge that has operational significance for that practice' (2006a, para. 4). Here, the artifact is not at the main focus of the research. The purpose behind this type of research is the advancement of knowledge about the practice, or the advancement of knowledge within practice. Contrary to practice-based research, this type of research may be solely described in text and inclusion of a creative outcome is not necessary – but artifacts may be included in order to better exemplify the practice in question if that is deemed necessary or appropriate.

7.2 ACTION RESEARCH

Action research is the most popular type of applied research. This type of research is an examination of the way in which practitioners reflect on their actions during and following their work (Schon, 1983). As such, action research can be described as an inquisitive process that leads to improvement and reform (Hopkins and Ahtaridou, 2006: 276). Action research can be easily integrated within the practice of design (Swann, 2002: 50), and can be a powerful tool for initiating change in the design profession (Crouch and Pearce, 2012: 143).

For example, as a designer, you can use action research as a way to improve your practical judgement in a real-world scenario. The validity of the theories that are generated by action research are not necessarily 'scientific', but nevertheless, the knowledge generated through this kind of research can help you to perform better in your professional environment (Burns, 2000: 443). Also, if you are able to coherently explain what are you doing and why, you will be better positioned to understand the significance of your work within your field. This, in return, can add more credibility to your work (McNiff and Whitehead, 2012: 14).

7.2.1 CONDUCTING ACTION RESEARCH

Action research is research about improving practice (McNiff and Whitehead, 2012: 14). This is a form of enquiry that enables practitioners to investigate and evaluate their own work. Unlike other types of research, action research does not necessarily need to begin with a clearly defined hypothesis or a research question. All you need is a general idea that some-thing in your existing practice can be improved, and you can refine things from there (Hopkins and Ahtaridou, 2006: 282). When beginning the action research process, according to Jean McNiff and Jack Whitehead (2012: 7), you should ask yourself the following questions:

- What am I doing?
- Do I need to improve anything?
- If so, what?
- How do I improve it?
- Why should I improve it?

The most important thing to remember here is that action research should be based around a problem, dilemma, or ambiguity from the situation in which practitioners may find themselves. Also, there are three things that need to be considered when conducting action research:

- The subject matter should be situated in a social practice that needs to be changed.
- This is a participatory activity where researchers collaborate among themselves or with the relevant stakeholders.
- The project proceeds through a cyclic spiral of planning, acting, observing, and reflecting in a systematic and documented way (see Figure 7.1).

This report should include commentary and interpretation of the whole action and research process. In return, this may lead to identification of a new problem (or problems) that may trigger a new cycle of planning, acting, observing, and reflecting (Swann, 2002: 55).

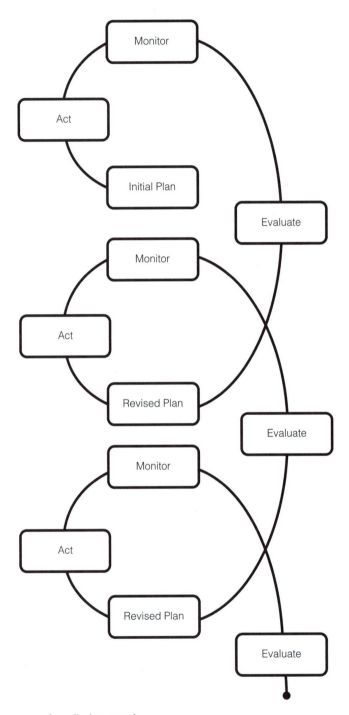

Figure 7.1 The process of applied research

Ultimately, the purpose of this type of research is to help you improve your own practice and by doing so to set new standards in the field. But in order for you to do so, you will need to demonstrate two things: how are you trying to improve what you are doing – which includes thinking about your work and learning how to do your work better; and how to influence others to do the same thing (McNiff and Whitehead, 2012: 7).

7.2.2 DATA COLLECTION

Data collection in action research in design is closely related to the design process itself. Considering that design is an outward-directed activity, in terms that it is others who often feel the consequences of the designers' actions, action research can often be participatory in nature when it comes to data collection. Therefore, participatory action research in design should engage various stakeholders who might be affected by the proposed solution (Crouch and Pearce, 2012: 151).

There are two ways of looking at this. If you are conducting a practice-led research and you are examining how your practice operates, then you may need to engage your co-workers to actively participate in the research process. In the case of individual practice, you can still engage any relevant stakeholders with whom you have any relevant interactions. If you are conducting practice-based research and you are examining how you can improve the design solution on which you are working, then you will also need to engage the broader public and your core audience. This is also called 'co-design', which stands for collaborative design.

As design develops as a discipline, the tasks that designers face are becoming increasingly complex. In many cases, complex problems, also referred to in the design community as 'wicked problems', cannot be addressed without some kind of research and collaboration with other people. Co-design was first introduced in architectural design, where cooperative and collaborative work by architects and end-users led to a new kind of designed environment that was distinct from the previous practice of rigid town planning. Co-design empowers the end user to actively participate in the design process. Working in this way, architects were able to bring a human dimension into the built environments, and have allowed the residents to influence the design rather than having the design directing the residents. While the nature of the design work is client-based and designers already try to incorporate the needs of the clients in their designs, co-design allows for this client–designer relationship to develop on a deeper and more intense level. This way of working is reminiscent of the era before the industrialization, where crafts people would have a close working relationship with the end users as they were producing tailor-made solutions rather than mass-produced products. In addition to this, co-design adds another dimension to the design process. Rather than just designing products (whether visual or tangible), designers will also have the opportunity to design systems that can address and facilitate a number of concerns, ranging from procurement and transport of raw materials, to production, distribution, marketing, and sales, as well as any associated environmental and social issues (Crouch and Pearce, 2012: 27–9).

Swann (2002: 56–7) supports the idea that design should be an inclusive process and argues that designers need to be accountable for what they do. This way of working also ensures that the research is relevant, democratic, and is there to meet people's needs (Crouch and Pearce, 2012: 151). That is why most definitions of action research incorporate three key elements. Action research should be participatory in character; it needs to have a democratic impulse; and it should contribute both to social science and to social change (Meyer, 2000: 178).

- **Participatory Research**: In a group practice where a number of people work together, joint participation is mandatory. All participants need to perceive the need to change and must be willing to play an active part in both the research and the change process. The distinction between 'researcher' and 'researched' in action research, as Meyer puts it, may not be so apparent, as is the case with other types of research. The way the research is conducted needs to be continually negotiated with the participants, and everyone will need to agree on what is the best way to go forward. Group participation in this kind of research is especially important, because this type of research leads to change and change can be threatening and obtrusive to everyone involved. In order for conflicts to be prevented, or at least minimized, a mutual trust must be obtained and a sense of teamwork needs to prevail (Meyer, 2000: 178).

- **Democratic Research**: In action research all participants should be seen as equals. The researcher works as a facilitator of change, consulting the participants on the action process and on the evaluation of that process. Throughout the study the findings are being fed back to the participants for validation so that informed decisions can be made about the next stage of the study (Meyer, 2000: 178).

- **Social Contribution**: Regardless of the field of study, there is always an underlying gap between theory and practice. Action research is seen as one way of dealing with this because it can generate findings that are meaningful and useful to practitioners. However, it has to be noted that generalizations made from action research differ from those made on the basis of more conventional forms of research. For example, the researcher will need to describe the work in rich contextual detail and will need to include the participants' perspectives and responses as new data in the final report. Any biases, such as the researcher's personal views, values, and beliefs, will need to be made explicit and evident. A good strategy to deal with this is by making self-reflective field notes during the research process. This process can initiate social or organizational change, but its success should not be judged in terms of how big the change was. Instead, as Meyer (2000: 180) points out, success can be viewed in relation to what has been learnt from the experience of undertaking the work.

Essentially, this is an eclectic and flexible type of research that can incorporate parts of other research methods when necessary. That is why there are a number of different approaches to action research. At one end of the spectrum, action research is seen as an individualistic or a person-centric activity, and on the other, action research is a participatory activity – a cooperative research that brings a range of people together in a collaborative manner.

7.2.3 DATA ANALYSIS

In the case of action research, both data collection and data analysis are intertwined with the design process. Therefore, the research process mirrors the design process. According to Cal Swann (2002: 53), there is a broad consensus in the field which has determined six basic steps that guide the design process:

Step 1: Problem identification

Step 2: Analysis of the problem

Step 3: Synthesis of possible solutions

Step 4: Execution of a design solution

Step 5: Production of the design

Step 6: Evaluation and revision of the process

While the design process presented in this way shows an empirical process, Swann (2002: 53) also points out that this process is not necessarily linear (see Figure 7.2). According to him, the process is iterative and this involves a constant review of the problem, repeated analysis, and synthesis of the revised solutions.

7.2.4 PREPARING A REPORT

Action research can be generally presented in a traditional thesis format or as a case study, and we should not have a problem with a written articulation of design. These are accessible formats that are capable of being read both by designers and by people outside the domain of design (Swann, 2002: 51; Crouch and Pearce, 2012: 147).

This type of systematic documentation of the design/research process can pose a challenge to most design practitioners who are not trained to work in this way, and do not have the will to change their working practices. This, according to Swann (2002: 58), is a failing that has been perpetuated in the practice of design for many years. While at the same time the design profession complains about the lack of understanding and appreciation of the social, cultural, and economic benefits of design to the community, little has been done for those benefits to be articulated and validated. For most part in the media, design is presented in superficial and sensationalist terms rather than intellectual. If design would like to mature as a profession, as Swann points out, then designers will need to be more self-critical and more systematic in providing evidence of the process of creation from beginning to end. This can only be done through methodologies that allow for objective evaluation and review (2002: 59).

In an emerging discipline such as design, a thesis format can help designers to achieve higher credibility and external validation. A thesis, of course, does not exclude the supplement of a

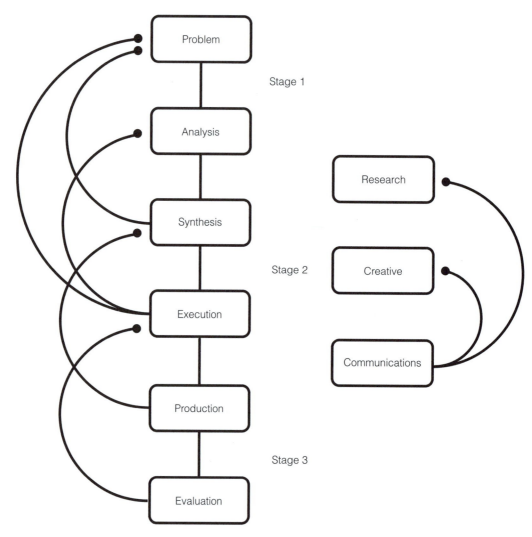

Figure 7.2 Illustration of Swann's diagram explaining action research and the practice of design

design project, or an artifact; and in the case of practice-based research, the artifact is the essential component of the presentation. The problem is not the work itself, but the theoretical component that needs to accompany their work. Designers are often unwilling to include a written report that supports their work. Many are more comfortable working in visual or tangible media, and written reports are often seem very literary based and unnecessary (Swann, 2002: 52).

The visual, or the physical, form can represent a valid form of knowledge, but this form can sometimes be difficult to be understood by audiences other than designers. Visual literacy, as Swann (2002: 51) argues, is the same as verbal, written, or audio literacy in a sense that it also requires practice and intelligence informed by the history and the concepts embedded in the form. New design forms, visual and tangible, are never truly original – they are always based on developments of existing forms and cultural contexts. In this way, as it has often been argued, trained observers can draw on familiar historical or conceptual references when evaluating a practical work. This is true in the sense that a trained eye can immediately 'read' the design, whereas others who do not share the same background will not be able to (2002: 51–2). The issue of whether designers are capable of explaining their research in purely visual or tangible terms continues to spark debates among academics and practitioners, and as Swann points out, there is a fierce defence of the idea that the artifact is sufficient evidence of its purpose and existence (2002: 52). This argument, however, can be refuted with some historical examples. For example, we can see the Egyptian pyramids and we understand their purpose, but we still do not fully understand how they were built, even though we have had centuries to study them. We can also see the Easter Island statues and we can understand how they were made, but we still do not know enough about them, nor do we know how they were transported to their locations. Even though our civilization is technologically far more advanced than those of the ancient Egyptians and the Rapa Nui people, we still cannot understand how they managed to do what they did – simply because there is no written explanation left behind. With this in mind, I believe that these two examples suffice to highlight the importance of documenting one's practical work in a written format.

7.3 HALLMARKS OF GOOD APPLIED RESEARCH

Even though applied research is a practice-driven research and at times the focus is on the artefact, the research is still defined in terms of process rather than outputs. There are four main features that must be taken into account:

- Purpose
- Context
- Rationale
- Artifact (Optional)

As is the case with any other type of research, applied research is also driven by research questions or problems. These questions need to be defined in such a way a to seek to enhance the knowledge in the field, and in this way, the purpose of the research is being set. Then, the context of the research also needs to be addressed:

- Why it is important that these particular issues are addressed?
- What other research has been done in this area?
- What kind of contribution will this project make to the advancement of this area?

The researcher then has to specify the methods for addressing and answering the research question(s). It is important that the researcher knows how to seek the answers, but it is also important for the researcher to explain the rationale of why these proposed methods are the most appropriate means by which these answers are sought. Then, once the study is complete, the work needs to be presented either as a case study or as a more substantial written thesis. In practice-based research, where the artifact is the main object of the study, the work itself needs to be presented alongside textual analysis that demonstrates critical reflection. In practice-led research artifacts may also be included, but the main focus of the study must remain the practice itself and not the outcome of that practice (see Candy, 2006b).

7.4 CONCLUSION

As a designer, you may need to investigate how to advance and transform your own practice, or to learn how to improve the organizational culture within your practice and make your day-to-day operations more efficient. This is where applied research comes into focus. Applied research can allow you to have more control over how you work and can help you to consolidate your practice in ways that better reflect what is important to you. The best way to do that is through action research. Action research empowers practitioners to research themselves. This, according to some experts in the field, is somewhat different from other types of research where a professional researcher would do research on practitioners – but not everyone agrees (see McNiff and Whitehead, 2012: 8). Meyer, for example, argues that practitioners can choose to engage external researchers in order to help them 'identify problems, seek and implement practical solutions, and systematically monitor and reflect on the process and outcomes of change' (2000: 178).

Then again, unlike the other research approaches that were previously discussed, action research is not always independently validated and then applied to practice; action research is validated *through* practice (Burns, 2000: 443). Therefore, it can be argued that action research is conducted 'within practice' and as such it is distinct from research that is 'about practice' (Crouch and Pearce, 2012: 145). Nevertheless, as with any type of research, applied research needs to be done in such a way that it can be disseminated further.

Sharing practical experiences in the form of substantive discourse, as Swann (2002: 61) puts it, will help design to progress as a discipline. As more and more design graduates progress to postgraduate study and develop research capabilities alongside their creative professional skills, we will increasingly see how this progress is taking place. Both practice-based and practice-led research can provide a platform for a systematic investigative process that could be easily adopted by progressive designers interested in converting their practice into a broader intellectual and public discourse. This is necessary for any profession that wants to provide evidence of the quality of the services it provides. In addition, greater collaboration between the profession and academia can establish a better understanding of research in practice, and it can instigate a change in the field of design.

7.5 SUMMARY

In this chapter I have introduced the use of applied research in design. While applied research may share some similarities with the other three research approaches (qualitative, quantitative, and visual), this type of research is significantly different when it comes to purpose. While the other research approaches are outer-directed – in the sense that you can use them to gain an understanding of the external factors associated with the problem that you are trying to resolve – applied research is inner-directed. Its main purpose is to help you improve your own creative work and/or design practice.

There are two types of applied research that may be relevant to you: practice-based research, where the focus is on the artifact, and practice-led research, where the focus is on the design practice itself. In either case the research is still defined in terms of process rather than outputs. The best way for conducting applied research in design is through action research.

Action research is an eclectic and collaborative research process that draws on a variety of data collection methods such as interviews and observations (Meyer, 2000: 180). The process of data collection and data analysis here are cyclical in nature, and they closely follow the design process. In terms of reporting and dissemination, action research can be generally presented in a traditional written format that follows the same principles that I have introduced with the previous research approaches.

RESEARCH AND DESIGN

KEYWORDS
Research Report	Design Brief
Executive Summary	Design Report

The final stage of your research involves writing a research report. The report is a straightforward document that introduces your research problem, outlines what you have done to resolve it, and presents your findings. A research report is not a work of literature – it is a factual, logical, and comprehensible document. When this document is written in the form of a postgraduate-level thesis, the report also becomes a reflection of your scholarship and it is used to measure your educational achievement (Leedy and Ormrod, 2010: 291).

Learning how to write professional research reports is a skill that you will find valuable in your professional life too, and not only within a university setting. The formal and impersonal style of writing that is characteristic to most research reports represents a model of writing and reporting that is often used in the corporate world as well. If, for example, your career takes you to the path of working for corporate or government clients, you will most certainly be expected to present your research and/or elaborate your design solutions in this way.

8.1 RESEARCH REPORT

Your research report should act as a documented record of your contribution to the knowledge in your field. Research reports can take many forms: theses, journal articles, conference presentations, business reports, and so on. This means that there are various ways of preparing and writing research reports. Therefore, here I will simply highlight the key principles that you should take into consideration when planning a research report, regardless of what your research is about (see Figure 8.1):

1. Introduction
2. Research Rationale
3. Research Methods and Methodology
4. Summary of Findings
5. Discussion
6. Conclusion

First you should begin by introducing your readers to the research problem. Then you will need to explain why this problem needs an in-depth investigation. Following this, you should describe how you attempted to resolve this problem (in other words, here you will need to explain your research procedure and discuss how you gathered the research data). Then you should present the research data. Finally, you should provide an interpretation of the data and conclude by demonstrating how your findings have resolved the research problem.

Approximate Content Distribution Ratio

Introduction ⎯⎯⎯⎯⎯⎯⎯⎯⎯⎯⎯⎯⎯⎯⎯⎯⎯⎯⎯⎯⎯⎯⎯

Research Rationale ⎯⎯⎯⎯⎯⎯⎯⎯⎯⎯⎯⎯⎯⎯⎯⎯

Research Methods and Methodology ⎯⎯⎯⎯⎯⎯⎯

Summary of Findings ⎯⎯⎯⎯⎯⎯⎯⎯⎯⎯⎯⎯⎯⎯⎯⎯

Discussion ⎯⎯⎯⎯⎯⎯⎯⎯⎯⎯⎯⎯⎯⎯⎯⎯⎯⎯⎯⎯⎯⎯

Conclusion ⎯⎯⎯⎯⎯⎯⎯⎯⎯⎯⎯⎯⎯⎯⎯⎯⎯⎯⎯⎯⎯⎯

Figure 8.1 Structure of a research plan

8.1.1 WRITING A RESEARCH REPORT

Once you have made a plan of how you will prepare your research report, you can start with your writing. The structure of your report should follow your plan, but in greater detail. This structure can also form the subheadings of your report (Figure 8.2):

1. Introduction
2. Research Problem
3. Research Objectives
4. Research Question
5. Knowledge Gap
6. Hypothesis
7. Research Rationale
8. Research Aims

9. Methodology and Methods

10. Review of the Literature

11. Theoretical Discussion

12. Summary of Key Findings

13. Conclusion

A typical stumbling block for most people is figuring out how to start writing – especially a formal report of such nature. In the first issue of the *Design Research Quarterly*, Eric J. Arnould (2006) provides a set of useful techniques on getting a typical research report to publication standards.

According to him, a good way of starting is by preparing a two- to three-page synopsis of the report that focuses on the highlights of your theoretical and/or practical contribution in design. The synopsis should begin with an opening sentence that introduces your field of study, states the purpose of your research, and makes links to existing key research in this area that is either canonical (accepted as being accurate and authoritative) or cutting edge – or covers both. Then, based on this, you should frame your research problem by including few sentences explaining what is known about the phenomenon in question, what yet needs to be established (what is the gap in the knowledge), and why this is important. This can be written in one or two paragraphs (Arnould, 2006: 21).

Next, you should state your objectives. Arnould (2006: 21) recommends that this should be done in three steps. The first step should state your long-term vision. What is your broad goal? Frame this within a broad problem area. Then, state your immediate research objective (this is your key research question), and explain how this relates to the knowledge gap that you have identified in your literature review. Following this, provide a hypothesis that states what needs to be done in order for this problem to be addressed.

Now, you will need to include a brief rationale, in one paragraph, that states what the outcome of your research will be, or explains how your research will enable any practical or theoretical steps that can follow in the future, if they cannot occur now. Also, here you should state why is this a feasible solution (Arnould, 2006: 21). Please note that it is perfectly fine if the information appears to be somewhat repetitive in a research report. As mentioned above, this is not a work of literature and different rules of writing apply.

Following this, you should state your conceptual aims. These are different from your descriptive aims, as their purpose is to explain *what* you aim to accomplish, rather than *how* or *why*. Anywhere between two and five aims is good. These aims should be logical, brief, concise, and hopefully exciting. Collectively, they should either test your hypothesis or fulfil the needs that you have identified. Then, you will need to describe your empirical studies, summarize your findings, and make an impact statement. You should begin by briefly explaining what is your methodology is and what research methods have you used. Then you need to set the theoretical context of your study. As Arnould (2006: 21–2) points out, the theorizing part consists of activities such as abstracting, generalizing, relating, explaining, synthesizing, and idealizing from contexts found in the relevant literature. The contexts will make your argument appear well rounded, reliable, and engaging. Then, you will need to outline your key results and findings, and elaborate on them without adding any irrelevant or unnecessary information. Be brief and to the point. If appropriate, include figures and tables that can visually aid the presentation of your results. Finally, write a concluding statement that sums up the impact of your study. Mainly, your conclusion should explain how your study advances theory or practice in your field (2006: 22).

Once you have completed your synopsis, Arnould suggests that you should share the synopsis with your peers and get feedback on it. Use this feedback to rewrite any parts that need improving. Finally, write your report as an extended version of your synopsis. The report can include more details, additional background information, detailed descriptions of your methodology and methods, and so on (Arnould, 2006: 22). In addition to this, you will often be asked to provide a list of keywords that best describe the topic of your research and to write an abstract outlining your report. Here, I will give you a brief introduction on what these are and why you need them. Also, I will provide you with a structure that you can use as a guide or a template when preparing your research report and the accompanying elements.

This type of research report is suitable for academic audiences, but if you need to prepare a research report for corporate clients, you may have to reformulate some components and perhaps include some additional information that may be of relevance to your clients. If the research is done primarily for the purpose of producing some kind of design outcome, then you will need to follow up on your research with some additional documentation that will support your design solution. The main purpose of this kind of research is for you to make informed design decisions. I will discuss this issue in more detail later in the chapter.

8.1.2 KEYWORDS

By looking at the keywords, the reader should be able to understand the key topics that you are addressing. Keywords are also useful for search engine purposes. Think about them in the following way: if you were trying to find something about your topic on the Internet, what terms would you search for in Google? The same principle applies here as well. In most cases anything between three and six keywords separated by commas is sufficient (e.g. aging, rural Australia, user-interface design).

8.1.3 ABSTRACT

An abstract is a condensed summary of your research report. The abstract is a stand-alone document that should provide clear and concise information about your research. This means that it should make sense on its own, even when it is not paired with the research study. For example, most academics will make a decision on whether to read a research paper or not on the basis of the abstract.

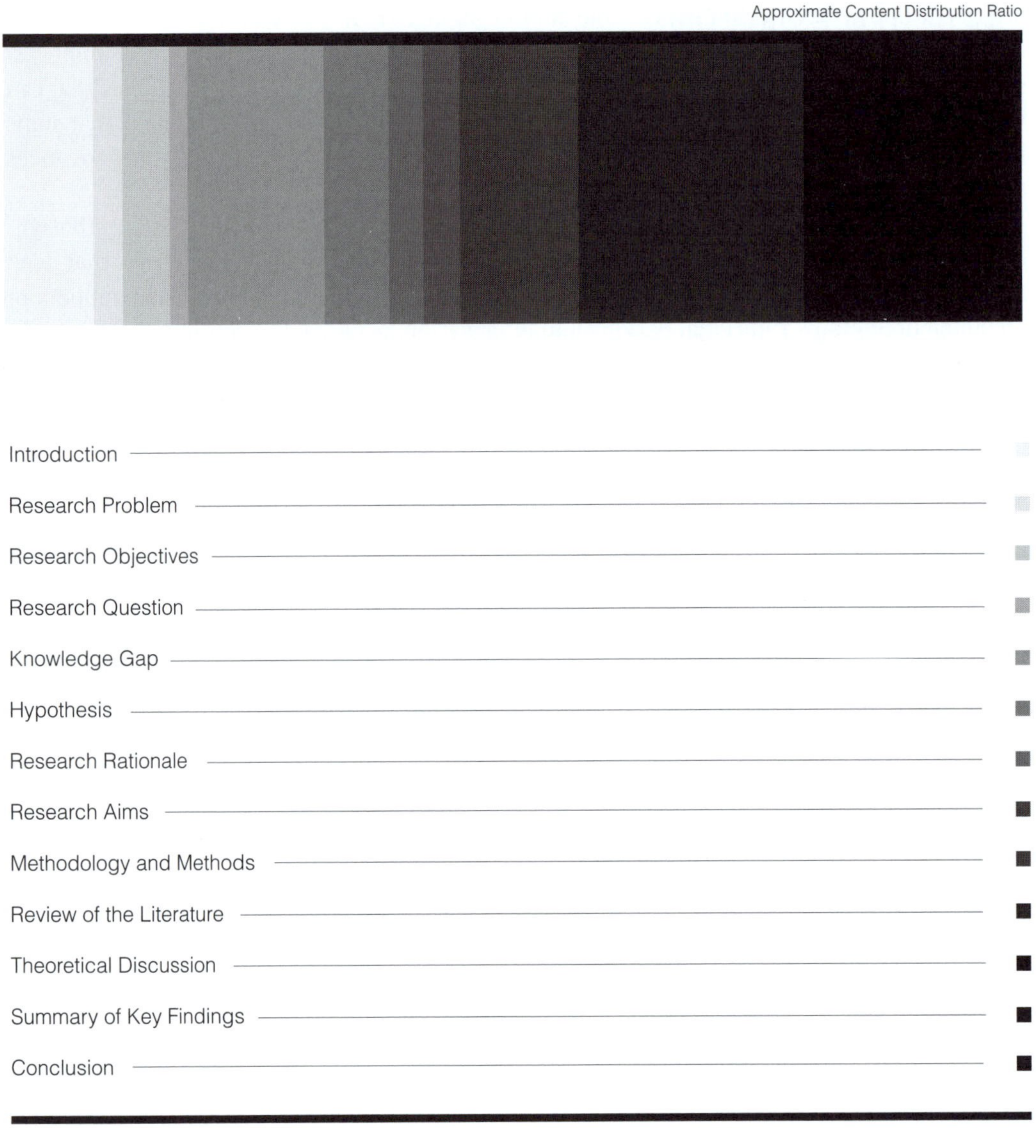

Approximate Content Distribution Ratio

Introduction ——————————————————————————————————————— ▪

Research Problem ———————————————————————————————— ▪

Research Objectives ————————————————————————————— ▪

Research Question ———————————————————————————————— ▪

Knowledge Gap ———————————————————————————————————— ▪

Hypothesis —— ▪

Research Rationale ———————————————————————————————— ▪

Research Aims ————————————————————————————————————— ▪

Methodology and Methods ————————————————————————— ▪

Review of the Literature ————————————————————————— ▪

Theoretical Discussion ——————————————————————————— ▪

Summary of Key Findings —————————————————————————— ▪

Conclusion ——— ▪

Figure 8.2 Structure of a research report

Abstracts are often used when submitting research papers for journals and conferences, or when preparing research proposals. Sometimes they can serve as a proposal as to what you intend to do research on, but most often their purpose is to describe your research after it is completed. Therefore, if you have begun your research with an abstract, you can continue to refine and update your abstract as you progress with your research and finalize your abstract once your research is completed.

8.1.4 ABSTRACT STRUCTURE

Writing an abstract is not easy for a novice, so I have developed a formula that you can follow. An abstract should be brief and to the point, so try to write your abstract in five sentences. Use the following instructions as a guide:

- **First sentence (the topic)**: What is this project about?

  You should begin by establishing your topic. Good abstracts often start with: 'This study examines . . .' Then, fill in the gaps. For example: '(. . .) the influence of social media on the Generation Y decision-making habits', or: '(. . .) the current trends in Australian wine label design and packaging for export purposes'.

- **Second sentence (conventional wisdom)**: Based on your literature review, what would you say the current situation on this topic is?

  Give very brief background information on the issue that you are addressing in one, or if necessary two sentences. Here is an example: 'The latest findings suggest that social media can influence the decision-making habits of Generation Y when it comes to travel choices, entertainment and clothing, but there is a limited information on how social media can influences their political preferences.' This sentence also moves into the next area – the research gap.

  Another example could be: 'The wine industry is one of the largest industries in Australia. The role that design and branding play in this industry is significant when it comes to maintaining the competitive advantage that Australian wines have on the domestic market; yet, the situation is different when it comes to foreign exports.'

- **Third sentence (gap in the knowledge)**: What unanswered questions remain in your literature review?

  Is there a particular issue that yet needs to be addressed? Often, in the conclusions of their research reports, researchers will highlight opportunities for further research. This is a good indication of the possible gaps in the knowledge that you can address. It is important that you find an area that has not been thoroughly examined and where more information is needed. This is an area where you can contribute with new research. This is the most important part of any research project. For example, you can write something along the following lines: 'A comparative case study analysis shows that the Australian wine industry can be more competitive on the European markets if it readjusted its branding strategy for export.'

- **Fourth sentence (the findings)**: What have you discovered in your research?

  Your findings need to be original and interesting. Explain how your findings contribute to the issue that you were examining. For example, you can say something like this: 'The research findings show that social media influences 68 per cent of the respondents when it comes to voting preferences', or: 'The key reason for this is the differences in the public expectations in Europe of how quality wine should be labelled and packaged, which is distinctively different from the that in Australia.'

- **Fifth sentence (social or practical implications)**: What are the implications for practice? Or, if applicable: What is the impact on society?

   What you need to address in this section is the 'So what?' factor. For example, you could say something along these lines: 'This means that social media can play a significant role in election campaigns, and this study provides a list of recommendations on developing social media communication strategies for political purposes, in addition to the overall printed and online campaigns', or: 'This study highlights the key design elements that need to be taken into consideration when developing wine branding strategies for European markets, both in terms of label design and packaging.'

Unless you are specifically asked to provide an extended abstract with references, try to limit your abstract to a maximum of 300 words and do not include any references in the abstract. Remember, the abstract is meant to work as a stand-alone document and may not be accompanied by the reference list that will follow your report. Based on the above comments, I have compiled the following two examples for your convenience. However, please note that these examples are fictional and are for illustration purposes only.

EXAMPLE

Abstract 1

Title and subtitle

Generation Y and Politics: The Influence of Social Media in the Election Process

Keywords

Generation Y, Politics, Social Media, Decision-Making, Elections

Abstract

This study examines the influence of social media on the Generation Y decision-making habits. The latest findings suggest that social media can influence the decision-making habits of Generation Y when it comes to travel choices, entertainment, and clothing, but there is limited information on how social media can influence their political preferences. The research findings show that social media influences 68 per cent of the respondents when it comes to voting preferences. This means that social media can play a significant role in election campaigns, and this study provides a list of recommendations on developing social media communication strategies for political purposes, in addition to the overall printed and online campaigns.

EXAMPLE

Abstract 2

Title and subtitle

Australian Wine in Europe: Design and Branding of Australian Wine for Exports

Keywords

Australian wine, Europe, Design, Packaging, Branding

Abstract

This study examines the current trends in Australian wine label design and packaging for export purposes. The wine industry is one of the largest industries in Australia. The role that design and branding play in this industry is significant when it comes to maintaining the competitive advantage that Australian wines have on the domestic market; yet, the situation is different when it comes to foreign exports. A comparative case study analysis shows that the Australian wine industry can be more competitive on the European markets if it readjusted its branding strategy for export. The key reason for this is the differences in the public expectations in Europe of how quality wine should be labelled and packaged, which is distinctively different from that in Australia. This study highlights the key design elements that need to be taken into consideration when developing wine branding strategies for European markets, both in terms of label design and packaging.

8.1.5 CONTENTS OF THE RESEARCH REPORT

The following is a contents list for a practice-based research report. This research report framework is accompanied by a framework on preparing a design brief, design report, and an executive summary – and I will present all of them below. As with the other examples in this book, you can also use this as a guide or a template, if you find it suitable (Figure 8.3):

1. Title and Subtitle

2. Abstract

3. Keywords

4. Introduction

5. Research Problem

6. Research Purpose

7. Stakeholders

   a) The Client

   b) Primary Audience

   c) Secondary Audience

8. Review of the Literature

9. Primary Research

10. Argument

11. Conclusion

12. Recommendations

13. Opportunities for Further Research

14. Reference List and a Bibliography

As with the research proposal, the research report should begin with a title and subtitle. Here you can use the same title and subtitle as for the proposal. However, it is common for your line of thinking to have changed after conducting your research and so you may need to change or refine the title and the subtitle of your project. This is perfectly normal. It means that you have broadened your understanding of the research problem and now you need to adjust your research report accordingly. Again, make sure that you use a clear title that sets the theme of your study and a subtitle that is descriptive in nature.

The introduction is next. The purpose of the introduction is to set the stage for the reader. Consider the following questions when writing the introduction:

- What is this study about?

- Why are you studying this?

- How will you go about this study?

- What should the reader expect to read?

- How is this study relevant, and to whom?

These are the things that you will need to reflect on in your introduction. Nevertheless, keep your introduction reasonably brief. You will explain all of this in more detail as you progress with the report. Then, you will need to reflect on the research problem by providing a clear statement:

- What is the problem that you trying to solve?

You should have already stated this in the first sentence of your abstract – repeat it here as well. If a client has commissioned the research, then you should consult the client prior to defining the research statement. If this is an independent research project, then you are expected to deliver the research statement. You can also formulate the problem as a research question or as a hypothesis. Following this, you also need to explain further why this issue is worthwhile exploring:

- What do you expect to achieve by resolving this problem?
- What is novel and interesting about this?
- What are your primary predications for the design outcome?
- Who will be affected by your work?

Everyone that has an interest in, or is directly or indirectly affected by, your research or the outcomes of your research should be treated as a stakeholder. Basically, you have to consider three key stakeholders: the client, and the primary and secondary audiences. First, you will need to provide details of your client, or a prospective client if you do not have a client yet. In other words, you will need to explain who has an interest in commissioning this type of research and associated design project, or may find it relevant, and why. This can be a company, a government agency, a non-government or not-for-profit organization, or an individual. Then, you will need to reflect on your primary target audience:

- Who will directly benefit from the findings of your research and who will be the end-user of the design outcome?

Often, the outcomes of any project or policy can affect third parties that are directly or indirectly associated with the client or with the key target audience. Here you should briefly outline any additional stakeholders that may be indirectly affected by the design outcome, both in a positive and a negative way. Once you have covered the practical aspects, you need to present what kind of research has already been conducted on this topic, or in this area so far:

- Are there some existing cases or historical examples that are related to your research question?
- Have there been any similar studies already conducted from which you have learned how this particular problem has been resolved?

Here you should focus on the most influential works in this field of research. Provide sufficient detail and reflection for each example:

- What makes these examples good or bad?
- How are they related to your research question?

Your literature review should be based on journals and books or official websites. The information that you are providing here should demonstrate that you have an in-depth understanding of the question that you have addressed. Do not use Wikipedia as a source of reliable information. Also, make sure that you have cross-referenced the information you have found in order to verify it.

Once you have completed the section for the literature review, you will need to discuss your primary research – the original data that you have gathered or created through applying different methods of empirical data collection. By 'empirical' I mean data collection 'based on, concerned with, or verifiable by observation or experience rather than theory or pure logic' (Oxford Dictionaries, 2013f).

As recommended earlier in the book, for this part of your research you will have conducted a triangulation of mixed methods. Here, you should briefly describe the methods that you have chosen, and why. Then, briefly describe the questions asked, the participant response, the strengths and weaknesses of each method, and the key findings. Explain why these findings are relevant to the development of your project. You can include the full documentation of your primary research as an appendix at the end of the research report. If ethics approval has been sought, in the appendix you can also include your ethics authorization letter, consent letters, and so forth.

Use the information you have gathered so far to advance or build your position. Agree with and/or challenge other researchers by questioning their position if you do not agree with it. Avoid faulty reasoning. Develop a strong argument by providing sufficient detail, comparisons, illustrations, and causal analysis. Be specific in your examples and restate your position in different ways to bring your message home to the reader. Maintain a coherent line of reasoning. Key questions to consider while structuring your argument are:

- What am I focusing on here?
- What am I talking about?
- Why am I focusing on this?
- What are my reasons?
- How do I want to develop this discussion?
- What do I want to discuss and in what order do I want to discuss these topics?

In the conclusion you should bring together the findings of your paper. Then, process your findings for the reader. Here you should ask yourself:

- What do I find most interesting or important about my findings?
- What is new about the idea and the position that I have developed?
- Who can benefit from this?

Then, proceed with recommendations and state clearly what the implications of your findings are. On the basis of what you have learned from this process, discuss what you think needs to be done – but make sure that you explain why you recommend this. This information should be further used for the development of the design brief, which will be discussed below. In the final section of your conclusion you can discuss what kind of opportunities for further research you envision:

- Is there a part of your study that can be further developed?
- If so, which part and why?
- What kind of other studies could benefit your project or the field of study in the future?

At the end of your report you will need to provide a list of your references or a full bibliography. A reference list includes all the sources that you have used and mentioned in your report, whereas a bibliography includes all the sources that you consulted for the preparation of your research, but not all of them are necessarily referenced in your report. In most cases, a reference list is mandatory and a bibliography is optional.

There are number of style guides that you can consult for this purpose. For example, some of the most commonly used referencing systems are *The Chicago Manual of Style*, *The Harvard System of Referencing*, and *The Publication Manual of the American Psychological Association*. If you are writing your report as a part of your studies, then check with your supervisor or the library on what is the preferred style of the university. If you are writing for a journal or a conference, check their requirements before you submit your study for review.

8.2 EXECUTIVE SUMMARY

The executive summary is a document that is usually required for business reports. Such documents are mainly read by business executives who do not have the time to read the full reports, but would like to be presented with enough details about ongoing or completed projects in order to stay fully informed.

You can think of the executive summary as an extended version of your abstract or a simplified synopsis of your research and/or design outcome. The executive summary can be presented alongside a formal report, but it should also be able to work as a separate document. Since this is a formal document, you should use the same impersonal writing style. There are two ways by which you can present your executive summary. Some prefer to present their findings/outcomes first and then to follow up with the rationale and the rest of the information, while others prefer to write the executive summaries by following the same order as the information appears in their abstract and in their study. The first approach is more attention grabbing (which is good for media releases, or for presenting it to people who are unfamiliar with the research project), while the second approach ensures that a logical flow and cohesion is maintained throughout the documents. It is up to you to make a decision as to what kind of executive summary is most suitable for your client.

Approximate Content Distribution Ratio

Title and Subtitle ——— ▪

Abstract ——— ▪

Keywords —— ▪

Introduction ——— ▪

Research Problem ——— ▪

Research Purpose —— ▪

Stakeholders ——— ▪

Review of the Literature ————————————————————————————————————— ▪

Primary Research ——— ▪

Argument ——— ▪

Conclusion ——— ▪

Recommendations ——— ▪

Opportunities for Further Research ——————————————————————————————— ▪

Reference List and a Bibliography ——————————————————————————————— ▪

Figure 8.3 Contents of a practice-based research report

8.2.1 CONTENTS OF THE EXECUTIVE SUMMARY

As discussed above, there are two ways in which you can prepare an executive summary. Here I will present you with a more traditional content structure that follows the rest of the documents (see Figure 8.4):

1. Title and Subtitle

2. Brief Introduction

3. Research Problem

4. Research Purpose

5. Research Methods and Methodology

6. Summary of the Literature Review

7. Summary of the Research Findings

8. Conclusion

9. Recommendations

As you will see, many of these points mirror those already discussed in your reports. The difference is that you will need to try to present these points in a simpler and more condensed form. The title of your executive summary can be the same as that in your research report. To begin with, you should provide a brief introduction of your research project:

- What is this study about?

The function of this introduction is to establish the context of the study. The introduction should be about 10 per cent of the overall word length of the document. For example, if your executive summary is 1,000 words, the introduction should be around 100 words. Following this, you should outline your research problem:

- What are you trying to solve?

You have already stated this in the first sentence of your abstract. Repeat it here as well. Then, explain why this issue is interesting and worthwhile exploring. Tell the reader what you expect to achieve by resolving this problem. In addition to this, you will need to explain briefly what methods and methodologies you have used to conduct your research, and why. Here is a fictional example of how this might look:

> This study is based on qualitative and quantitative research that incorporates a hermeneutic and semiotic analysis of collected data. This means that this study is based on interpretation of information from both a historical and theoretical perspective based on a literature review, case studies, and interview data, based on methods triangulation (focus group interviews, survey, cultural probes). The study includes problem identification, data gathering, data analysis, interpretation, and a report of the analysis results to support decision making.

Once you have established this, you will need to discuss briefly the key findings in the field so far. At the beginning of your research, you conducted a review of the literature (secondary research); tell the reader what have you learned from your literature review, but focus only on the key points. Highlight the gap in the knowledge and explain how your research fills this gap. You should follow up on this by providing a brief summary of your research findings (the primary research). Again, focus only on the key points of your research and whenever possible use visually appealing media to present the information.

In your conclusion you should restate the main ideas that you have developed. Remember that this is only a summary of your argument in the research report. Therefore, remove any minor points and focus on the key issue. Ensure that your conclusion is clear and concise. Do not leave the reader saying: So what?

Finally, discuss the main implications of your research and say what kind of action you would recommend. Write your recommendations clearly and in a concise manner. Use

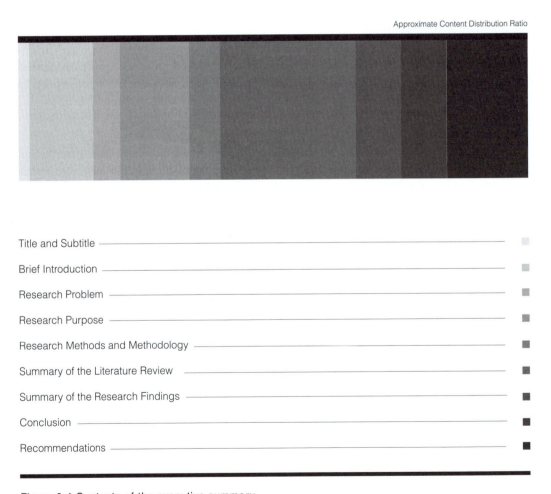

Approximate Content Distribution Ratio

Title and Subtitle

Brief Introduction

Research Problem

Research Purpose

Research Methods and Methodology

Summary of the Literature Review

Summary of the Research Findings

Conclusion

Recommendations

Figure 8.4 Contents of the executive summary

numbered bullet points (e.g. Recommendation 1, Recommendation 2, and so on). These recommendations can set the framework for the design brief.

8.3 DESIGN BRIEF

Once you have completed your research, you can begin making informed design decisions about the problem that you have been tasked with resolving. The next stage would be for you to prepare a design brief. A design brief is a written document that outlines the expectations for a design project.

Many designers are often tempted to begin their projects straight from this stage, without conducting a proper research on the problem that they have address beforehand. It is quite common in the design industry for designers to ask their clients to provide a design brief for them. I will encourage you to do the opposite. Design briefs are much more effective when designers work with the clients on developing a final design brief after the research has taken place. In other words, the client's initial design brief should not be the final design brief. Instead, this should serve as a first point of discussion about the problem that the client wants to be resolved.

This is somewhat different approach to the 'traditional' model, where the client identifies a problem and then thinks of a solution in the form of a 'brief' that is then suggested to the designer, who in return decides how this idea is best realized. The problem with this approach is that the client may not always have the research skills or the design background to identify the core of the problem or the most appropriate design solution. In other words, the client is not necessarily qualified to drive the design thinking process. To better exemplify this, I will draw a parallel with medical practitioners or attorneys. While a patient or a person in a need of a health advice or legal assistance may be well aware that they have a problem, they are not qualified to suggest types of medications or legal actions to their doctors or lawyers – nor does anyone expect them to do so. The same principle of work should be applied in the design profession. That is why it is better if the design brief is based on a research report. Professional designers should be able to identify the problem, suggest solutions, provide expert advice, and deliver design outcomes.

8.3.1 CONTENTS OF THE DESIGN BRIEF

There is not one standardized way in which you can prepare a design brief. In order to help you get started, here is a content structure that you may use when preparing one (see Figure 8.5):

1. Project Title
2. Problem Statement
   a) Client Profile
   b) Client's Needs

    c) Target Audience

    d) Key Competitors

3. Proposed Outcome

    a) Design Consideration

    b) Design Constraints

4. Budget

5. Timetable

The title can be the same as the one that you are using in your research report, or you can provide a new title that describes the project rather than the research. Then, begin by providing brief information of what the project is that you are working on. Follow this by providing some background information about your client. This can include information related to the client's business history, areas of operation, brand values, key objectives, and future vision. Next, explain what the problem is that you are addressing:

- What are your client's needs?

If necessary, include a list of sub-problems. Here you should also provide a brief analysis of the primary target audience (end-users and/or consumers). Also, you should provide some information on the client's key competitors by listing any competing organizations and/or products.

    The problem statement can simply be based on the problem stated in your research report. However, based on the findings of your research, here you can realign the focus of the problem if necessary. The purpose of this information is for you to show that you understand the context in which you are working and by doing that to reassure your client that you understand their business and their expectations. Once you have established this, you should discuss what kind of design outcome you propose to deliver:

- What is the design solution that you believe will work best, and why?

Answer this by explaining how this solution will address the above-mentioned problem. Here you can discuss similar examples from industry – but only if necessary. In addition to this, you need to be aware that there may be a number of things that you need to take into consideration while working on this project. Therefore, you should also provide brief information on the issues that you will take into consideration when designing. Depending on what the client's primary needs are, some of these issues may be related to the following:

- Function
- Purpose
- Aesthetics
- Key Design Elements

- Environment
- Sustainability
- Performance
- Materials
- Production
- Manufacture
- Human Factors and Ergonomics
- Semantics and Semiotics
- Marketing and Communications
- Packaging
- Distribution
- Design and/or Trademark Registration

Please note that this is not a definitive list and that all considerations may not be applicable to your project or some possibilities might not have been included in this list. Also, design

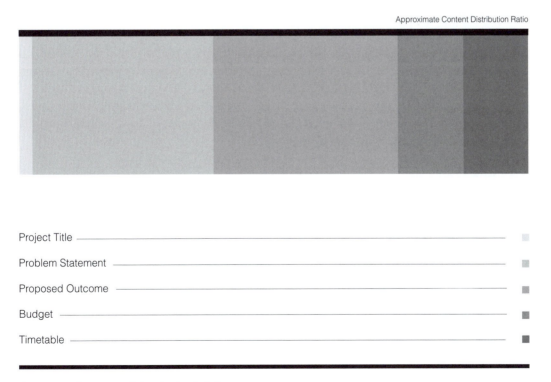

Approximate Content Distribution Ratio

Project Title

Problem Statement

Proposed Outcome

Budget

Timetable

Figure 8.5 Contents of the design brief

considerations may vary from project to project. Therefore, it is best to frame the design considerations in consultation with your client.

Once you have listed the design considerations, you should also list whether there are any constraints in terms of production, colours, or materials that you also need to take into consideration. Likewise, design constraints may vary from project to project and there are many factors that you will need to be made aware of before you address this issue. Therefore, you should consult your client on this as well.

Another thing that you need to discuss with your client is the budget. As with any design project, there will be either a set budget allocated up front, or you will need to calculate a budget based on the expected expenses. If you are preparing a design brief as a part of your studies, budgeting might be an unrealistic expectation and it is rarely a necessary component of any student project. However, a timetable is often required in both cases. Therefore, here you should present a timeline of your activities. What you need to include is information on when you expect to complete the project, and what are your milestones (the different stages of your project).

8.4 DESIGN REPORT

Once the design work is completed, you will need to prepare a report that outlines what you have done and for whom. Your design solution or an artifact should be accompanied by a design report. The purpose of the report is to provide an explanation of the work that you have done and to justify your design decisions. Ideally, your design report should be stylistically well designed, and well written. The design of the report should reflect the proposed design solution and the writing style of the design report should be similar to the writing style of the research report.

8.4.1 CONTENTS OF THE DESIGN REPORT

There are no standardized ways of preparing design reports. Nevertheless, here is a content structure that you may use when preparing a design report (see Figure 8.6):

1. Project Title
2. Project Summary
   a) Client Profile
   b) Client's Needs
   c) Target Audience
   d) Key Competitors

3. Project Presentation

    a) Design Specifications

    b) Design Rationale

    c) Design Evaluation: SWOT Analysis

4. Costing

5. Appendix 1: Research Proposal

6. Appendix 2: Research Report

7. Appendix 3: Design Brief

8. Appendix 4: Design Documentation

9. Appendix 5: Invoice

The way you present your project is very important. The production values of your presentation and of your design report should match the production values of your design outcome. The title of the design report should be the same as the title of your design brief. At the beginning of your design report, provide a brief project summary. Here you can refer back to the design brief and you can sum up key details from your client's profile, their needs, their key target audiences, and key competitors. You can present most of this information as bullet points. Then, once you have set the context of the project, you should present your design solution. Here you can include visuals such as drawing, renderings, and photographs of the design artifact, or of prototypes and models. In addition to this, you should provide a list of the design specifications, such as technical information related to size, dimensions, production technologies, materials, mediums, and so on. Then, you will need to provide a justification of the design solution by writing a design rationale. Following this, provide an evaluation of the design solution. There are several ways by which you can do this, such as conducting user testings or focus groups. You can report on this by proving a SWOT analysis – a brief outline of the strengths, weaknesses, opportunities, and the threats associated with this project. Following this, include a list of expenses and associated costs. Here you can provide a breakdown of your activities, list of the materials and the resources that were necessary for the completion of this project, and any other expenses that you have incurred by working on this project. This, of course, will need to be linked to the original budget that was approved by your client.

    In addition to your design report, you can gather together all of the materials that you have produced so far – the research proposal, the research report, and the design brief – and include them as an appendix. In addition to this, you can also include any supporting design documentation, such as copies of your sketches, drawings, photographs, and notes from meetings with the client. This is very important for record-keeping purposes, both for you and your client. At the end, you can include your invoice.

Approximate Content Distribution Ratio

Project Title ─── ▪

Project Summary ──────────────────────────────────── ▪

Project Presentation ──────────────────────────────── ▪

Costing ─── ▪

Appendix 1: Research Proposal ─────────────────────── ▪

Appendix 2: Research Report ──────────────────────── ▪

Appendix 3: Design Brief ───────────────────────────── ▪

Appendix 4: Design Documentation ───────────────────── ▪

Appendix 5: Invoice ───────────────────────────────── ▪

Figure 8.6 Contents of the design report

8.5 CONCLUSION

The research report is a report on what you have done over the course of your research effort. The purpose of the report is for you to help the reader understand:

- What was the problem you were trying to resolve?
- What was the data that have led to the resolution of that problem?
- What were the means by which these data were gathered?
- How were these data analysed?
- What conclusions were reached?

The interpretation and presentation of the findings should be written in the *present tense.* The writing style of the report must be formal and impersonal – with the exception of reports written as a part of ethnographic or historical studies, which may be written in personal and literary (storytelling) fashion (Leedy and Ormrod, 2010: 304). In addition to the research report, you can also prepare an executive summary. This is a simplified synopsis that can be presented alongside your reports or as an independent document that sums up your activities. The main purpose of conducting research in a design context is either to help you improve your design practice, or to help you make informed design decisions that will result in high-quality design outcomes. Therefore, the research report can help you draft a better design brief, which can lead to a more appropriate design solution. Also, you should be able to use your research report when writing your design report.

8.6 SUMMARY

In this chapter I have highlighted the key points that you will need to take into consideration when preparing research and design reports, including supporting documentation such as abstract, keywords, and executive summaries, as well as a design brief. In this book I have covered some of the key essentials that you need to know when embarking on a research path, and why these things are relevant to design practice. However, I have not focused on the practical aspects of working on a design project because this falls outside the scope of this book.

CONCLUSION

For the most part of its short history, design has been seen as a field of practice. Nevertheless, things are changing. Design has evolved and it is increasingly becoming a field of thinking and research as well. Design has moved on from being merely a hands-on arts and crafts practice and has become an academic field in its own right. The increasing use of research in design represents a willingness to look beyond the basic concern of 'crafting a project'. A good understanding of production techniques, material properties, and technical skills are still very important for designers, but this is simply not enough if we want the field to progress further. For that reason, designers also need to learn to ask the 'right' questions and develop a keen understanding of people, cultures, and even belief systems. This is why introduction of research in design education is becoming increasingly important.

In today's complex environments, design aspires to become a process that delivers new solutions to existing problems, or at least to become a process that can transform less preferred solutions to more desirable ones. In order for designers to be accepted as effective problem-solvers by their clients and the society at large, the field of design needs to be revisited and cross-disciplinary research methods will need to become a regular part of the design process. Introduction of cross-disciplinary research in design is a complex long-term process and designers will need to develop relevant skills over time. However, with such a set of skills, designers will not only be able to react to existing problems, as is the case now, but they will also be able to prevent many new problems from occurring in the first place. Therefore, before designers start introducing solutions, they will first need to learn to anticipate and understand problems. That is why this is a process that always begins with the question: What is it that we are trying to resolve here? The answer to this question is rarely straightforward, and pursuing it can best be described as a journey through the field of knowledge. This investigative process leads designers not only through the creative industries – where they look for inspiration – but also through many other disciplines that may never have been associated with design before.

Contemporary design is both a problem-finding and a problem-solving process. Once the problem is identified and placed within a given context, the search for gaps in the knowledge and possible resolutions follows. Once sufficient information is gathered, a process of analysis and interpretation begins, and design solutions should follow. This way of conducting design may appear at odds with the 'traditional' way of designing, where design was seen as an artistic discipline driven by the technical skills and the creative zeal of individuals. Nevertheless, times have changed and the tasks for many designers are shifting from 'product creation' to 'process creation'.

While the demand for traditional designers with 'old school' skills (now enhanced with proficiency in design software) is constant within the design industry, both business and society today demand a new generation of designers who can design not only products and visuals, but systems for living as well. This calls for designers who are not only providers of creative services, but also strategic planners, managers, business entrepreneurs, human factor specialists, and social scientists. While this brings new opportunities for the profession, it also brings new challenges. Design skills need to progress from artistic and technical to conceptual and analytical. Therefore, if designers want to be competitive, their knowledge will need to come from areas that go far beyond arts and crafts.

This way of thinking about design is necessary when contemporary problems associated with economic crises, globalization, multiculturalism, terrorism, overpopulation, and environmental issues demand new solutions, innovative concepts, and alternative approaches. A shift in the profession is inevitable if designers want to deliver better design outputs – solutions that are not simply aesthetic refinements, but also meaningful contributions to business and society.

Then again, this is not such big leap forward as it may appear at first glance. In many cases, designers already act as social scientists and business strategists – even though they might be unaware of this. In practice, designers already identify problems, select appropriate goals, and deliver various social or business solutions. Nevertheless, what many fail to recognize is that most of these problems involve multifaceted societal, political, and economic issues that are interlocked with complexities of commerce, technology, and innovation. Understanding and applying a variety of research methods can help designers understand their tasks better and make informed decisions that will lead towards new and original outcomes.

The future challenge for designers will not be to recognize obvious problems after they occur and then to solve them, but rather to prevent problems from occurring in the first place. Shaping new, but well-informed processes and linking them to effective methods of design development is necessary. A systematic research-based approach can offer a level of robust understanding that can do this. This, in return, will lead not only to a better and more empathetic design practice, but also to a richer relationship with other disciplines and to new design knowledge. Hopefully, *Research for Designers* has guided you through this process and has served you as a useful resource and a study companion.

REFERENCES

Aagaard-Hansen, J. (2007) 'The Challenges of Cross-Disciplinary Research', *Social Epistemology* 21(4): 425–38.

Aagaard-Hansen, J. and Ouma, J.H. (2002) 'Managing Interdisciplinary Health Research: Theoretical and Practical Aspects', *International Journal of Health Planning and Management* 17(3): 195–212.

Abras, C., Maloney-Krichmar, D. and Preece, J. (2004) 'User-Centered Design' in W. Bainbridge (ed.), *Berkshire Encyclopedia of Human–Computer Interaction*. Thousand Oaks, CA: SAGE, p. 767.

Aguinis, H. and Henle, C.A. (2004) 'Ethics in Research' in G. Adams and M. Berzonsky (eds), *Blackwell Handbook of Adolescence*. Oxford: Blackwell, pp. 34–56.

Almquist, J. and Lupton, J. (2010) 'Affording Meaning: Design-Oriented Research from the Humanities and Social Sciences', *Design Issues* 26(1): 3–14.

Alreck, P. and Settle, R. (1985) *The Survey Research Handbook*. Homewood, IL: Irwin.

American Psychological Association (2009) *Publication Manual of the American Psychological Association*, 6th edn. Washington, DC: APA.

Arnould, E.J. (2006) 'Getting a Manuscript to Publication Standard', *Design Research Quarterly* 1(1): 21–3.

Barrett, T. (1994) *Criticizing Art: Understanding the Contemporary*. Mountain View, CA: Mayfield.

Barrett, T. (2000) 'About Art Interpretation for Art Education', *Studies in Art Education* 42(1): 5–19.

Bateson, M.C. (1972) *A Metaphor of Our Own: A Personal Account on the Effects of Conscious Purpose on Human Adaptation*. New York: Knopf.

Baudrillard, J. (1998) *The Consumer Society: Myths and Structures*. London: SAGE.

Baxter, P. and Jack, S. (2008) 'Qualitative Case Study Methodology: Study Design and Implementation for Novice Researchers', *The Qualitative Report* 13(4): 544–59.

Bayazit, N. (2004) 'Investigating Design: A Review of Forty Years of Design Research', *Design Issues* 20(1): 16–29.

Bell, J. (2005) *Doing Your Research Project: A Guide to First-Time Researchers in Education, Health and Social Sciences*. Maidenhead: Open University Press.

Belli, G. (2009) 'Nonexperimental Quantitative Research' in S.D. Lapan and M.T. Quartaroli (eds), *Research Essentials: An Introduction to Designs and Practices*. San Francisco, CA: Jossey-Bass, pp. 59–77.

Bengtsson, S. (2013) *IKEA the Book: Designers, Products and Other Stuff*. Stockholm: Arvinius Förlag AB for IKEA FAMILY.

Berger, J. (1972) *Ways of Seeing*. London: Penguin.

Bignell, J. (1997) *Media Semiotics: An Introduction*. Manchester: Manchester University Press.

Bryman, A. (2006) 'Integrating Quantitative and Qualitative Research: How Is It Done?', *Qualitative Research* 6(1): 97–113.

Buchanan, R. (1998) 'Education and Professional Practice in Design', *Design Issues* 14(2): 63–6.

Buchanan, R. (1999) 'The Study of Design: Doctoral Education and Research in a New Field of Inquiry' in *Proceedings from the Doctoral Education in Design Conference*, Pittsburgh, USA, 8–11 October, School of Design, Carnegie Mellon University, pp. 1–29.

Buchanan, R. (2001) 'Design Research and the New Learning', *Design Issues* 17(4): 3–23.

Bunge, M. (1999) *The Dictionary of Philosophy*. Amherst, NY: Prometheus.

Burdick, A. (2003) 'Design (as) Research' in B. Laurel (ed.), *Design Research: Methods and Perspectives*. Cambridge, MA: Massachusetts University of Technology, p. 82.

Burns, R.B. (2000) *Introduction to Research Methods.* Frenchs Forest: Longman.

Candy, L. (2006a) 'Differences Between Practice-Based and Practice-Led Research', *Creativity and Cognition Studios*. Broadway: University of Technology, Sydney. Retrieved 14 February 2013 from www.creativityandcognition.com/research/practice-based-research.

Candy, L. (2006b) 'Practice Based Research: A Guide', *Creativity and Cognition Studios*. Broadway: University of Technology, Sydney. Retrieved 29 November 2013 from www.creativityandcognition.com/research/practice-based-research.

Chicago Press (2010) *The Chicago Manual of Style: The Essential Guide for Writers, Editors and Publishers*, 16th edn. Chicago, Il: Chicago University Press.

Cooper, R. and Press, M. (2006) 'Academic Design Research'. London: Design Council. Retrieved 1 September 2009 from www.designcouncil.org.uk/en/About-Design/Design-Techniques/Academic-Design-Research-by-Rachel-Cooper-and-Mike-Press/.

Cottrell, R.R. and McKenzie, J.F. (2011) *Health Promotion & Education Research: Using The Five-Chapter Thesis/Dissertation Model.* London: Jones and Bartlett.

Coulter, J. (1989) *The World's Great Cars*. London: Marshall Cavendish.

Cranston, M. (1995) 'Ideology', *The New Encyclopaedia Britannica: Macropaedia* 20(1): 768–72.

Creswell, J.W. (2003) *Research Design: Qualitative, Quantitative and Mixed Methods Approaches.* Thousand Oaks, CA: SAGE.

Crouch, C. and Pearce, J. (2012) *Doing Research in Design.* London: Berg.

Cutler, T. (2009) *Designing Solutions to Wicked Problems: A Manifesto for Transdisciplinary Research and Design*. Melbourne, VA: RMIT University.

de Saussure, F. (1983) *Course in General Linguistics.* London: Duckworth.

Del Favero, M. (2014) 'Academic Disciplines – Disciplines and the Structure of Higher Education, Discipline Classification Systems, Discipline Differences', *Education Encyclopedia*. Retrieved 12 January 2014 from http://education.stateuniversity.com/pages/1723/Academic-Disciplines.html.

Design Council (2010) *Multi-Disciplinary Design Education in the UK: Report and Recommendations from the Multi-Disciplinary Design Network*. London: Design Council.

Dilnot, C. (1984a) 'The State of Design History, Part I: Mapping the Field', *Design Issues* 1(1): 4–23.

Dilnot, C. (1984b) 'The State of Design History, Part II: Problems and Possibilities, *Design Issues* 1(2): 3–20.

Dorst, K. (2008) 'Design Research: A Revolution-Waiting-to-Happen', *Design Studies* 29(1): 4–11.

Downton, P. (2003) *Design Research.* Melbourne: RMIT University Press.

Durling, D. and Griffiths, B. (2001) 'From Formgiving to Braingiving' in *Proceedings from the Re-Inventing Design Education in the University Conference,* Perth, Australia, 11–13 December, School of Design, Curtin University of Technology, pp. 29–36.

Engeler Newbury, B. (2012) 'Design Thinking and Futures Thinking, Strategic Business Partners or Competitors? Exploring Commonalities, Differences and Opportunities' in G. Muratovski (ed.), *agIdeas Research: Design for Business, Volume 1.* Melbourne: agIdeas Press, pp. 26–41.

Fadayev, A. (1971) 'Socialist Realism', *Encyclopedia of World Literature in the Twentieth Century* 3(1): 298–301.

Formosa, D. (2012) 'Design Thinking', *Keynote Address at agIdeas 2013 Advantage, part of the 2013 agIdeas International Design Week,* Design Foundation, Melbourne, Australia, 2 May. Retrieved 4 May 2013 from www.agideas.net/coming-event/business-breakfast.

Fowles, J. (1996) *Advertising and Popular Culture*, London: SAGE.

Friedman, K. (1997) 'Design Science and Design Education' in P. McCrery (ed.), *The Challenge of Complexity*. Helsinki: University of Art and Design, pp. 54–72.

Friedman, K. (2002) 'Conclusion: Toward an Integrative Design Profession' in S. Squires and B. Byrne (eds), *Creating Breakthrough Ideas: The Collaboration of Anthropologists and Designers in the Product Development Industry*. London: Bergin & Garvey, pp. 199–214.

Friedman, K. (2003) 'Theory Construction in Design Research: Criteria, Approaches, and Methods', *Design Studies* 24(6): 507–22.

Friedman, K. (2012) 'Models of Design: Envisioning a Future for Design Education', *Visible Language*, 46(1–2): 128–51 and 135–54.

Friedman, K., Lou, Y., Norman, D., Stappers, P.H., Voûte, E. and Whitney, P. (2014) *DesignX: A Future Path for Design*. Shanghai: DesignX Collaborative. Retrieved 15 May 2015 from www.linkedin.com/pulse/20141204175515-12181762-designx-a-future-path-for-design?trk=prof-post.

Gaver, B., Dunne, T. and Pacenti, E. (1999) 'Cultural Probes', *Intersections* 6(1): 21–9.

Gaver, W.W., Boucher, A., Pennington, S. and Walker, B. (2004) 'Cultural Probes and the Value of Uncertainty', *Intersections* 11(5): 53–6.

Gimbel, S. (2011) 'Introduction' in S. Gimbel (ed.), *Exploring the Scientific Method: Cases and Questions*. Chicago, IL: University of Chicago Press.

Given, L.M. (2008) *The SAGE Encyclopedia of Qualitative Research Methods*. Thousand Oaks, CA: SAGE.

Goldammer, K.M.A. (1995) 'Religious Symbolism and Iconography' *The New Encyclopaedia Britannica: Macropaedia* 17(1): 591–600.

Hanington, B.M. (2005) 'Research Education by Design: Assessing the Impact of Pedagogy on Practice' in *Proceedings from the Joining Forces: International Conference on Design Research*, Helsinki, Finland, 22–4 September, University of Art and Design. Retrieved 14 April 2011 from www.uiah.fi/joining forces/papers/Hanington.pdf.

Hanington, B.M. (2010) 'Relevant and Rigorous: Human-Centered Research and Design Education', *Design Issues* 26(3): 18–26.

Harvard (2015) *The Harvard System of Referencing*. Retrieved 30 May 2015 from www.library.dmu.ac.uk/Images/Selfstudy/Harvard.pdf.

Hatch, M.J. and Shultz, M. (2008) *Taking Brand Initiative: How Companies Can Align Strategy, Culture, and Identity Through Corporate Branding*. San Francisco, CA: Jossey-Bass.

Heckman, M.A., Sherry, K. and Gonzalez de Mejia, E. (2010) 'Energy Drinks: An Assessment of Their Market Size, Consumer Demographics, Ingredient Profile, Functionality, and Regulations in the United States', *Comprehensive Reviews in Food Science and Food Safety* 9: 303–17.

Higgin, T. (2009) 'Blackless Fantasy: The Disappearance of Race in Massively Multiplayer Online Role-Playing Games', *Games and Culture* 4(1): 3–26.

Hines, L.M. (2009) 'Evaluating Historical Research' in S.D. Lapan and M.T. Quartaroli (eds), *Research Essentials: An Introduction to Designs and Practices*. San Francisco, CA: Jossey-Bass, pp. 145–64.

Holt, S.S. (2000) 'Beauty and the Blob: Product Culture Now' in D. Albrecht, E. Lupton and S.S. Holt (eds), *Design Culture Now: National Design Triennial*. New York: Princeton Architectural Press, pp. 21–4.

Hopkins, D. and Ahtaridou, E. (2006) 'Applying Research Methods to Professional Practice' in S.D. Lapan and M.T. Quartaroli (eds), *Research Essentials: An Introduction to Designs and Practices*, San Francisco, CA: Jossey-Bass, pp. 275–93.

Huppatz, D.J. and Lees-Maffei, G. (2013) 'Why Design History? A Multi-National Perspective on the State and Purpose of the Field', *Arts & Humanities in Higher Education* 12(2–3): 310–30.

IBM (2007) 'User-Centred Design', *IBM Design*. Retrieved 21 April 2013 from www-01.ibm.com/software/ucd/ucd.html.

Ireland, C. (2003) 'The Changing Role of Research' in B. Laurel (ed.), *Design Research: Methods and Perspectives*. Cambridge, MA: MIT Press, p. 22.

Jhally, S. (2000) 'Advertising at the Edge of the Apocalypse' in R. Andersen and L. Strate (eds), *Critical Studies in Media Commercialism*. Oxford: Oxford University Press, pp. 27–39.

Jones, M.L., Kriflik, G. and Zanko, M. (2005) 'Grounded Theory: A Theoretical and Practical Application in the Australian Film Industry' in A. Hafidz Bin Hj (ed.), *Proceedings of the International Qualitative Research Convention 2005 (QRC05)*. Kuala Lumpur: Qualitative Research Association of Malaysia. Retrieved 20 February 2013 from: http://ro.uow.edu.au/commpapers/46.

Jowett, G.S. and O'Donnell, V. (2006) *Propaganda and Persuasion*. London: SAGE.

Jung, C.G. (1964) *Man and His Symbols*. London: Aldus.

Kilbourne, J. (2013) *Jean Kilbourne*. Retrieved 15 December 2013 from www.jeankilbourne.com.

Kristensen, T. (1999) 'Research on Design in Business'. Keynote paper delivered at *Useful and Critical: The Position of Research in Design*, International Conference, University of Art and Design UIAH, Helsinki, Finland, 9–11 September 1999.

Larson, K. (2009) 'Research Ethics and the Use of Human Participants' in S.D. Lapan and M.T. Quartaroli (eds), *Research Essentials: An Introduction to Designs and Practices*. San Francisco, CA: Jossey-Bass, pp. 1–17.

Laurel, B. (2003) 'Introduction: Muscular Design' in B. Laurel (ed.), *Design Research: Methods and Perspectives*. Cambridge, MA: MIT Press, pp. 16–19.

Laverty, S.M. (2003) 'Hermeneutic Phenomenology and Phenomenology: A Comparison of Historical and Methodological Considerations', *International Journal of Qualitative Methods* 2(3): 1–29. Retrieved 20 February 2013 from www.ualberta.ca/-iiqm/backissus/2_3final/pdf/laverty.pdf.

Lawrence, R. and Després, C. (2004) 'Introduction: Futures of Transdisciplinarity', *Futures* 36(4): 397–405.

Leedy, P.D. and Ormrod, J.E. (2010) *Practical Research: Planning and Design*. Boston, MA: Pearson.

Leiss, W., Kline, S. and Jhally, S. (1997) *Social Communication in Advertising*. New York: Routledge.

Leonard, D. and Rayport, J.F. (1997) 'Spark Innovation Through Empathic Design', *Harvard Business Review*. Retrieved 3 March 2013 from http://hbr.org/1997/11/spark-innovation-through-empathic-design/ar/1.

Lester, S. (1999) 'An Introduction to Phenomenological Research', *Stan Lester Developments*. Retrieved 22 February 2013 from www.sld.demon.co.uk/resmethv.pdf.

Levin, D.E. and Kilbourne, J. (2009) *So Sexy So Soon: The New Sexualized Childhood and What Parents Can Do to Protect Their Kids*. New York: Ballantine.

Lewis-Beck, M., Bryman, A.E. and Liao, T.F. (2004) *The SAGE Encyclopedia of Social Science Research Methods*. Thousand Oaks, CA: SAGE.

Love, T. (2001) 'New Roles for Design Education in University Settings' in *Proceedings from the Re-Inventing Design Education in the University Conference*, Perth, Australia, 11–13 December, School of Design, Curtin University of Technology, pp. 249–55.

Madden, R. (2010) *Being Ethnographic: A Guide to the Theory and Practice of Ethnography*. London: SAGE.

Margolin, V. (1992) 'Design History or Design Studies: Subject Matter and Methods', *Design Studies* 13(2): 104–16.

Margolin, V. (2010) 'Doctoral Education in Design: Problems and Prospects', *Design Issues* 26(3): 70–78.

McAllister, G. and Furlong, A. (2009) 'Understanding Literature Reviews' in S.D. Lapan and M.T. Quartaroli (eds), *Research Essentials: An Introduction to Designs and Practices.* San Francisco, CA: Jossey-Bass, pp. 19–33.

McNiff, J. and Whitehead, J. (2012) *All You Need to Know About Action Research.* London: SAGE.

Merriam-Webster (1993) *Merriam-Webster's Collegiate Dictionary*, 10th edn. Springfield, MA: Merriam-Webster, Inc.

Meyer, J. (2000) 'Using Qualitative Methods in Health Related Action Research', *British Medical Journal*, 320: 178–81.

Mirzoeff, N. (1999) 'What is Visual Culture?' in N. Mirzoeff (ed.), *The Visual Culture Reader.* London: Routledge, pp. 3–13.

Mirzoeff, N. (2009) *An Introduction to Visual Culture.* London: Routledge.

Mitchell, C. (2012) *Doing Visual Research.* London: SAGE.

Mithen, S. (1998) *The Prehistory of the Mind: A Search for the Origins of Art, Religion and Science.* London: Phoenix.

Mollerup, P. (2005) *Wayshowing: A Guide to Environmental Signage Principles and Practices.* Zürich: Lars Müller.

Moore, N. (2000) *How to do Research: The Complete Guide to Designing and Managing Research Projects.* London: Library Association.

Muratovski, G. (2006) *Beyond Design.* Skopje: NAM Print.

Muratovski, G. (2010a) 'Design and Design Research: The Conflict Between the Principles of Design Education and Practices in Industry', *Design Principles and Practices: An International Journal* 4(2): 377–86.

Muratovski, G. (2010b) 'Design Research: Corporate Communication Strategies – From Religious Propaganda to Strategic Brand Management', PhD dissertation, University of South Australia, Adelaide.

Muratovski, G. (2011a) 'In Pursuit of New Knowledge: A Need For a Shift From Multidisciplinary to Transdisciplinary Model of Doctoral Design Education and Research'. Paper presented at the 2011 *Doctoral Education in Design*, Hong Kong Polytechnic University, Hong Kong, China, 22–25 May 2011. Retrieved 15 July 2012 from www.sd.polyu.edu.hk/DocEduDesign2011/proceeding.php.

Muratovski, G. (2011b) 'Challenges and Opportunities of Cross-Disciplinary Design Education and Research'. Paper presented at the 2011 *Australian Council of University Art and Design Schools (ACUADS) Conference: Creativity: Brain, Mind, Body*. Australian National University and the University of Canberra, Canberra, Australia, 21 September 2011. Retrieved 26 February 2013 from http://acuads.com.au/conference/2011-conference.

Muratovski, G. (2012a) 'What is Design, and Where it is Going?', *Between Design Journal* 5: 44–7.

Muratovski, G. (2012b) 'The Importance of Research and Strategy in Design and Branding: Conversation with Dana Arnett' in G. Muratovski (ed.) *Design for Business, Volume 1.* Melbourne: agIdeas Press/ Bristol: Intellect, pp. 16–23.

Norman, D. (2010) 'Why Design Education Must Change', *Core77*, 27 November. Retrieved 15 January 2014 from www.core77.com/blog/columns/why_design_education_must_change_17993.as.

Norman, D. (2013) *The Design of Everyday Things*: *Revised and Extended Edition.* New York: Basic Books.

Ochoa, G. and Corey, M. (1995) *The Timeline Book of Science.* New York: Ballantine.

Olins, W. (1995) *The New Guide to Identity.* London: The Design Council.

Owen, C.L. (1989) 'Design Education and Research for the 21st Century' in *Design, Your Competitive Edge – Proceedings of the First International Design Forum*, Singapore, 20 October, Singapore Trade Development Board. Retrieved 13 January 2014 from www.id.iit.edu/media/cms_page_media/.../ Owen_singapore88.pdf.

Oxford Dictionaries (2013a) 'Research', *Oxford University Press.* Retrieved 21 December 2013 from www. oxforddictionaries.com/definition/english/research.

Oxford Dictionaries (2013b) 'Method', *Oxford University Press.* Retrieved 15 February 2013 from http:// oxforddictionaries.com/definition/english/method?q=method and 'Methodology' from http:// oxforddictionaries.com/definition/english/methodology?q=methodology.

Oxford Dictionaries (2013c) 'Culture', *Oxford University Press.* Retrieved 15 December 2013 from www. oxforddictionaries.com/definition/english/culture.

Oxford Dictionaries (2013d) 'Image', *Oxford University Press.* Retrieved 14 December 2013 from www. oxforddictionaries.com/definition/english/image.

Oxford Dictionaries (2013e) 'Sign', *Oxford University Press.* Retrieved 26 December 2013 from www. oxforddictionaries.com/definition/english/sign.

Oxford Dictionaries (2013f) 'Empirical', *Oxford University Press.* Retrieved 31 December 2013 from www. oxforddictionaries.com/definition/english/empirical.

Oxford Dictionaries (2014a) 'Form', *Oxford University Press.* Retrieved 8 July 2014 from www.oxford dictionaries.com/definition/english/form.

Oxford Dictionaries (2014b) 'Object', *Oxford University Press.* Retrieved 8 July 2014 from www.oxford dictionaries.com/definition/english/object?q=object.

Plowman, T. (2003) 'Ethnography and Critical Design Practice' in B. Laurel (ed.), *Design Research: Methods and Perspectives.* Cambridge: MIT Press, pp. 30–38.

Punch, K.F. (2005) *Introduction to Social Research: Quantitative and Qualitative Approaches.* London: SAGE.

Ramberg, B. and Gjesdal, K. (2013) 'Hermeneutics', *The Stanford Encyclopedia of Philosophy.* Retrieved 13 December 2013 from http://plato.stanford.edu/entries/hermeneutics/.

Reeves, S., Kuper, A. and Hodges, B.D. (2008) 'Qualitative Research Methodologies: Ethnography', *British Medical Journal* 337: 512–14.

Riemer, F.J. (2009) 'Ethnography Research' in S.D. Laplan and M.T. Quartaroli (eds), *Research Essentials: An Introduction to Designs and Practices.* San Francisco, CA: Jossey-Bass, pp. 203–221.

Rittel, H.W.J. and Webber, M.M. (1973) 'Planning Problems are Wicked Problems' in N. Cross (ed.), *Developments in Design Methodology.* New York: Wiley, pp. 135–44.

Rose, G. (2012) *Visual Methodologies: An Introduction to Researching with Visual Materials.* London: SAGE.

Rosenfield, P.L. (1992) 'The Potential of Transdisciplinary Research for Sustaining and Extending Linkages Between the Health and Social Sciences', *Social Science and Medicine* 35(11): 1343–57.

Sandström, C. (2009) 'The Rise of Digital Imaging and the Fall of the Old Camera Industry', *The Luminous Landscape.* Retrieved 26 February 2013 from www.luminous-landscape.com/essays/rise-fall.shtml.

Sato, S. and Mrazek, D. (2013) *Measuring the Impact of Design on Business*, seminar presented at the Design Management Institute, Seattle, 11–12 April.

Schon, D. (1983) *The Reflective Practitioner: How Professionals Think in Action.* New York: Basic Books.

Schönberger, A. (1990) 'Preface' in A. Schönberger (ed.), *Raymond Loewy: Pioneer of American Industrial Design.* Munich: Prestel, pp. 7–8.

Schudson, M. (1993) *Advertising, the Uneasy Persuasion: Its Dubious Impact on the American Society.* London: Routledge.

Schutz, P.A., Nichols, S.L. and Rodgers, K.A. (2009) 'Using Multiple Methods Approaches' in S.D. Lapan and M.T. Quartaroli (eds), *Research Essentials: An Introduction to Designs and Practices.* San Francisco, CA: Jossey-Bass, pp. 243–58.

Simon, H. (1982) *The Sciences of the Artificial.* Cambridge, MA: MIT Press.

Smith, D.W. (2008) 'Phenomenology', *Stanford Encyclopedia of Philosophy.* Retrieved 13 February 2013 from http://plato.stanford.edu/entries/phenomenology/.

Stevens, J.S. (2009) *Design as a Strategic Resource: Design's Contributions to Competitive Advantage Aligned with Strategy Models.* PhD dissertation, University of Cambridge, Cambridge.

Stokes, J. (2011) *How to Do Media & Cultural Studies.* London: SAGE.

SurveyMonkey (2012) '99designs Shares Insights with Their Users', *SurveyMonkey Audience.* Retrieved 13 April 2013 from www.surveymonkey.com/mp/audience/insights/case-study/99designs/.

Swann, C. (2002) 'Action Research and the Practice of Design', *Design Issues* 18(2): 49–61.

UXPA (2010) 'What is User-Centered Design?' *User Experience Professionals Association.* Retrieved 13 February 2013 from www.upassoc.org/usability_resources/about_usability/what_is_ucd.html.

van Riel, C.B.M. and Fombrun, C.J. (2007) *Essentials of Corporate Communication.* London: Routledge.

Watson, P. (2005) *Ideas: A History of Thought and Invention from Fire to Freud.* New York: HarperCollins.

WGSN (2013) 'About WGSN', *Worth Global Style Network.* Retrieved 26 February 2013 from www. wgsn.com.

Whicher, A., Raulik-Murphy, G. and Cawood, G. (2011) 'Evaluating Design: Understanding the Return on Investment', *DMI Review* 22(2): 44–52.

Williams, C. (2007) 'Research Methods', *Journal of Business & Economic Research* 5(3): 65–71.

Williamson, J. (1978) *Decoding Advertisements: Ideology and Meaning of Advertising.* London: Marion Boyars.

Woodward, I. (2007) *Understanding Material Culture.* London: SAGE.

Wyeth, P. and Diercke, C. (2006) 'Designing Cultural Probes for Children', *OZCHI '06 Proceedings of the 18th Australia Conference on Computer–Human Interaction: Design: Activities, Artefacts and Environments,* 20–24 November, Sydney, Australia. Retrieved 15 January 2013 from http://dl.acm.org/citation.cfm?id=1228252.

Yin, R.K. (1994) *Case Study Research: Design and Methods.* Thousand Oaks, CA: SAGE.

Zec, P. (2011) 'Design Value', *DMI Review* 22(2): 36–42.

Zimmerman, E. (2003) 'Creating a Culture of Design Research' in B. Laurel (ed.), *Design Research: Methods and Perspectives.* Cambridge, MA: MIT Press, pp. 185–92.

INDEX